The Town Hall, otherwise Court-house, Compter and Borough gaol (c.1797).

The Abbey Gateway, otherwise House of Correction and Liberty gaol (c.1787).

Hertfordshire Record Publications, Volume 7

(Hon.General Editor: A.W.Mabbs)

St.Albans
Quarter Sessions Rolls
1784 - 1820

A Calendar of Rolls of the General Court of Quarter Sessions
for the Borough of St.Albans

Edited with an introduction by

David Dean

Hertfordshire Record Society

1991

Hertfordshire Record Society

The publication of this volume has been
assisted by generous grants from:

Robert Kiln Charitable Trust
Hertfordshire County Council
St.Albans Museums
St.Albans and Hertfordshire Architectural and Archaeological Society
P.W.Barrows Charitable Trust
and sponsorship by Lionel and Diana Munby and Mrs.Dorothy Pelham.

ISBN 0 9510728 6 2

Printed by
E. & E. Plumridge Ltd.,
High Street, Linton, Cambridge, England

Contents

(continued)

Contents (continued)

Illustrations

Frontispiece   The Town Hall, otherwise Court-house, Compter and Borough Gaol.
The Abbey Gateway, otherwise House of Correction and Liberty Gaol.

The illustration of the old town hall (c.1797) is attributed to H.G.Oldfield and shows the view looking East from Market Place at its intersection with Dagnal Street.

The engraving of the abbey gateway (c.1787) shows the view looking from the South. The high wall adjoining the gateway on the right hand side surrounds a yard. The Abbey Church is further to the right.

Acknowledgements

I wish to thank and to acknowledge the dedicated work and support of my colleagues Eveline Alty, the late Donald Ashby, Ann Dean, Kathleen Goad, Evelyn Isherwood and Maureen Jacques with assistance from Pat Grigg and Pamela Smith for producing the more extensive edited transcripts upon which this calendar is based.

I thank also Peter Walne and Alfred Mabbs for their invaluable advice, and the latter for his contribution to the indexes.

My thanks are due also to The City and District Council of St.Albans and the staff of the Central Library, St.Albans, for access to the Sessions Rolls, to The City and District Council for permission to publish and to the Hertfordshire County Record Office for permission to reproduce the illustration of the old town hall, St.Albans.

Introduction

The Sessions Rolls

The Sessions Rolls consist of the documents filed at each sitting of the General Court of Quarter Sessions for the Borough of St.Alban and relate to the judicial and administrative business before the justices.

The numeration of the rolls is that assigned to them in serial order in the inventory of the City Archives of St.Albans compiled in 1948 by the late Col.W.H.C.le Hardy. The item number for each document is assigned by this calendar. It covers rolls nos. 407A to 549 (1784 to 1820). No rolls earlier than the first one, no.407A for Michaelmas 1784 are thought to survive but earlier records are available in the form of Sessions Books and Minute Books etc. (see under Supplementary sources). Rolls 550 to 607 continue the series from 1821 to 1836.

As an outcome of the operation of the Municipal Corporations Act, 1835 (5 & 6 Will.IV.c.76), the General Court of Quarter Sessions for the Borough of St.Alban was abolished in 1836. Although Lord John Russell, Secretary of State for the Home Department, offered to renew the Commission of the Peace, the Borough magistrates declined the offer and their jurisdiction was merged with that of the Liberty.

Each roll typically contains 10 to 20 documents, here referred to as 'items'. At the close of the Sessions, the items were placed together, threaded through one corner on a tape, rolled into a tight roll and bound with the long tape end. The most commonly reoccurring items are:-

The Writ proclaiming Quarter Sessions is almost invariably the outer item on each Roll. Dated at the previous Sessions, it required in the King's name that certain actions to be taken. Principally, that the Sergeants at Mace make proclamation, gather two juries, each of twelve men, and together with other specified officers, meet on a given date at the town hall for holding the General Quarter Sessions for the Borough.

The jury lists provide the names of the all male Grand and Petty juries. They usually include a few extra names and identify those sworn, excused or fined for non attendance. The qualifications for Grand and Petty jurors were the same, but the Grand jury was 'selected from the most respectable class'.[1] It could in law consist of up to 23 men, but was specified as 12 in the proclamations used in St.Albans. The function of the Grand jury was to determine whether there was a *prima facie* case to answer and to endorse the Indictment accordingly. The case would then be tried before the Petty jury (see under The judicial process).

The Gaol and House of Correction Calendars list the names of all prisoners held or bailed out, with appropriate dates. For those under sentence it usually includes the nature of the crime and sentence. For those awaiting trial it includes reason for committal, by which magistrate committed and upon whose complaint.

'Information', 'Information and Complaint', 'Examination', 'Examination and Confession' etc. were roughly equivalent to the modern 'Statement of Witness'. They inform us that on a given date and before a named magistrate the facts related in the document were sworn to. The items are normally endorsed with the signature or mark of the examinant. Occasionally they are endorsed with the names of witnesses and notes of recognisances.

Recognisances are dated items giving names, occupations and the amount of money by which bound to adhere to certain requirements, usually to appear at the next Quarter Sessions in connection with a specified charge. Similar details are included in respect of any sureties, usually one or perhaps two in number. Recognisances were normally set between £5 and £100. Since, in law, married women normally owned no property, their attendance was ensured by recognisances entered into by husband, other male relative or employer.

The 'Presentment of the Jury' concerns the findings of the Grand jury upon the indictments preferred. They are usually endorsed on the back with the verdict of the Grand jury, sometimes with that of the Petty jury and occasionally with the names of witnesses. (See difference between 'presentment' and 'inquisition' under Judicial process).

'Sacrament Certificates' were documents witnessed by the minister and churchwardens of a named church. They stated that the named person, on a given date, 'did receive the Sacraments of the Lords Supper'. The certificates were a requirement for those holding certain public offices.

'Bills', otherwise accounts or claims for expenses, were submitted by Clerks of the Peace, constables, gaolers and others. Their chief value lies in the information which they give about the duties and activities of the claimants, the extent of military activity (e.g. by virtue of local transport supplied), the extent of vagrancy, the cost of maintaining prisoners, the outcome of some of the criminal cases etc. Bills are occasionally the only source of such information in the Rolls.

Supplementary sources

The calendar contains only information derived from the Borough rolls. These are held in the City Archives, St.Albans. The archives are supervised by a part time archivist under the direction of the Museums Service and can be consulted at the Central Library in St.Albans.

There are other Borough Quarter Sessions records in the City Archives which supplement this calendar:-

Sessions Rolls 1821-1836.	(City Archives 550-607)
Recognizance Book 1829-1839	(City Archives 355)
Gaol and House of Correction	
Calendars 1819-1828	(City Archives 36)
Draft Minute Books 1819-1836	(City Archives 363-365)
Sessions Books	(City Archives 366-367)
Justices Oath Roll 1753-1816	(City Archives 1378)
Commissions of the Peace, 1800, 1825, 1836	(City Archives 1379-1382)

Other Borough Quarter Sessions records, together with those for the Liberty, are to be found in the County Record Office, County Hall, Hertford. Both Borough and Liberty shared a number of record books in which successive records for each jurisdiction usually alternate. These date from 1758 and continued in shared use until 1819. They include Minute Books, Sessions Books, Gaol Books and Estreats of Fines and are valuable supplements to the calendar. Some decisions of the court which do not appear in the rolls are recorded in these sources.

The Quarter Sessions records for the Liberty and Borough are described in Guide to the Hertfordshire Record Office, Volume I (1961), pp.47-58[2] and listed in more detail in the inventory of this archive group available in the Record Office search room.

The rolls, Draft Sessions Books, Sessions Books and other miscellaneous Liberty documents, 1758-1840 have been calendared and published as Hertfordshire County Records, Volume IV (1923). These two volumes should be consulted in parallel with each other. The corresponding records for the Borough have not been comprehensively published.

Administrative areas

To understand the business of the Quarter Sessions it is helpful to know something about the relationship between the Borough of St.Alban, its constituent parishes, and the surrounding Liberty of St.Alban.

The boundary of the Borough almost certainly corresponded to that of monastic times and remained unchanged until 1835. It embraced 320 acres and a population of 3,038 in 1801. The Borough consisted of parts of four parishes: St.Michael's, St.Peter's, St.Alban's and a small uninhabited part of St.Stephen's. The parish of St.Alban, otherwise known as the Abbey Parish, lay almost totally within the Borough, but the three larger parishes lay mainly in the Liberty. The Liberty of St.Alban surrounded the Borough and extended into some 22 parishes, nearly a quarter of the County of Hertfordshire. No part of the Borough was in the Liberty and no part of the Liberty in the Borough.

The Borough and Liberty had both been in the jurisdiction of the pre-dissolution Monastery of St.Alban and a charter of Edward VI granted the Liberty certain privileges within the Borough. Both Borough and Liberty held separate Quarter Sessions courts at the Town Hall in the Borough, both had separate gaols in the Borough and both shared a common House of Correction in the Borough. Expenses mutually incurred were met one third by the Borough and two thirds by the Liberty.

Increasingly from the reign of Henry VIII, ecclesiastical parishes also became units of civil government responsible for the administration of duties and functions placed upon them by statute. Amongst the many responsibilities of parishes, under their vestries, were maintenance of highways, levying local poor rates, appointing parish constables and administering parish workhouses. Although four parishes lay part in the Borough of St.Alban and part in the Liberty, there is no evidence in the Sessions Rolls of any conflict over administrative responsibilities.

Some Borough matters, notably the payment of certain taxes, appointment of constables and matters relating to the Court Leet, were based not upon parishes within the Borough, but upon 'wards'. The Borough consisted of four wards: [3] St.Peter's, Fishpool, Middle and Holywell. The parish of St.Peter within the Borough corresponded with St.Peter's Ward, but the other ward boundaries have not been accurately determined.[4]

The Borough and people

The inhabitants of St.Albans relied upon trade, agriculture and such cottage industry as straw plaiting. These sustained a weekly market for the area, [5] two annual fairs and the requirements of travellers using the busy coaching routes through the town. In 1820 the ratio of adult male inhabitants to licenced ale houses and inns was 25:1.

Government of the Borough was invested in the mayor and twelve aldermen. The aldermen, from amongst whom the mayor was elected, served for life and appointed replacements when one of their number died or moved away. Their involvement in activities in the Borough was extensive, their influence offering every opportunity for self serving enterprise. The mayor was *ex officio* chief magistrate for the Borough and a magistrate for the Liberty. 'The privileges granted by the charters were very great, rendering the Mayor, who was chief magistrate, little if at all inferior to a petty prince both in pomp and power.' [6]

The small electorate for the Borough returned two members to parliament; and the 17th, 18th and 19th centuries saw both doubtful and illegal electioneering practices. A parliamentary commission found that nearly two thirds of the electorate had been bribed in the election of 1847[7] and the Borough was disenfranchised. This was a time in which every petty official expected fees and gratuities for doing his job. Many, including parish constables and, until the late 18th. century, gaolers, received no salary but relied upon statutory, customary or occasional fees and perhaps some other remunerative activity, as a means of earning their livelihoods. The electorate probably saw charging parliamentary candidates, who were eager to pay for the privilege of feathering their own nests, as a legitimate perquisite. The situation in St.Albans was far from exceptional.

The Borough courts

The General Court of Quarter Sessions met four times a year with additional 'Adjourned Sessions' if required. It was concerned both with administrative matters and with crimes not sufficiently serious to incur either the death penalty or transportation for life.

By virtue of its charters, several other courts were held within the Borough. These were the Petty Sessions, Court of Record, View of Frankpledge or Court Leet, the Court of the Clerk of the Market and the Court of Pie Poudre. In 1834 the Court of Pie Poudre was described as being 'totally disused' and the Court of the Clerk of the Market as being concerned with the annual checking of weights and measures used in the market.[1] A 'Mayor's Court' was also held, but its role was chiefly that of a town council.

The Court Leet met once a year and was concerned with appointing a constable for each of the four wards and with presenting matters of nuisance and obstruction. Although appointed on behalf of each ward, the constables acted throughout and on behalf of the Borough.

The Court of Record, held weekly, was concerned with actions for debts up to the value of £50. The use of this court declined following an Act establishing a Court of Requests for St.Albans in 1752 and was finally discontinued in 1789. The Court of Requests met once a week and was concerned with the recovery of small debts amounting to less than 40/-.

The Petty Sessions were held once a week. This was a court of summary jurisdiction held before one or more magistrates and dealt with some of the crimes classified as misdemeanours, e.g. minor assaults.

The Gaols and House of Correction

The Gaol of the Borough was housed in the Town Hall, a large 16th. century timber frame building in the Market Place.[8] The upper floor was used for holding judicial proceedings and in the winter season, occasional balls and assemblies. The lower floor was used as the gaol, with a residence for the gaoler and a (fire) engine house.[9]

The Liberty Gaol and House of Correction for both Borough and Liberty were housed in the old Abbey Gateway, a large stone structure rebuilt in the 14th.century. The eastern half, nearest the Abbey Church, was the Liberty Gaol. The other half of the Gateway was the House of Correction or Bridewell.

By the 18th.century the distinction between gaols and houses of correction was gradually being lost. In St.Albans, both vagrants and other offenders were committed to the House of Correction where there was the means of keeping them to hard labour.

John Howard, the tireless campaigner for prison and law reform, reported on five visits he made to St.Albans between 1776 and 1782. He visited both gaols and bridewell and his comments are of some interest. [10]

He reported of the Borough Gaol, or Compter:- 'Debtors have sometimes the use of the town-hall in the day-time: the lodging-room of those that pay joins to it. Felons and poor debtors have two day rooms, and two close offensive night-rooms: no fire-place. Allowance to felons, a pound of bread a day. No straw: no court: no water. Fees for felons, 13s.4d. Licence for beer. Clauses against spirituous liquors hung up. - The debtors from the court of requests (debts under 40s.) are confined here with felons. Though the act of 25th.Geo.II. clears them in forty-two days, yet as it does not specify the gaoler's fee, and here is no table, they must continue in prison till they can pay whatever the keeper demands.'

Of the Liberty Gaol Howard reported:- 'For debtors, two spacious day-rooms, and three lodging-rooms. - For felons, three offensive rooms. When there are men and women, they cannot be properly separated. - No straw: no court. Licence for beer. Clauses against spirituous liquors not hung up. Fees, 13s.4d. no table.'

And of the Bridewell for the Liberty and for the Borough. 'One large work-room, and two lodging-rooms; all up stairs, and airy. No court: no water; no allowance: no straw. Prisoners have their earnings. Clauses against spirituous liquors not hung up. No fees. In 1779, I found a girl, who was sentenced for a year's imprisonment, locked up all day with two soldiers in the work-room: and at my last visit, a girl and a boy were confined together.'

The calendar reveals (452/5) that at least as early as 1796, visitors had been appointed for the Borough Gaol, and the Liberty records show that medical men were already in attendance at the Liberty Gaol. Even so, the Liberty gaoler was accused in 1800 of ill treatment of a prisoner who died shortly after release. The accusations seem upon investigation to have been well founded and he was lucky to escape with mere dismissal, being found to be 'a very unfit person to have the care of any person committed to that prison any longer.'[11]

The gaoler for the Borough and the keeper of the House of Correction were appointed by the Borough. The gaoler for the Liberty was appointed by the Lord Lieutenant of the County.

Prisoners were allowed one pound of bread per day: this being increased by half a pound in 1812.[9]

Capital crime

It would be wrong to believe that because the Quarter Sessions did not pass capital sentences, such matters were not of significant concern to the court. The reason for this is not hard to understand given that the law had become exceedingly complicated and that the offence with which a suspect might be charged depended upon how one chose to interpret the circumstances. Consider for example, larceny (theft), the frequency of which is second only to assaults in the calendar. Larceny could be a capital offence depending upon the value of the goods stolen. This critical value depended in turn upon the place from whence the goods were stolen and the circumstances in which the theft took place; upon whether by day or night, whether near a highway, whether from a house, shop or boat, whether with face blackened (disguised), with or without the knowledge of the victim etc. Thus the capital nature of an offence could turn upon a word in the indictment or the indulgence of the court.

From the reign of Henry I in the 11th. century, theft of goods worth more than one shilling had been made a capital offence [12] and this remained a basic premise until the early 19th.century. The effect was modified over the centuries by the way in which goods were valued and by 'benefit of clergy'. Bracton, the great legal commentator of the 13th.century, had argued that the value of money had changed with the passage of time and that account should be taken of this in determining the value of a stolen item. [13] There are numerous instances in the calendar of items being valued at less than a shilling when they clearly cost more. Theft to a value not exceeding one shilling was known as Petty Larceny. Theft above that value was Grand Larceny.

Capital offences were either within 'benefit of clergy' or non-clergyable. An act of 1692 (3 W.&M.c.9) extended to women the privileges which men enjoyed from benefit of clergy and in 1707 (5&6 Ann.c.6) the qualifying reading test was abolished. Benefit of clergy (which could only be claimed once) became little more than a formula by which first time offenders might have their capital sentences commuted. Applying this to the case of larceny discussed above, theft up to the value of one shilling (petty larceny) might be punished by whipping, gaol, a fine or transportation, usually for seven years. Theft above the value of one shilling (grand larceny), but below some higher value, might be within benefit of clergy. Theft from the person, privily, (e.g. picking pockets) was capital above the value of a shilling and totally excluded from clergy until 1808 (48 G3.c.129). Clergy was extended to: stealing from a shop or breaking into a house and stealing to a value of less than 5/- (3 W.&M.c.9 and 10&11 W3.c.23) 1691&1699: stealing from a house, without breaking in, to a value less than 40/- (12 Ann.c.7) 1712: stealing from places for drying or processing linen, 10/- (18 G2.c.27) 1744, and so on.

Having been admitted to their clergy, prisoners were supposed to be branded on a thumb in open court, then at the discretion of the justices, to be put to hard labour in the House of Correction for a period of six months to two years. An act of 1717 (4 G.c.11) stated that those convicted within benefit of clergy and liable only to be whipped or burnt in the hand may instead be transported for seven years. The act implied that whipping was an alternative to branding, an interpretation regularised by an act of 1779 (19G3.c.54). This acknowledged that branding was frequently neglected and offered the alternatives of a moderate fine or public or private whipping. Second time offenders and those found guilty of any non-clergyable offences might be capitally convicted at the Assizes. The only hope for those so sentenced was the Royal Mercy which could be granted on recommendation of the judge. In the last quarter of the 18th.century, of 2,218 capital convictions in London and Middlesex, slightly less than 40% were executed,[14] an average of about 35 per year.

Statutes increased the number of capital offences throughout the 18th.century from some 50 in 1727 [15] to approximately 200 by the year 1819.[16] The scale of this increase should not be taken as an index of repression. Laws were passed on an *ad hoc* basis in response to real or assumed threats. There are many examples of laws which could have been grouped together under a comprehensive heading, thus reducing their number. For example, one year it might be made a capital offence to forge an official stamp on one type of document, the next year to forge the stamp on another, whilst similar documents might or might not be covered by some earlier legislation. By the end of the 18th. century the law had become complicated by numerous fine distinctions and exclusions.

Although Quarter Sessions did not pass capital sentences, at the Hertfordshire County Sessions in 1773 a man claimed benefit of clergy[17] and in the Liberty Sessions in 1774 and 1775 two prisoners were branded.[11] Preliminary examination would have been before a justice and the fact that each was tried at the Sessions suggests at least a marginal encroachment upon the prerogative of the Assize Courts.

Crime in the Rolls

The Rolls mention eleven different instances of prisoners being removed to Hertford Gaol. Apart from two unnamed prisoners for an unspecified offence,[18] all were for capital crimes. Five were for horse stealing,[19] one for the theft of a watch, clothing and 13 guineas,[20] one for burglary,[21] one for uttering forged banknotes,[22] one for escaping from the Borough gaol where he was held for an unspecified offence[23] and one, the only female in the group, for stealing 21 yards of cotton. [24]

In the period of a little over 36 years covered by the calendar, only three prisoners are recorded as having been transported, each for 7 years. The first[25] was Elizabeth Prudden who was committed in 1797 for the theft of a pair of pattens worth 6d. She spent 15 months in the gaol before being removed for transportation. The second case[26] was that of James Harding committed in 1800 for the theft from his employer of 20 items of silver cutlery and two of clothing. He spent nearly 18 weeks in gaol before being removed to the hulks to await transportation. The third case[27] was that of Charles Louch, committed in 1816 for picking the pocket of a man in a drunken slumber. He stole a purse containing bank notes and silver to the value of £12..6s. He too spent nearly 18 weeks in gaol before being removed to the hulks.

Some prisoners mentioned in the Rolls may not have appeared at the Sessions in person. These include prisoners of war, some of the prisoners committed on suspicion of an offence but later released, for example deserters, and those committed for minor acts of vagrancy. It is unlikely that prisoners sent to the Assizes first made an appearance at Quarter Sessions since they would already have been examined by a magistrate.

Examination of the first 200 cases in the calendar, ignoring minor acts of vagrancy, deserters and prisoners of war, yields some interesting results. Eighty two cases (41%) were assaults or bindings to keep the Peace. Mere threats can amount to an assault, whilst an exchange of blows constitutes battery. Although the word 'battery' rarely appears in the calendar, many of the cases were clearly 'assault and battery'. Some of the assaults might have been more appropriately dealt with summarily, at Petty Sessions.

Sixty of the surveyed cases (30%) were for various forms of larceny and include most of the cases sent to Hertford. Considering merely what was stolen causes few surprises. Watches, silver spoons, tankards and the like might be expected to raise small sums from pawn or sale. Materials, tools and food might be for personal use or sale. The theft and occasional sale of minor items of wearing apparel is of some interest. It reminds us that there has in the past been a ready market for the meanest items of second hand clothing and that a significant number of the poor might own little more than that in which they stood.

Sixteen cases (8%) concerned begetting bastards upon females. There were eight cases of fraud or misrepresentation, five of uttering false coin, five of disturbance or riot and five of misbehaviour. Misbehaviour took several forms from 'getting drunk' to 'wandering in a idle and disorderly manner'. Four cases might be described as 'against statutes' e.g. non payment of stamp duty. There were three cases of receiving stolen goods. Of the sixteen assorted cases remaining, two of the charges were not specified.

Coining (counterfeiting) and uttering (passing) false coins occurs several times in the calendar. Uttering was normally only a misdemeanour, the seriousness of which depended upon how many such coins were in the possession of the accused or how many passed in one day etc. An Act of 1741 (15 G2.c.28) made the counterfeiting of gold or silver coin, high treason. Until 1771 (11 G3.c.40), counterfeiting halfpennies and farthings had been a misdemeanour, but by this act was made a felony. It was not extended to pennies and other copper coins until 1797 (37 G3.c.126). In the first such case to occur in the calendar (407A/7), James Batchelor confessed to uttering a counterfeit shilling and implicated his wife, Ann, and two others with coining. Ann was lucky to be indicted only for uttering. James Batchelor was committed to gaol for six months. Ann was acquitted and discharged in court.[28] The others were found guilty of high treason at the Assizes and condemned to death. [17] A woman similarly convicted would have been charged with petty treason, the penalty for which was, until 1790, to be publicly burnt (as in burnt at the stake, not branded). By the late 18th.century she would normally have been hanged before her body was burnt.

Coining and uttering offences at this time were quite common. By the end of the 18th.century, the coinage had long been deficient in quantity and quality. A large proportion of that in circulation was underweight by virtue of clipping or having been worn down to mere blanks, was counterfeit or of foreign origin.[29]

Vagrancy represented a problem of which there is ample evidence in the Rolls. A convenient starting point is to consider the poor in general, whether the industrious deserving or otherwise. One was normally expected to have a parish of legal settlement. Settlement qualifications might be acquired in numerous ways: by birth, marriage, apprenticeship, service, forty days overt habitation etc.[30] A poor person wishing to work or stay in another parish would normally be required to furnish a certificate stating the willingness of his home parish to take him back should he become chargeable to parish relief. Failure to produce a certificate or committing a vagrancy offence led to individuals and families being removed to their last place of legal settlement, conducted from parish to parish, sometimes to distant parts of the country.

Vagrancy was an offence covered by numerous Acts, perhaps the most relevant being 17 G2.c.5 (1744) and 32 G3.c.45 (1792). Vagrants were classified under three headings:-

(a) Idle and disorderly persons. Amongst these were persons found begging in their own parish, those refusing to work and permitting their families to become chargeable to the parish and those who returned to a parish from which they had been removed, without bringing a certificate. The punishment was a maximum of one month hard labour in the House of Correction. The reward for apprehending was five shillings.

(b) Rogues and vagabonds. This class included those begging outside their own parish, street players without a licence, those lodging in barns etc. and not giving a good account of themselves and those running away and leaving their wives and children chargeable to the parish. The punishment was to be publicly whipped or committed to the House of Correction until the next Sessions or for a period of not less than 7 days (with certain exceptions). At the Sessions they could be committed for a further period of not more than six months. The reward for apprehending was ten shillings.

(c) Incorrigible rogues. These could, for example, be persons repeating the offences of rogues and vagabonds or escaping after being apprehended. The punishment was whipping or committal to House of Correction for a period from six months to two years.

An Act of 1597 (39 Eliz.c.4) concerning vagrants, required that when whipped they be naked from the waist up and whipped only until their back be bloody. An Act of 1792 (32 G3.c.45) abolished the whipping of female vagrants. The Rolls make frequent mention of whipping vagrants and the Gaol Book contains further information concerning one Elizabeth Maccarty who in 1785 was convicted as 'an incorrigible rogue - to be publicly whipped ....from the Market Cross of St.Albans round the same up the back street down by the Market House and around the cross again and then to be passed to her last legal settlement which she has already sworn to be in the County of Clare in Ireland.'[31]

The unsympathetic attitude towards vagrants, suggested by contemporary legislation, would seem to have been shared by a significant proportion of common people. Carl Moritz noted several examples of the indignities heaped upon the travelling pedestrian during his visit to England in 1782,[32] including being hissed at as he walked through a village. Samuel Bamford suggested stratagems for the foot traveller wishing to obtain reasonable treatment at wayside hostelries in 1819.[33]

There are 36 cases in the calendar concerning children likely to be born bastards. Under an Act of Elizabeth I, women with child likely to be born a bastard, and chargeable to the parish, were required to name the father and have the matter presented before Quarter Sessions where maintenance requirements would be settled.

Six suicides are recorded in the calendar. Three hanged themselves and three cut their throats. A seventh may have attempted to cut his throat.

The judicial process

Offenders against whom an indictment was to be preferred normally came before the Quarter Sessions as the result of an 'Information' or 'Complaint' sworn before a Justice of the Peace, commonly by the injured party. A possible exception to this might arise from the findings of a coroners court

xvi

(435/7 to 10), the papers for which appear in the Rolls unheralded and no further proceedings in the matter are recorded.

The judicial process can be illustrated by means of a hypothetical case. Suppose that an inhabitant living within the Borough boundary missed a pair of breeches from his dwelling and that a suspect could be identified. The injured party would proceed to a magistrate and swear out a complaint. Whether this most commonly occurred at the town hall during specified hours, or at the magistrates dwelling, has not been determined. The suspect would be summoned or perhaps brought before the magistrate by a constable who could also have been armed with a search warrant. The suspect would be examined by the magistrate and an 'Examination' possibly taken down in writing. An accused person could not give evidence under oath and was not required to swear to his examination. The majority of cases in the Rolls do not contain a written Examination of the accused.

Since the example concerns a case of larceny, the matter would be destined for Quarter rather than Petty Sessions. Both complainant and suspect would be bound in recognisance of say £10, with possible sureties, to appear at the next Quarter Sessions: one to prefer a Bill of Indictment, the other to answer the indictment. If recognisances could not be found, the suspect might languish for anything up to three months in gaol, awaiting trial at the next Sessions.

At some stage, the Clerk of the Peace would draw up the Bill of Indictment for which he would be paid two shillings by the prosecutor (usually the injured party). This would be worded in accord with legal requirements, mentioning that the breeches had been *feloniously* taken and carried away. Indictments could fail on technicalities in the wording. The value of the item stolen had also to be entered, but might commonly be scaled down to take into account the change in value of money. This scaling down was accepted legal practice.

An alternative approach to framing a charge against a suspect *may* have been more common. Where the Grand jury pronounced upon a formally worded charge, the findings of the jury were 'more properly' called an 'inquisition'. Each count of the indictment had to be accepted in its entirety and could not be modified by the jury. The alternative was for the evidence and nature of the complaint to be considered by the jury who would then formulate the indictment, no doubt with legal guidance. Their pronouncement would then be the 'presentment' of the jury. Under these circumstances, the value attributed to a stolen item, for example, could be set by the jury. Throughout the calendar the findings of the jury are referred to as the 'presentment of the jury'. Various conflicting pointers in the rolls and contemporary legal books make the correct nomenclature slightly uncertain.

The case would be heard at the Quarter Sessions, before a bench of perhaps three justices and the Grand jury. There is no evidence from the Rolls to suggest that the prosecutor was legally represented and it seems unlikely that many defendants were represented.[34] The magistrate was required to look after the defendants interests. Both prosecutor and defendant could be questioned by the Grand jury.[13] The defendant could not give evidence under oath, but could make a statement. The duty of the Grand jury was to determine whether a *prima facie* case had been established and to record their verdict on the back of the Indictment as 'A true Bill' or as 'No true Bill' (or 'Ignoramus'). In the event of 'No true Bill' the prisoner was required to be discharged and set free in open court, without paying the gaoler's fee (14G3.c.20) (1744), a maximum of 13/4d. In the event of 'A true Bill' the case would be tried before the Petty jury who, on the basis of the evidence, would find the defendant 'guilty' or 'not guilty'.

Poor prosecutors who *succeeded* in their prosecution of a *felon* could claim reasonable expenses (25 G2.c.36)(1751) and by the Act of 18 G3.c.19 (1778) they could claim, whether successful or not, provided that prosecution was justified. By the latter act poor witnesses could also claim expenses. Expenses were awarded at the discretion of the court and to secure them the prosecutor had to pay one shilling to each of the Treasurer and Clerk of the Peace. Witnesses had to pay 6d. to each. There are several examples of claims for expenses in the Rolls.

Editorial note

In order to publish in this one volume the proceedings of Quarter Sessions for a period of 36 years, editing has been necessary. For the rolls covered, *all* documentary items have been included in the text. 'Examinations', 'Complaints' etc have been edited only by the omission of names of justices and common form as well as of repetitious and less relevant words and phrases. All entries in the gaol and House of Correction calendars have been included together with the numbers of vagrants, but omitting the names of vagrants who are not also mentioned elsewhere. Jury lists and recognisances are mentioned, but names etc. omitted. Some documents were able to withstand severe editing with little or no loss of useful information, for example proclamations and Sacrament Certificates. It was principally in the editing of bills and accounts that the greatest difficulty was encountered. From these it was only possible to include entries of particular interest and relevance.

The more complete edited transcripts, upon which this volume is based, were made by members of St.Albans and Hertfordshire Architectural and Archaeological Society. Copies will in due course be deposited with the Hertfordshire County Record Office and with the Central Library at St.Albans. They are not indexed, but have the advantage of naming all jurors, justices, those bound in recognisance and many vagrants. Occupations and parishes of residence are also included.

Notes and references

1. Reports from commissioners on municipal corporations in England and Wales. 1834.

2. The list of entries concerning Borough records given on page 49 of the cited guide, erroneously omits entry 167 for Minute Books (Draft Sessions Books).

3. Upon the technicality of having four wards, the borough police force avoided amalgamation with the county force until 1947. The story of Hertfordshire police. Neil Osborn. Hertfordshire Countryside. 1969.

4. The report given as reference 1 states 'The boundaries of the wards are described in the charter of Edward 6th.' This is not true. Only their extremities at the four compass points of the Borough boundary are defined.

5. Four fairs and two markets were granted by the charters but, at least by the early 19th. century, only two fairs and one market were being held.

6. Topographical and statistical description of the county of Hertford. Cooke. Published between 1806 and 1811.

7. Report of the commissioners to inquire into the existence of bribery in the Borough of St.Alban's. HMSO 1852.

8. This building is commonly believed to date from about the 14th. century, but has now been more accurately dated. English Houses 1200-1800: the Hertfordshire evidence. J.T.Smith. (HMSO, forthcoming, 1991); Also, Inventory (RCHME, forthcoming, 1991)

9. History of Verulam and St.Albans. Anon. 1815.

10. The state of prisons in England and Wales 3rd. edit. Howard. 1784.

11. Hertfordshire County Records. Vol. IV. Notes and extracts from the Sessions records of the Liberty of St.Alban Division. 1770 to 1840. William Le Hardy. Longmore. 1923.

12. English legal history. 2nd. edit. L.B.Curzon. MacDonald and Evans. 1979.

13. The Justice of the Peace and Parish Officer. 22nd.edit. R.Burn. 1814.

14. How they lived. Vol.III 1700-1815. Asa Briggs. Blackwell. 1969.

15. The English Bastille. Anthony Babington. MacDonald. 1971.

16. <u>Punishment in former days</u>. Ernest W.Pettifer. E.P.Publishing. 1974.

17. <u>Hertfordshire County Records. Notes and extracts from the Sessions Rolls 1699 to 1850. Vol. II.</u> W.J.Hardy. Longmore 1905.

18. Item 547/14.

19. Items 417/2, 427/2, 444/6, 467/3 and 496/9.

20. Item 450/2.

21. Item 453/2.

22. Item 516/14.

23. Item 522/16.

24. Item 462/2.

25. Item 459/2.

26. Item 471/4.

27. Item 533/3.

28. Sessions Minute Book, 1776-1786. (LSMB 1) Hertfordshire County Record Office.

29. <u>'Our traitorous money makers': The Yorkshire coiners and the law, 1760-83</u>. John Styles. Published in <u>An ungovernable people</u>. Edited by John Brewer and John Styles. Hutchinsons. 1980.

30. <u>The Justice of the Peace and Parish Officer</u>. 18th.edit. R.Burn. 1797.

31. Gaol Book 1770-1814. (LSGB) Hertfordshire County Record Office.

32. <u>'Journeys of a German in England'</u> Edited by Reginald Nettle 1965. See pages 110, 111, 113-115, 117 and 118 for relevant examples.

33. <u>'Passages in the life of a Radical'</u> OUP 1984.

34. <u>Crime and authority in Victorian England</u>. David Philips. Croom Helm/Rowan and Littlefield 1977.

SESSIONS ROLL 407A, Michaelmas 1784

407A/1 Complaint of Ralph Page, Deputy Postmaster of the Borough, 26th.July 1784. Who saith that on Tuesday evening last between 7 and 8 o'clock as he was sitting in his gateway in the Woolpack Inn, two officers of His Majesty's Royal Regiment of Horse Guards came to put a letter at the General Post Office box, when one of them looking in and reading the directions of several letters that lay there and calling the other back saying "Jack, here is a direction you know". This informant, as Deputy Postmaster, thought it his duty to take notice thereof and accordingly walked down the yard and said "Gentlemen, that is not a gentlemanly action", upon which one of them whose name is John Reade, a lieutenant, asked the other, what this informant said and run after him and struck him immediately two violent blows on the face near his eye and the second blow knocked him down which totally stunned him, and upon attempting to get up, the said Reade hit him and struck him several times, and the other, whose name is Boarde, a Cornett, was present during the whole time of this assault and drew his sword almost out of the scabbard in order to prevent any person coming to this informants assistance, and they both called out for some troopers to come to help them, and this informant further says that there were several of this informants servants who see this informant assaulted, but were afraid to come to his assistance.
Recognisances <u>407A/14 & 15</u>.

407A/2 The Information of Peter Gibbons, ratcatcher, 4th.September 1784, who saith that about 18 years ago, he apprehended one Joseph Ayre upon White Coat Hill near Leeds in the West Riding of the County of York, for a highway robbery. That in consequence, Joseph Ayre was committed to York Castle and took his trial at the Assizes and was condemned for death, but was afterwards reprieved upon condition of Transportation for Life. And that he was transported. And this examinant further saith that on the 31st.August, as he was at the sign of the Valiant Trooper, in the Borough, he saw Joseph Ayre sitting on the table, that he said to Joseph Ayre, "What countryman are you?" to which he answered, "Yorkshire, near Leeds". And to several questions that this examinant asked him respecting the neighbouring places of Leeds, he pretended not to know any of them, and particularly denied any knowledge of White Coat Hill. That he afterwards went to the constable of the Borough and with him again apprehended the said Joseph Ayre.
407A/3 Similar to above, but dated 1st.Sept. and not written on official form.
Recognisances <u>407A/18 & 19</u>.

407A/4 Examination of Joseph Ayre, labourer, taken this 4th. day of September 1784. ----- being charged upon the oath of Peter Gibbons for being at large in the Borough after Transportation for Life for a felony committed in the County of York, saith that his name is John Wainwright, lives at Riston in the County of York, never was transported for felony and

1

is not guilty of the ------ charged on him by Peter Gibbons.

407A/5 Examination of Mary, the wife of John Placket, victualler. Taken the first day of September 1784, who upon her oath saith, to the best of her knowledge, that Joseph Ayre was about eighteen years ago tried at the Assizes for the County of York for a highway robbery, was condemned to death and afterwards reprieved upon the condition of being transported for life. And this examinant further saith that she can the more clearly speak to the aforesaid circumstances from her having personally known Joseph Ayre long before his trial, and that she was in court when he was tried and was present when he received sentence of death and saw him after he was reprieved and saw him set out in the wagon to be transported.

407A/6 Information of James Paling, labourer. Taken the 21st.July 1784. Who on his oath saith that last night he apprehended Mary White in the Borough, widow, who had in her custody part of a striped linen window curtain with a load and line ----- the property of Ralph Page of the Borough, Innholder.
Recognisances 407A/12 & 13.
Presentment of the jury 407A/9 concerning theft to the value of six pence. Endorsed 'A true Bill'.

407A/7 The Examination and Confession of James Batchelor, taken this 11th. August 1784, who saith that for about three weeks past, John Walsh, Patrick Walsh and Ann, the wife of James Batchelor, did make sundry counterfeit half crowns, shillings and sixpences, in the house of Patrick Walsh, situated in the Parish of Hatfield in the County of Hertford, called The Paper Mills, and that John and Patrick Walsh and Ann Batchelor were all concerned in filing and fabricating the counterfeit money. That Patrick Walsh and Ann Batchelor gave him at different times some of the counterfeit shillings in order to pay away, in pursuance whereof, he, James Batchelor, did yesterday pay to the son of Daniel Gold, one of the shillings, and three other of the shillings were found in his pocket when apprehended.
Recognisances 407A/16 & 17.
Presentment of the jury 407A/10 & 11 concerning a charge against James and Ann Batchelor for uttering false money. Endorsed 'A true Bill'.

407A/8 Sacrament Certificate of Francis Kingston.

407A/20 & 21 Recognisances concerning an assault upon James Marston, in the execution of his office as one of the constables of the Borough, by John Siggins.

407A/22 & 23 Recognisances concerning an assault upon John Peele by John Sharpless.

407A/24 & 25 Recognisances concerning John Sharpless locking up a certain door leading to the town hall of the Borough, obstructing the Justices for the Liberty in the execution of their office from access to the town hall and breaking of the locks from the Borough Gaol.

SESSIONS ROLL 407, Epiphany 1785   (14th.Jan.)

407/1   Writ proclaiming Quarter Sessions and Gaol Delivery.

407/2   Calendar of prisoners for the Borough Gaol.
Robert Tanner, Convicted at Christmas Sessions 1784 for two years. Remains in gaol.
John Wilson, Convicted at Christmas Sessions 1784 for one year. Remains in gaol.
James Batchelor, Convicted at Michaelmas Sessions 1784 for six months. Remains in gaol.
John Burgess, Committed of stealing sundry rafters, the property of William Wells.
William Major, Committed of stealing a purse containing 5/3d from John Welch.

407/3 & 407/4   Lists of jurors for the Grand and Petty juries. (Similar list 407/5)

407/6   Information of Thomas Walker, shoemaker, 9th. November, 1784, who saith about 19 months ago, he delivered some shoes *(12 pairs)* to one Coventry Harbridge, labourer, of the value of £14..11..4. Who gave a direction to him at No.135 Bishopsgate Street, London. And that he was to have some --- ----- in return. That he would not have delivered the said shoes but on that condition. That on enquiry there was no such person lived at the said place nor did he ever receive the said --- --- defrauded of them by Coventry Harbridge -------.
Recognisances 407/18 & 19.
Presentment of the jury 407/13 Endorsed 'No true Bill'.

407/7   Information of Winch Wells of Hitchin, labourer, 27th. November last. *(Who)* Came before me, one of His Majesty's Justices for the Peace, and informed me that Roger Thorn of Hexton in the Liberty, tanner, did keep and use a waggon and had not given notice to the proper officer of keeping and using such waggon and had not paid down the rates and duties imposed by the Act, whereupon the said Roger Thorn, voluntarily confessed the same to be true. I do hereby convict him of the offence and that he have forfeit the sum of £5. *(This item has been considerably edited).*

407/8   Complaint of James Eldridge taken 5th. December 1784. Who on his oath saith he has heard and believes that about the first day of September last, one Joseph Ayre, styling himself John Wainwright, was committed to the common gaol of the said Borough, charged on oath with being at large in Great Britain, after transportation for life, and that he was detained by a detainer for the said offence. And this informant further saith that between the first and twenty ninth of September, whilst the detainer was in force, he

3

has seen Joseph Ayre, otherwise John Wainwright, at large and without the gaoler being with him. And in particular that he has seen Joseph Ayre go by himself from the gaol to the Kings Head alehouse and stay 10 or 15 minutes and come back again by himself to the gaol.
Recognisances 407/15 & 16. See also 408/9.

407/9   Bill of John Sharpless, Keeper of His Majesty's Gaol for the Borough 1783. Including Subsistence of four pence per day per prisoner and fees of 13/4d for each prisoner.
John Wilson committed 28th.Dec.1783 for theft of one silver salt and one silver spoon, the property of Ralph Page. Subsistence for 165 days.
Robert Tanner committed 28th.Dec.1783 for breaking open a chest and stealing £3..0..6. Subsistence for 165 days.
Mary White committed 25th.July 1784 for stealing a piece of curtain and lead. Subsistence for 71 days.
Ann Welch committed 10th.August 1784 for offering to pay bad silver. Subsistence for 41 days.
Joseph Ayre committed September 1784 for returning from transportation. Subsistence for 29 days.

407/10   Presentment of the jury concerning William Major, labourer, on December 20th. feloniously stealing five pieces of silver coin called shillings and six pieces of copper coin called halfpennies, the monies numbered of John Welch.   Endorsed 'No true Bill'.
Recognisances 407/21 & 22.

407/11   Presentment of the jury concerning John Burgess, labourer, on November 29th. feloniously stealing nine oak rafters of the value of 5/-, the goods and chattels of William Wells. Endorsed 'No true Bill'.
Recognisances 407/20.

407/12   Bill of Geo.Whitbread for medicines for Robert Tanner and John Wilson.

407/14   Bill for maintaining prisoners. 15th.Jan.1785. Entries include:-
Sept.29th.1784 received Robert Tanner into custody and   £.. s .. d
remains in prison. Maintaining him one quarter.   1..12.. 6
Sept.29th.1784 received John Wilson into custody,
to be discharged Jan.7th.1785. Maintaining him,
whipping and fees.   2..15..10
Sept.29th.1784 received Joseph Ayre into custody.
Discharged Oct.7th.1784. Fees.   13.. 4
Sept.29th.1784 received Ann Welch into custody.
Discharged Oct.7th.1784. Fees.   13.. 4
Aug.11th.1784 received James Batchelor into custody.
Remains in prison. Maintaining him one quarter.   1..12.. 6

407/17   Recognisance concerning William Agglington, labourer, being required to keep the peace especially towards his wife Rachel.

SESSIONS ROLL 408, Easter 1785 (8th. April)

408/1 Writ proclaiming Quarter Sessions and Gaol Delivery.

408/2 Calendar of prisoners for the Borough Gaol.
Robert Tanner, convicted Jan.15th.1784 for two years, remains in gaol.
James Batchelor, convicted Oct.8th.1784 for six calendar months, remains in gaol.
Ann Agglington, committed Jan.23rd.1785 on the oath of William Archer, with privately stealing out of his shop, one Quartern loaf.
Elizabeth Rush, committed March 21st.1785, charged with stealing a handkerchief from the house of John Kent.

408/3 & 408/4 Lists of jurors for the Grand and Delinquent juries.

408/5 Presentment of the jury concerning Ann Agglington of the Parish of St.Alban, wife of John Agglington, on 23rd. January, feloniously stealing one Quartern loaf of the value of one penny, the goods of William Archer Junior. Endorsed 'A true Bill'.
Recognisances 408/8.

408/6 Presentment of the jury concerning Elizabeth Rush, of the Parish of St.Peter, in the Borough, singlewoman, feloniously stealing two linen handkerchiefs, value of six pence, a pair of worsted stockings of the value of two pence and a pair of drill pockets valued at two pence, the goods of John Kent. Endorsed 'A true Bill'.
Recognisances 408/13.

408/7 February 25th.1785. Information and complaint of Mathew Brickland, breeches maker, who on his oath saith that he is a constable of the Borough and that this day he had a warrant from Lord Chief Justice Mansfield for not appearing and pleading to an indictment in the Court of Kings Bench. And that he, having heard that John Sharpless should say at diverse and sundry times that he would kill the first person that offered to take him with a Judges Warrant and which he, Mathew Brickland, verily believed to be true, thought to in executing the warrant to get a sufficient number of people to prevent him putting the threats in execution and that he, John Hevans a constable and James Deayton a strong man whom they charged to aid and assist, went to the house of John Sharpless in a public house and called for a pint of beer. And that he, Mathew Brickland asked a little boy in the house, where his father was, who replied, "In the stable". He told the boy he would go with him to his father and went together to the stable door of the said John Sharpless, whose wife stood at the stable door and seeing him coming, endeavoured to shut it, but that he run in and immediately told him he was his prisoner and had a warrant against him, or words to that effect. On this John Sharpless took a large stable fork that

5

stood in the stable and this he immediately ---- up, endeavoured with a straight thrust and great strength, to have run it through the said Mathew Bricklands body, and that he verily believes he intended to have done, to have made his escape, as no one was in sight at the time. And that he positively swears that had not James Deayton come to the door in the very critical moment of time, the fork must have run through his body, but for James Deayton catching hold of the end of the fork and it ---- ------ his breast run through his great coat and undercoat.
Recognisances 408/10, 11 & 12.

408/9   Recognisances concerning item 407/8.

408/14 & 15   Recognisances concerning an assault upon John Peele, by William Baker.

408/16 Recognisances concerning James Batchelor being of good behaviour for six months.

SESSIONS ROLL 409, Midsummer 1785   (15th.July)

409/1   Writ proclaiming Quarter Sessions and Gaol Delivery.

409/2   Calendar of prisoners for the Borough Gaol.
Robert Tanner, convicted for two years, remains in gaol.
William Alexander committed 12th.April 1785, charged on the oath of Patrick Kennedy and his own confession, with defrauding Patrick Kennedy of a quantity of buttons, Irish Holland etc.

409/3 & 409/4   Lists of jurors for the Grand and Delinquent juries.

409/5   Calendar of the prisoners for the House of Correction.
Beace McKarlie, committed the 7th.June, charged with returning from her pass as a rogue and vagabond, wandering in the Parish of St.Alban, that not being the place of her settlement.
Joseph Wheeler, one of the poor in the workhouse of the Parish of St.Peter, committed for disorderly behaviour in refusing to work and running away.
John Harding, committed as an incorrigible rogue. Ordered to remain in the House of Correction for twelve months.

409/6   The Information and Complaint of Patrick Kennedy, tailor, 12th.April, 1785. Who saith that yesterday in the forenoon, he discharged a servant named William Alexander for misconduct and that this morning a Mrs.Selby called on him and informed him that William Alexander had been at her husbands house the evening before and asked for a quantity of buttons. These she delivered to him and likewise for some Brown Holland and several other things. That he told Mrs.Selby they were for his master and that Patrick Kennedy immediately on receiving this information, made enquiry concerning him and found that he was gone for Ireland. On which he pursued him and catched him in this Borough and they found on him a quantity of Irish cloth.

409/7 Examination of William Alexander, charged by Patrick Kennedy, April 12th.1785, for going to the house of J.Sealby, mens mercer, and taking up in his name a quantity of buttons, Brown Holland, Irish cloth etc. And saith that he went to the house of J.Sealby, and had in his ----- ------ one dozen and a half of copper buttons and two yards and a half of Irish and three yards of cotton and these they delivered to him, and that he pawned the cotton at a pawn broker in the city for 3/6 and that he sold the buttons to a stranger in Oxford Road for 2/-.
Recognisances 409/9.

409/8 Bill for carpenters work done at the Bridewell.

409/10 Recognisance concerning William Gower the Younger begetting a bastard on the body of Mary Peacock.

409/11 & 12 Recognisances concerning an assault upon James Marston by Mary Thrale.

409/13 & 14 Recognisances concerning an assault by James Topham upon Mathew Brickland, a constable of the Borough.

409/15 Recognisance concerning Richard Tearle being licensed to keep a common inn and alehouse called the Crabtree.

SESSIONS ROLL 410, Michaelmas 1785 (7th.Oct.)

410/1 Writ proclaiming Quarter Sessions and Gaol Delivery.

410/2 Calendar of prisoners for the Borough Gaol.
Robert Tanner, convicted Jan.16th.1784 for two years, remains in gaol.
George White, committed July 16th.1785, bailed out.
Thomas Halmer and William Gregory, Charged on the oath of Richard Mason on suspicion of stealing one silver spoon, the property of a person unknown.
William Brown, bailed out, committed July 28th.1785 for assaulting and beating Charles Brackley.
James Brace, committed August 6th.1785, charged on the oath of Thomas Caulkington and others, with feloniously stealing one linen shirt, his property.
John Smith, committed August 6th.1785, charged on the oath of Levi Curtis and others, with feloniously stealing one linen table cloth.
Thomas Wilowby, bailed out, committed August 20th.1785 for assaulting and beating Thomas Walker.

410/3 Lists of jurors for the Grand and Petty juries.

410/4   Information and Complaint of Edward Poulton, baker, 23rd.July 1785. Who saith that he has looked upon a five gallon cask bound with iron hoops and marked in sundry places with the letters EP, which has been produced and shown to this complainant and the same is his property.

410/5   The Information of William Dalton of the Borough, driver of the coach of Ralph Page, 23rd.July 1785. Who saith that on Monday 18th.July, in the evening, William Marston, baker, came to this informant who was then at the turnpike near the Borough with the coach of Mr.Page, and asked for a cask which was to come by the coach to the said William Marston. And this informant bid him get up and if he had any cask, to take it. And this informant being thus engaged in taking the fare of a passenger did not give that observation as otherwise he should have done, but on speaking to William Marston, he replied it was not his, but as he had got it, would keep it. And this informant further saith that the next morning, he looked into the basket of the coach in which he brought down the casket so taken by William Marston and there did not appear to this informant that any yeast was spilt.
Recognisances 410/22, 23 & 24.
Presentment of the jury 410/19, concerning the theft of a five gallon cask containing yeast to the value of 2/-. Endorsed 'A true Bill'.

410/6   Examination of Mary Tapster, widow, 19th.August 1785. Who saith that on Monday evening last, the 12th.day of August, that this examinant in the evening did see James Brice and John Smith on premises belonging to William Ward of the Borough, innholder, and John Smith had something white tucked in his bosom, and James Brice had in his possession a shirt which he flung away and which was picked up by this examinant and delivered to William Bigg.
Recognisances 410/32 & 33.

410/7   Examination of Thomas Cockington, labourer, 6th.August 1785. Who saith that on monday morning last, ----- ----- had in his possession one shirt, his property, and which has now been produced by William Geffard, one of the constables of the Borough, and this examinant saith the shirt is his property and is marked with the initial letters of his name, TC.

410/8   Examination of William Morris, keeper of the tollgate, August 1785. Who saith that on monday evening last the 12th.August, this examinant, at six in the evening, did see John Smith fling away a table cloth into a hedge in Key Field, whereupon this examinant went to the hedge and took into his possession the table cloth and that same evening delivered it to William Geffard, one of the constables of the Borough.

410/9   Examination of Mary Vaughan, spinster, 6th.August 1785. Who saith that she has now looked upon one linen table cloth produced and shown to her at the time of examination, and she well knows the same which was formerly the property of the late Mrs.Mary Longford, widow deceased, and is marked with the letter L and is now the property of Levi Curtis.

410/10 Examination of William Bigg, 6th.August 1785. Who saith that on Monday last 17th.August, this examinant about six in the evening, did see John Smith take from off a hedge belonging to Levi Curtis, a piece of linen and throw the same again on the hedge and the complainant did pursue and take the said John Smith and did also apprehend James Brice who was an accomplice.
Recognisances 410/30 & 31.
Presentment of the jury 410/20. Endorsed 'A true Bill'.

410/11 Examination of Thomas Walker. This examinant on his oath saith that on Wednesday 19th.October 1785, he saw Joseph Godwin take from the bench at the door of Thomas Ansell, four pattens and put them under his coat and went away with them. And this examinant acquainted Mr.Archer who went after the prisoner and took him in the Red Lion Yard.
Recognisances 410/40.
Presentment of the jury 410/21 concerning the theft of four womens pattens worth 10d. Endorsed 'A true Bill'.

410/12, 13 & 14 Sacrament Certificates of John Osborn, Thomas Kinder and Joseph Gape.

410/15 Presentment of the jury concerning an assault upon Francis Shakespeare by Thomas Everstaffe and William Bunnage, labourers. Endorsed 'No true Bill'.
Recognisances 410/36 & 37.

410/16 Presentment of the jury concerning an assault upon Alice Clarke by Thomas Everstaffe and William Bunnage, labourers. Endorsed 'No true Bill'.
Recognisances 410/36 & 37.

410/17 Presentment of the jury concerning an assault upon Charles Brackney by William Brown. Endorsed 'Assault was done in the Liberty'.
Recognisances 410/25 & 26.

410/18 Presentment of the jury concerning William Bigg and John Fly, labourers, feloniously stealing one fowl valued 6d, the property of John Day. Endorsed 'A true Bill'. 'William Bigg committed to gaol for 7 days.'
Recognisances 410/34 & 35.

410/27 Recognisance concerning the suspicion of George White having stolen a silver spoon.

410/28 & 29 Recognisances concerning an assault and battery on Thomas Walker by James Willouby.

410/38 Recognisance concerning John Munt being licensed to keep a common alehouse, or victualling house, known by the sign of 'The Dog'.

410/39 Recognisance concerning William Higbid being licensed to keep a common alehouse, or victualling house, known by the sign of 'Saint Christopher'.

SESSIONS ROLL 411, Epiphany 1786   (13th.Jan.)

411/1 Writ proclaiming Quarter Sessions and Gaol Delivery.

411/2 Calendar of prisoners for the Borough Gaol.
Robert Tanner, convicted for two years. Remains in Gaol.
Joseph Godwin, committed October 20th.1785 for stealing four patterns, the property of Thomas Ansell.

411/3 & 411/4 Lists of jurors for the Petty and Grand juries.

SESSIONS ROLL 412, Easter 1786   (28th.April)

412/1 Writ proclaiming Quarter Sessions and Gaol Delivery.

412/2 & 412/3 Lists of jurors for the Petty and Grand juries.

412/4 Calendar of prisoners for the Borough Gaol.
William Wheeler, committed 9th.Feb.1786, on the oath of William Kinder with stealing three whips, the property of William and Thomas Kinder.
The said Wm.Wheeler, committed 9th.Feb. on the oath of George East and on his own confession, with stealing one whip, the property of George East.
Joseph Gregory, committed 3rd.April 1786, on the oath of John Knowles and John Staples, with feloniously taking and carrying away a quantity of iron chain from off the posts of the premises of the Revd.Thomas D'Oyly.
(The following entry was crossed out). James Whalley, otherwise Worley, committed 7th.April 1786 for further examination and until discharged by due course of law, charged on the oath of Thomas Asprey with having feloniously assaulted him on the Kings highway and put him in bodily fear of his life.
William Ewington, committed 15th.April 1786 on a charge of defrauding William Chennills of three shillings and six pence.

412/5 The Information and Complaint of William Kinder, common brewer, taken on oath 9th.February 1786. Who saith that on Monday morning last, he missed three waggon whips he provides his servants to drive the difficult teams and that he yesterday, in the evening about 8 o'clock, met William Wheeler the prisoner, with a whip. That this informant stopped him and asked him where he got the whip which was

10

then in his hand. He answered, "On the other side of St.Stephens", but that this informant suspecting the whip to be his property, he took William Wheeler into custody who then confessed that he stole the whip together with two other out of the stables of the said William Kinder, one of which he directed this informant where to find, which he accordingly found, and the other he confessed he sold to a hostler at the Goat Inn.

Presentment of the jury 412/12. Concerning the theft of 3 whips to the value of 1/-. Endorsed 'A true Bill'.

412/6 The Information of George East, servant to Thomas and William Kinder, taken upon oath, 9th.February, 1786. Who saith that on Saturday evening last, he left his whip in the stable of Thomas and William Kinder. That when he went to his work on Monday morning he missed the whip and believes it was stolen from the stable by some person or persons unknown.

The Examination of Thomas Wheeler, servant to William House, of the Parish of Wheathamstead, farmer, who said that on Monday morning last, at about 8 o'clock, William Wheeler, the prisoner, came to this examinant whilst he was at work and offered a whip which is now produced and which whip is claimed by George East as his property for sale and which this examinant bought for eighteen pence.

Recognisances 412/13 & 14.

412/7 The Examination of Moses Warner and John Underwood, two of the servants of Thomas and William Kinder of the said Borough, 9th.February 1786. Moses Warner said that a certain waggon whip now produced and shown to this examinant by William Kinder and which William Kinder says he found in a certain field called Wallnut Tree Field, was the whip which Mr.Kinder furnished him with to drive his team and which was stole and taken away from the stable of William Kinder on Sunday evening or Monday morning last. And John Underwood saith the whip which is now produced and shown to him and which William Kinder says he took from the prisoner William Wheeler, was the whip which William Kinder furnished this examinant with to drive his team and which was stole and taken away from the stable sometime on Sunday evening last.

Recognisances 412/15 & 16.

412/8 The Examination and Confession of William Wheeler, labourer, who saith that on Sunday evening last at about 7 o'clock, he stole and took away from the said stables of Thomas and William Kinder, four waggon whips.

412/9 Information and Complaint of the Revd.Tho.D'Oyly, Clerk of the Borough, 3rd.April 1786. Who on his oath saith on Sunday morn last, he lost a quantity iron chain that was fixed to the posts before his dwelling house in the said Borough.

The Examination of John Knowles, labourer, 3rd.April 1786. Who on his oath saith that Saturday night last between 10 & 11 o'clock he saw two men rattling the chains against the posts of Mr.D'Oyly in St.Peters Street. He hallowed to them and then went to the watchman and told him of them. They both went to the place and the men was gone. They then hid themselves behind a Pollard when one of the men came down Dearmans Lane opposite the house. The man on being asked where he was going said, home to Saundridge. On searching his pockets they found a pair of pinchers and chisel and he afterwards told them the chains were hid behind Mr.Dearmans barn, and that himself (Joseph Gregory) and another man named Taylor, took them from off the posts of Mr.D'Oyly. He went to the place aforesaid and found the said chains.

The Examination of John Staples, watchman of the Borough, 3rd.April 1786. This examinant on his oath saith on Saturday night past, between 10 & 11 o'clock John Knowles came to him as he was standing at the watch-house door in St.Peters Street and told him he saw two men rattling the chains opposite Mr.D'Oylys and that he went with Knowles but the men were gone. That he found a small parcel of chain upon the ground. He said to Knowles, stop, if they are gone away with any they will come back for these. That he stood a few minutes when a man named John Gregory came down Dearmans Lane to the parcel of chains and was stooping down to take them when he laid hold of him and he then informed him of the other parcel of chain which Knowles went and found.
Recognisances 412/17 & 18. (See also 413/10 & 11).
Presentment of the jury 412/11 concerning the theft of chain to the value of 1/-. Endorsed 'A true Bill'. (See also 413/14).

412/10 Presentment of the jury concerning William Ewington obtaining from William Chinnells, three shillings and six pence by false pretences. Endorsed 'A true Bill'.
Recognisances 412/19 & 20.

412/21 to 412/30 inclusive. Bills for sundry expenses including those for:-
The death and burial of Cuthbert More from the Liberty gaol. (412/22)
The death of James Hilsdon in the Borough gaol. (412/24)
Digging a boghouse at the Borough gaol. (412/27)
The Prosecutors costs for the trial at the last Assizes, of John Sharpless, who was to have appeared at the Assizes before. (412/28)
Fees for Joseph Godwin, 6/8, committed for felony and discharged by proclamation. (412/30)

412/31 Expenses incurred by the late John Hall, Clerk of the Peace. Entries mention:-
Concerning the Indictment of John Sharpless.
For the fees of Ann Agglington, convicted of petty larceny.
For the fees of Elizabeth Rush.
Drawing an order that all horse passes be directed to the constable of St.Michaels.
Drawing an order concerning paying rewards for apprentice vagrants.

Drawing an order concerning the committing of several vagrants taken up.
Drawing an order concerning vagrants removed from Middlesex to this Borough.
Drawing an order concerning contractors who shall improperly bring vagrants into this Borough.
Drawing an order concerning expense to the Borough of idle and disorderly people.
Drawing an order that a maximum of 5/- be allowed for apprehending vagrants.
Drawing an order that all apprehended vagrants be kept to hard labour.
For the fees of George White & John Fly, acquitted of felony. For John Smith, convicted of felony. For Thos.Halmer, Wm.Gregory, Jas.Braw, William Bigg & William Marston.
For drawing an order concerning the punishment to be inflicted upon Elizabeth Maccarty, an incorrigible rogue.

SESSIONS ROLL 413, Midsummer 1786 (14th.July)

413/1   Writ proclaiming Quarter Sessions and Gaol Delivery.

413/2   Calendar of prisoners for the Borough Gaol.
Benjamin Tatlock, committed on suspicion of stealing one black silk handkerchief.
Peter Taylor, committed 10th.July 1786, charged with stealing a quantity of iron chain, the property of the Rev.Thomas D'Oyly or Mr.Boradale.

413/3   List of jurors for the Grand and Petty juries.

413/4   Estimate of repairs to be done to the House of Correction belonging to the Liberty. (Mention made of the Day Room over the kitchen).

413/5, 6 & 7   Bills for bricklaying work at the town hall, clothing for prisoners and expenses relating to Elizabeth Dickinson being with child by John Henshaw.

413/8   Bill of fees of the Clerk of the Peace including:-
The fees of James Godwin, Joseph Gregory and Benjamin Tatlock. All discharged by proclamation, 6/8 each.

413/9   Estimate of work to be done at the House of Correction. Mention is made of the Day Room, the room over the gateway and of Mrs.Twitchells bedroom.

413/13   Presentment of the jury concerning the theft by Benjamin Tatlock of a silk handkerchief valued at 4d., the property of Edward Walton. (A corporal in the 65th.Regiment of Foot). Endorsed 'No true Bill'.
Recognisances 413/12.

413/14 Presentment of the jury concerning the theft of iron chain valued at 10d. Endorsed 'Not a true Bill'. (See 412/9).
Recognisances 413/10 & 11.

413/15 Bill for building work at the Liberty Gaol.

SESSIONS ROLL 414, Michaelmas 1786 (6th.Oct.)

414/1 Writ proclaiming Quarter Sessions and Gaol Delivery.

414/2 Lists of jurors for the Grand and Petty juries.

414/3 Bill for carpenters work done at the gaol.

414/4 Presentment of the jury concerning Thomas Birch assaulting William Marston. Endorsed 'No true Bill'.

SESSIONS ROLL 415, Epiphany 1787 (12th.Jan.)

415/1 Writ proclaiming Quarter Sessions and Gaol Delivery.

415/2 Calendar of prisoners for the Borough Gaol. (No prisoners).

415/3 List of jurors for the Grand and Petty juries.

415/4 Report of Justices certifying that :- 'We have viewed the public highway leading from St.Peters Street within the said Borough, through a certain farmyard called Folly Yard, and that the obstruction which was presented at the Court Leet held for the Borough .... is effectually removed and the said highway made safe and convenient.'

SESSIONS ROLL 416, Easter 1787 (20th.April)

416/1 Writ proclaiming Quarter Sessions and Gaol Delivery.

416/2 Calendar of prisoners for the Borough Gaol.
John Lane committed the oath of John Attersoll of the Parish of Shenley, innholder, and his own confession, with stealing out of the dwelling house of John Attersoll, two callico muslin stocks and one linen handkerchief.

416/3 Lists of jurors for the Grand and Petty juries.

416/4 Presentment of the jury concerning John Lane stealing two callico muslin stocks and one linen handkerchief, valued at 10d. Endorsed 'A true Bill, Guilty'.

416/5   Receipt of Thomas White for £3..2..3, paid to Bethlam Hospital for clothing.

416/6   Receipt for 2 weeks and 3 days board and care of Thomas White £1..2..0.

416/7   Bill for clothes for Thomas White. (Written on the back of a printed price list for clothing supplied by Bethlam Hospital).

416/8, 9 & 10   Bills of Richard Huggins, constable of Fishpool Ward, Joseph Pew, constable of St.Peters Ward and Humphry Alansell, constable of Middle Ward.

SESSIONS ROLL 417, Midsummer 1787   (13th.July)

417/1   Writ proclaiming Quarter Sessions and Gaol Delivery.

417/2   Calendar of prisoners in the Gaol of the Borough.
Robert Dean, otherwise Robert Shead, committed for 3 months, charged with having offered himself to serve in the Hertfordshire Militia as a substitute and sworn in the said militia and having on his own confession sworn at Dunstable as a substitute in the Bedfordshire Militia. Remains in Gaol.
Thomas Pratt committed June 10th., charged with stealing a scythe and two hand staves, the property of J.Markham and J.Benning.
Henry Eastwell and Thomas Carter committed on June 20th., charged with stealing sundry fowls.
John Hodges alias Richard Charlton committed 23rd.June on strong suspicion of stealing a black mare, the property of J.Beauchamp.

417/3   Lists of jurors for the Grand and Petty juries.

417/4   Recognisance concerning William Archer of St.Albans, baker. To be of good behaviour especially towards John Lewin.

417/5   Presentment of the jury concerning Thomas Pratt of the Parish of St.Peter, stealing a scythe and two handstones of the value of ten pence, the goods of John Markham. Endorsed 'A true Bill'.

SESSIONS ROLL 418, Michaelmas 1787   (5th.Oct.)

418/1   Writ proclaiming Quarter Sessions and Gaol Delivery.

418/2   Calendar of prisoners for the Borough Gaol. (No prisoners).

418/3   Lists of jurors for the Grand and Petty juries.

418/4   Recognisance of John Henshaw of Northampton, labourer, for having begat a bastard child upon the body of Elizabeth Dickinson, a singlewoman of St.Peters Parish, the said child being chargeable to the parish.

418/5 & 6   Recognisances of William Marston of the Borough, baker, and Thomas Birch of the Borough, basket maker, concerning an assault by Thomas Birch upon William Marston.

418/7 & 8   Recognisances of William Wills of the Parish of Redbourn, leather dresser, and William Long of of the Borough, baker, concerning an assault by William Long upon William Wills.

418/9 & 10   Recognisances of William Spicer of the Borough, labourer, and William Corby of the Borough, whitesmith, concerning an assault and ill treatment by William Corby upon William Spicer.

SESSIONS ROLL 419, Epiphany 1788   (18th.Jan.)

419/1   Writ proclaiming Quarter Sessions and Gaol Delivery.

419/2   Calendar of prisoners in the Borough Gaol. (No prisoners).

419/3   Lists of jurors for the Grand and Petty juries.

419/4   Bill for 4 constables, an assistant and 10 men, sitting up all night for a fowl stealing. £1..3..0.

419/5 & 6   Sacrament Certificates of John Kentish and Thomas Kinder.

419/7   Bill of James Deayton which includes maintenance of Edward Doyle for 21 days, 7/1d.

SESSIONS ROLL 420, Easter 1788   (4th.April)

420/1   Writ proclaiming Quarter Sessions and Gaol Delivery.

420/2   Calendar of prisoners for the Borough Gaol. (No prisoners).

420/3   Lists of jurors for the Grand and Petty juries.

420/4   Bill of Mary Twitchell, 4th.April 1788.
John Pestell committed 21st.February 1788 maintained in the Smallpox a fortnight at 20/- per week.   Total £2.
Keeping John Pestell a fortnight after the Smallpox before he was fit to be moved, at 6/- per week.   Total 12/-.

SESSIONS ROLL 421, Midsummer 1788   (18th.July)

421/1   Writ proclaiming Quarter Sessions and Gaol Delivery.

421/2   Calendar of prisoners for the Borough Gaol.
Henry Chapman charged on the oath of Ann Chapman, his wife, with violently assaulting, beating and bruising her.
James Bibbey committed on the oath of George Fisher, gardener of the said Borough, with feloniously taking and carrying away out of the tool house at Holywell, two scythes and a small snaith, being the property of the Countess Dowager Spencer.

421/3   Lists of jurors for the Grand and Petty juries.

421/4   Presentment of the jury concerning James Bibbey stealing 2 scythes and a snaith of the value of 5/-. Endorsed 'A true Bill'.
Recognisances <u>421/5 & 6</u>.

SESSIONS ROLL 422, Michaelmas 1788   (10th.Oct.)

422/1   Writ proclaiming Quarter Sessions and Gaol Delivery.

422/2   Calendar of prisoners for the Borough Gaol.
Henry Chapman ordered to be confined in the gaol until he shall have entered into a recognisance himself of £20 and two sureties of £10 each. Remains in gaol.

422/3   Lists of jurors for the Grand and Petty juries.

422/4 Bill of James Deayton,	£ .. s .. d
To whipping and discharging James Bibbey.	10 .. 0
To 4 days pay to William Dick, a deserter, but not owned.	2 .. 0
To public whipping of said William Dick.	10 .. 0
To maintenance of Johnathan Wright under an execution from the Court of Requests.	5 .. 0
To maintenance of Johnathan Weedon under an execution from the Court of Requests.	5 .. 0
To 12 weeks maintenance of Henry Chapman at 2/4 per week.	1.. 8 .. 0
To pens, ink and paper.	1 .. 0
To one fire.	2 .. 6
To the fees of Henry Chapman.	<u>13 .. 4</u>
Total	£3.. 16..10

422/5   Sacrament Certificate of William Kinder.

423/1   Writ proclaiming Quarter Sessions and Gaol Delivery.

423/2   Calendar of prisoners for the Borough Gaol.
James Wilson committed on the oath of William Kilby of the Borough, carpenter, for breaking into his workshop with intent to steal.
Richard Ing committed on the oath of John Hewes of St.Albans, chimney sweeper, with stealing several bushels of oats to the value of 10/-, the property of James Proctor of Dunstable.
Thomas Jeffries and Thomas Smith charged on the oath of John Hewes with stealing several bushels of oats to the value of 10/-, the property of Thomas Wilson of London.
John Peters charged on the oath of James Painter of Edgware and Thomas Hewes of St.Albans, chimney sweepers, of receiving certain stolen goods, viz several bushels of oats to the value of 10/-, the property of Thomas Wilson of London and James Proctor of Dunstable in the County of Bedford.

423/3   Lists of jurors for the Grand and Petty juries.

423/4   Information and Complaint of William Kilby of the Parish of St.Alban, carpenter. Who on his oath saith that between the hours of 3 & 4 o'clock in the morning on the 12th.Oct., he was called upon by his servant girl and informed that some men were in the yard belonging to the dwelling house, that he got up and called out of the window but no-one answered. He then came down stairs and went into his shop, which adjoined his dwelling house, with a pistol in his hand and there found the prisoner James Wilson standing in his shop against the working bench. That he the said William Kilby went up to him and took him into custody. That to the recollection and belief he had as he usually did, locked and fastened the door of his shop and he believes that James Wilson had broken into his shop without *(sic)* an intent to steal. *('with intent to steal' in the indictment.)*
Recognisances 423/8 & 9.
Presentment of the jury 423/22. Endorsed 'A true Bill'.

423/5   The Examination of Thomas Smith of the Parish of St.Alban, horsekeeper. The said Thomas Smith being charged on the oath of John Hewes for feloniously stealing several bushels of oats the property of Thomas Wilson of the City of London, of the value of 10/-, denieth that he stole the said goods.

423/6   The Examination of Thomas Jefferys of the Parish of St.Peter in the Borough, horsekeeper. He denieth that he stole the goods.
Presentment of the jury 423/17 concerning both Thomas Smith and Thomas Jefferys. Endorsed 'Not a true Bill'.

423/7   The Examination of Richard Ing of the Parish of St.Alban in the Borough, horsekeeper. He denieth that he stole the goods.

18

Recognisances 423/11 & 12.

Presentment of the jury 423/18 concerning the theft of oats to the value of 5/- by Richard Ing. Endorsed 'No true Bill'.

Presentment of the jury 423/19 concerning the theft of oats to the value of 5/- by John Peters Endorsed 'No true Bill'.

423/10 Recognisance of John Breech jun.& John Breech sen., both of the Borough, peruke makers, concerning John Breech jun. begetting a bastard on Ann Veasy of St.Michaels.

423/20 Presentment of the jury concerning John James preferring a bill of indictment against Jane, wife of Richard Turner, for an assault. Endorsed 'A true Bill. Pleaded guilty, fined 6d'.
Recognisances 423/15 & 16.

423/21 Presentment of the jury concerning Thomas Everstaff preferring a bill of indictment against James Cummins for an assault. Endorsed 'A true Bill. Guilty, fined 4d'.
Recognisances 423/13 & 14.

423/23 Expenses of William Kilby. 16s..6d.

SESSIONS ROLL 424, Easter 1789   (24th.Apr.)

424/1 Writ proclaiming Quarter Sessions and Gaol Delivery.

424/2 Calendar of prisoners for the Borough Gaol. (No prisoners).

424/3 Lists of jurors for the Grand and Petty juries.

424/4 Bill of Mary Twitchell.
To privately whipping of Thomas Saveall.   5s..0d.

424/5 Borough of St.Albans to the Churchwardens and Overseers of the Poor of the Parish of St.Michael in the Borough and the Churchwardens and Overseers of the Poor of the Parish of Flamstead. Whereas complaint has been made to us by the Churchwardens and Overseers of the Poor of the Parish of St.Michael that Francis Hudnal, Sarah his wife and Mary their daughter aged 6 years have lately intruded and come into the said Parish of St.Michael and are likely to become chargeable to the same workhouse. Said Justices do ajudge the same to be true and that the place of the last legal settlement of Francis Hudnal etc. to be the Parish of Flamstead. The Churchwardens and Overseers of the Poor of St.Michaels are instructed to remove Francis Hudnal etc. to the Parish of Flamstead.

424/6 To the Churchwardens and Overseers of the Poor of the Parish of St.Michael in the Borough. This is to give notice that we the

Churchwardens and Overseers of the Poor of the Parish of Flamstead do intend at the next Quarter Sessions of the Peace to be held in St.Albans to appeal against an order of removal concerning the removal of Francis Hudnal, Sarah his wife and Mary their daughter from your Parish of St.Michael to our Parish of Flamstead.

424/7 The examination of Sarah Hudnall the wife of Francis Hudnall, who on her oath saith that she hath heard her husband declare that he was born in the Parish of Flamstead in the County of Hertford. Mary the daughter, aged 6.

SESSIONS ROLL 425, Midsummer 1789 (17th.July)

425/1 Writ proclaiming Quarter Sessions and Gaol Delivery.

425/2 Calendar of prisoners for the Borough Gaol. (No prisoners).

425/3 Lists of jurors for the Grand and Petty juries.

425/6 Presentment of the jury concerning an assault upon John Lewin by William Archer. Endorsed 'Not a true Bill'.
Recognisances 425/4 & 5.

SESSIONS ROLL 426, Michaelmas 1789 (9th.Oct.)

426/1 Writ proclaiming Quarter Sessions and Gaol Delivery.

426/2 Calendar of prisoners for the Borough Gaol. (No prisoners).

426/3 Lists of jurors for the Grand and Petty juries.

426/4 Sacrament Certificate of John Harrison Esq.

SESSIONS ROLL 427, Epiphany 1790 (15th.Jan.)

427/1 Writ proclaiming Quarter Sessions and Gaol Delivery.

427/2 Calendar of prisoners for the Borough Gaol.
Job Cox committed for stealing a bay mare, the property of Peter Harvey of Birmingham. Ordered to be removed from the gaol of this Borough to the gaol in Hertford in order to take his trial at the next Assizes.

427/3 List of jurors for the Grand and Petty juries.

427/4 Sacrament Certificate of Thomas Allen.

427/5 & 6   Recognisances concerning an assault upon John Platt, labourer, by Richard Turner who is meanwhile required to keep the peace.

427/7   Bill of James Deayton. Including:-

		s .. d
To the maintenance of George Theobald under an execution from the Court of Request.		5 .. 0
To pens, ink and paper.		1 .. 0
Two fires for the day.		5 .. 0
To fire and candles at the examination of Job & Richd.Cox.		2 .. 6
To removing Richard Cox to Warwick Gaol.	£4..	0 .. 0
To the fees of Richard Cox.		13 .. 4
To the maintenance of Charles Ward on suspicion of stealing a silver teaspoon.		1 .. 0
The maintenance of Wm.Jeffard under an execution from the Court of Requests.		5 .. 0
The fees of Job Cox.		13 .. 4

SESSIONS ROLL 428, Easter 1790   (16th. April)

428/1   Writ proclaiming Quarter Sessions and Gaol Delivery.

428/2   Calendar of prisoners for the Borough Gaol.
Elizabeth Stevens committed on the oath of Ann Potton with stealing her check apron.

428/3   Lists of jurors for the Grand and Petty juries.

428/4   Note.   Committed, John Scanlon, a deserter, discharged.
Committed, Mary McQuire and Ann her child, discharged
Committed, Henry Kelly for one calendar month.

428/5   Information and Complaint of Ann Potton of the Borough, spinster, Who on her oath saith that she lost a check apron which she had hung upon the bar door of her masters house at the Boot ---- in the Borough. And this informant further saith, one Elizabeth Stevens, a woman who had arranged to call soon after she had hung up the apron, came into the house soon after which she missed her apron and further saith that Elizabeth Stevens this day came to her masters house with the apron tied around her and from the above circumstances this informant verily believes Elizabeth Stevens stole the apron.

428/6   Examination of Elizabeth Stevens who saith that she bought it off a woman she ---- ---- ----met near the Market Place and paid 9d. for it at least 3 weeks ago, but she did not know the said woman of whom she bought it and five ---- -----.
Recognisances 428/12.
Presentment of the jury 428/8 concerning the theft of an apron valued at 10d. Endorsed 'No true Bill'.

428/7   The several Examinations of Thomas Pearce and William Brown. Thomas Pearce saith that he is a watchman in the Borough and was attending his duty between 12 and 1 o'clock this morning. He observed several persons standing in the street making a noise and disturbance at the back part of The Crown ground. That he went up to them to see who they were and asked them what they wanted and requested them to go about their business, when Joseph Beech came up to him and knocked him down and repeated his blows so as to knock him down three times. That he took this examinants staff out of his hands and broke it and threatened to murder him and the other watchman too, if he was further interrupted.

The examinant William Brown saith that he is a watchman and, attending his duty as such, was by the above named Thomas Pearce, informed of a disturbance near the Crown. That he went with Thomas Pearce to the place aforesaid and enquired into the cause of the disturbance, wherein Joseph Beech came up to him and swore several oaths and then struck him and knocked him down several times and kicked him whilst on the ground very violently on the ribs and side.

Recognisances 428/13 & 428/14.

Presentment of the jury 428/11 concerning an assault upon Thomas Pearce. Endorsed 'A true Bill, guilty'.

Presentment of the jury 428/10 concerning an assault upon William Brown. Endorsed 'No true Bill'.

428/9 Bill of James Deayton. Including:-	£ .. s .. d
To the maintenance of Job Cox, 46 days.	15 .. 4
Moving Job Cox to Hertford.	12 .. 0
Going to London after James Manley, self & horse, two days.	1 .. 1 .. 0
To the fees of James Chester and Ann Chester.	1 .. 6 .. 8
Removing James Chester and Ann Chester to Hertford.	1 .. 4 .. 0
To fees of Elizabeth Stevens.	13 .. 4

SESSIONS ROLL 429, Midsummer 1790   (16th.July)

429/1   Writ proclaiming Quarter Sessions and Gaol Delivery.

429/2   Calendar of prisoners for the Borough Gaol.
Burton Woodward, bailed out, committed by the oath of Jabez Hirons, Johnathan Boys and Joseph Reay for forging a certain paper writing, purporting to be the certificate of the age of Joseph Reay and uttering the same knowing it to be forged with the intent to defraud the Mayor, Aldermen and Burgesses of the Borough of St.Alban.

429/3   Lists of jurors for the Grand and Petty juries.

429/4   The Examination of Joseph Reay, who saith that he is the only son of Thomas Reay, late of the Borough, staymaker and Freeman of the Borough, deceased. That last summer being informed by Burton Woodward, cordwainer, that he was entitled to his freedom by virtue of his fathers copy and that Burton Woodward promised to get him his freedom for which he, Burton Woodward, applied to the Rev.Mr.Jabez Hirons for a certificate of baptism and that Burton Woodward did give this desponent a certain paper writing, purporting to be a certificate of his baptism to be produced to the court of Mayor and Aldermen. And this deponent further saith that he did immediately after receiving the paper, present the same to the court in the same state as that in which he had received it and he does not know nor is privy to an alteration that appears to be made in the date of the paper writing.

429/5 Examination of the Revd.Jabez Hirons and John Boys, gentlemen. Jabez Hirons for himself saith that he did make out a certificate and did deliver the same to the said Burton Woodward which said certificate being now produced further saith that since the certificate was so made out, the same appears to be altered by an erasure made in two of the ---- the same being made out by this deponent to the best of his knowledge and belief in the figures of his '1770' and that it now appears to bear the date 1768 and this deponent further saith that the said paper writing or certificate being this day brought to him for the purpose of ascertaining whether he had wrote the figures 68 or not, he did thereunder write 1770 by way of rectifying what he deemed a mistake being desired so to do by Richard Mason.
And this deponent John Boyes saith that he was this day present at the court of the Mayor and Aldermen when Joseph Reay produced a certain paper writing purporting to be a certificate of his age for the purpose of obtaining his freedom, which said paper writing appears to be altered in the date. Recognisances 429/6.

429/7 Declaration dated 16th.June 1790. I John Harrison Esquire Mayor of the Borough of Saint Alban in the County of Hertford Do solemnly swear that I have not directly nor indirectly received any sum or sums of money Office Place or Employment Gratuity or Reward or any Bond Bill or Note or any Promise of Gratuity whatsoever either by my self or any other person to my use or Benefit or Advantage for making any Return at the present Election of Members to serve in Parliament And that I will return such Person or Persons as shall to the Best of my Judgment appear to me to have the Majority of Legal Votes.

429/8 James Smith to Churchwardens and Overseers of the Poor of the Parish of St.Michael in the Borough. Notice of appeal against the rate assessment made for the relief of the Poor 'as assessed and rated at more money than ought to be for the Messuage and Premises which I hold'. And requiring the records for the past 20 years to be produced at the Quarter Sessions.

SESSIONS ROLL 430, Michaelmas 1790   (8th.Oct.)

430/1 Writ proclaiming Quarter Sessions and Gaol Delivery.

430/2   Lists of jurors for the Grand and Petty juries.

SESSIONS ROLL 431, Epiphany 1791 (14th.Jan.)

431/1   Writ proclaiming Quarter Sessions and Gaol Delivery.

431/2   Calendar of prisoners for the Borough (No prisoners) and lists of jurors for the Grand and Petty juries.

431/3   Recognisances concerning Joseph Beech appearing at the next Quarter Sessions and until then to be of good behaviour.

431/4   Recognisances concerning Abraham Milemore, sawyer, appearing to answer for begetting a child on the body of Elizabeth Bigg.

431/5   Recognisances concerning Samuel White appearing at the next Quarter Sessions and until then to be of good behaviour.

SESSIONS ROLL 432, Easter 1791 (6th.May)

432/1   Writ proclaiming Quarter Sessions and Gaol Delivery.

432/2   Calendar of prisoners for the Borough Gaol.
George Day committed for want of proper securities, he having a bastard child sworn to him by Elizabeth Downing of the Parish of St.Michael, a singlewoman.

432/3   List of jurors for the Grand and Petty juries.

432/4, 5 & 6   Recognisances concerning James King answering an indictment for taking 23 bushels of coals.

SESSIONS ROLL 433, Midsummer 1791 (15th.July)

433/1   Writ proclaiming Quarter Sessions and Gaol Delivery.

433/2   Calendar of prisoners for the Borough (No prisoners) and lists of jurors for the Grand and Petty juries.

433/3   Order concerning Abraham Milemore begetting a bastard child upon the body of Elizabeth Bigg, the said child being a female and likely to become chargeable to the Parish of St.Peter. Ordered that Abraham Milemore pay 40/- towards the lying in and 1/6d.weekly maintenance. Further, that Elizabeth Bigg shall pay 1/- weekly unless she takes care of the child herself.

SESSIONS ROLL 434, Michaelmas 1791   (7th.Oct.)

434/1   Writ proclaiming Quarter Sessions and Gaol Delivery.

434/2   Calendar of prisoners for the Borough Gaol.
Jeremiah Puddephatt committed on the oath of George Kippings for having assaulted him and refusing to find sureties for his appearance in the next general Quarter Sessions. Similarly for his assault upon John Breech.

434/3   List of jurors for the Grand and Petty juries.

434/6   Presentment of the jury concerning Samuel Wildbore assaulting Jane Stocks, daughter of James Stocks.   Endorsed 'A true Bill, guilty'. Recognisances 434/4 & 5.

SESSIONS ROLL 435, Epiphany 1792

435/1   Calendar of prisoners in the Gaol of the Borough. Jan.13th.
Henry Spleving committed Dec.1st.1791 by Johnathan Osborn charged on the oath of James Palin and others of the Borough with stealing one shirt of the value of 4/- the property of James Palin.

435/2   Lists of jurors for the Grand and Petty juries.

435/3 & 4 Recognisances concerning Christopher Poutney answering a bill of indictment presented by Samuel Corfield for an assault.

435/7   Information of witnesses severally taken and acknowledged on behalf of Our Sovereign Lord the King, touching the death of Thomas Humbley at the dwelling house of Thomas Norris known by the sign of the Black Lion in the Parish of St.Michael in the said Borough before me John Boys, Gentleman Coroner, on an inquisition then and there taken on the view of the body then and there lying dead as follows. William Brown of the Borough, shoemaker, on his oath deposeth and saith that on the 5th. day of January 1792, between the hours of 9 and 10 in the morning, he was coming out of his house into the street. That just as he was coming out he heard a drum beat belonging to some soldiers who were coming by the corner of Mr.Smiths Wall. That he at the same time saw Adams's waggon coming down the town. That the horses seemed frightened. That the deceased ran and caught hold of the fore horse with one hand holding the other up endeavouring to stop the horses. As the drum came opposite them, the horses came towards the rails and rubbed the deceased against them so as to oblige him to quit his hold. The chains or some part of the tackle then caught hold of him and nearly pulled him down. Whereupon the deceased tried to catch hold of the rails. He then fell down and the horses went over him and likewise both the near wheels of the waggon went over his head by which he was instantly killed. That the drum was beating all the time and the party of soldiers had not fairly cleared the waggon when the wheels were going over the body of the deceased. That this witness called out "The man is killed you rascals". That when he so called out he was at his own door and the party of soldiers opposite to him in the street about 12 or 14 yards. That they made no reply, but proceeded on. That several other persons screamed out as well as this witness. That he went to the spot and saw the deceased lying dead with his head smashed to pieces and his brains lying near a yard from the body. That the noise of the drum before the waggon frightened the horses and was the cause of the accident. That he thinks the Sergeant must have seen the horses running away and also the danger the deceased was in before the accident, the street being very narrow and not above 12 yards wide.

435/8 Thomas Wimbush, mealman, on his oath deposeth and saith that .... coming out of Mr.Bourns to see the recruiting party come by He saw a waggon opposite Mr.Wellinghams coming full trot down the town with the deceased endeavouring to stop the horses. The third and forth horses went over him and likewise both the wheels of the waggon on the near side went over his head. The waggon passed this witness and he endeavoured to stop it. The party when he first saw them were in the middle of the road. They gave way to the horses in some degree, but not so much as they might have done. They were nearly opposite the fore wheels of the waggon when the accident happened, but they neither desisted drumming nor did they take in their colours or take any notice of the matter except that one of the recruits in a brown coat stopped or was going to stop and the one behind pushed him forward. That this witness is certain the recruit must have seen the deceased killed. There was a great confusion of cries at the moment the accident happened and the witness is positive that the recruit saw the man lay dead in the road after the waggon had gone over him as well as the one who was behind him.

Joseph Kentish, labourer, on his oath saith that as he stood at Mr.Perrots mill door, he heard the noise of the drum and saw the party of recruits go by the fore horses. That he saw the deceased between the horses and the rails and that he fell. The drum and colours frightened the horses, but he was at some distance when the accident happened.

Thomas Gregory, labourer, on his oath deposeth and saith, that yesterday he saw a drum and flag belonging to a recruiting party coming along by the corner of Mr.Smiths. That it was a blue flag with different colours on it. That he saw the deceased then about the Angel Inn lower gate endeavouring to stop the horses which were frightened by the drum and flag. When the deceased was opposite Mr.Browns House he held up his hand and said something which this witness could not hear owing to the noise of the drum. As they came on the horses went faster. The deceased tumbled down from the fore horse and got up again and caught hold of the body horses chains. They threw him down against the rails. He tumbled down twice and as he tumbled a second time he fell with his head exactly under the fore wheel which went over his head and killed him on the spot. The drummer did not desist the whole time and this witness is certain the party saw the deceased killed. That one of them turned back and laughed. That none of them stopped. That he was very near the deceased when he ran and stopped the horses.

435/9   Mary the wife of George Deacon, labourer, on her oath deposeth and saith that she was standing at her own street door in St.Michaels in the said Borough. That she saw a party of soldiers coming up the town. That the soldiers were in the High Road, but on the opposite side to her when she first saw them. They had a flag flying and a drum beating. That a waggon was coming down the town. That the soldiers came on the other side the road and fronted the horses as they were coming along. The horses were much frightened and drove the deceased up against the rails. That he fell back under the near wheel and was instantly killed. Both near wheels went over his head and arm. That the party as near as she can recollect was as far as Mr.Marstons when the waggon went over the body. That the party consisted of about four or five or most likely more. They were near together following each other up the street in single rank. That the party were as near as she can recollect about 12 or 14 yards past the waggon at the instant the wheel was going over the body, but she cannot say positively as it might be something more or perhaps less. That the party drum continued beating without stopping. That they certainly were past the waggon when the accident happened.

William Skelton, private in the Royal -----on his oath saith that he, in company with the rest of his party, came into St.Albans. That they spread their colours on coming into St.Albans from Redbourn about the smith shop in St.Michaels. They came over the bricked bridge with drum beating and colours flying. That they kept the horse path. That. when they came about the Black Lion this witness first saw a waggon coming down the road meeting the party. That when he first saw the waggon the horses did not seem frightened. They were at the distance of the Angel. The party consisted of one sergeant, one drummer, three privates, one corporal and three recruits. They kept about three paces distant from each other. The sergeant first, then the drummer. The witness was the last but one. That they passed the waggon in single file. That after the sergeant saw the waggon, he gave way and came into the footpath as near the houses as possible. This witness in his rank came into the footpath about the Black Lion. That this witness in his rank was about the centre of waggon at the instant the wheel went over the deceased. That his sergeant was nigh upon thirty or forty yards before him at the moment the accident happened. This witness will not pretend to say that there was or was not any outcry at the time the accident happened. He did not see that his sergeant turned his head. He did not quit his rank because he deemed it contrary to orders. Cannot say whether the drum stopped. The colours were not taken in. That he saw the wheel go over the deceased's head, but did not say anything to his sergeant about it.

435/10   An inquisition indented taken for our Sovereign Lord the King ....to enquire for our said Lord the King when where how and in what

manner Thomas Humbley came to his death........upon their oath say that
the said Thomas Humbley on the 5th. day of January being carefully
driving of a waggon drawn by eight horses. It so happened that the horses
took fright by the beating of a drum and the flying of a flag belonging to a
certain recruiting party. Thomas Humbley in endeavouring to stop the
horses was thrown down and the near wheels of the waggon accidentally
casually and by misfortune went over the head of Thomas Humbley whereby
he was instantly crushed to death. And that the said accident happened
through the inhumanity of the Sergeant commanding the said recruiting
party at that time. That the two near wheels of the waggon were moving to
the death of the said Thomas Humbley and are of the value of one shilling
and the property and in the possession of John Adams of Daventry in the
county of Northampton, carrier.

435/11 The Examination of James Pallin, labourer and William Smith,
victualler, who on their oath saith that a shirt marked IP3 the property of
this examinant James Pallin was taken away by some person or persons
unknown from the hostelry belonging to the Woolpack Inn and this
examinant further saith that the shirt now shown to him found in the
possession of one Henry Splevings is the same shirt which he lost. And
that this examinant William Smith saith that a person who says his name is
Henry Spleving came to his house at the Lamb in the Borough about 8
o'clock last night and offered the aforesaid shirt for sale, telling him he
brought the same from Baldock.
Recognisances 435/5 & 6.
Presentment of the jury 435/12. Endorsed 'A true Bill'.

435/13 Be it remembered that a retail dealer in gloves was convicted
before me John Osborn Esq. residing near the place where the offence
hereafter mentioned was committed. That Samuel Farren did lend utter and
sell to one Thomas Treeyern one pair of leather mittens exceeding the value
of 1/4d., and subject to the stamp duty of 3d., without a stamp ticket
contrary to the statute. And I do declare and ajudge that Samuel Farren hath
forfeit the sum of £10 for the offence and also the sum of 4/6 for costs.

SESSIONS ROLL 436, Easter 1792   (20th.April)

436/1   Writ proclaiming Quarter Sessions and Gaol Delivery.

436/2   Calendar of prisoners for the Borough Gaol.
William Sloper committed on the oath of James Perceval with assaulting
him and cutting the nose of the said James Perceval with a stone mug.
Richard Kible committed on the oath of Richard Leonard Kent with
obtaining three ells of Dowlas and sundry other goods the property of
William Lawson, draper, under false pretences.

436/3   List of jurors for the Grand and Petty juries.

436/4 & 5   Recognisances concerning James Perceval appearing to prefer a bill of indictment against William Sloper for an assault.

436/6   Recognisances concerning William Day begetting two female bastards upon the body of Ann Hicks.

436/9   Information and Complaint of Mr.Lawson, draper, who saith on affirmation that this afternoon Richard Kible came to his shop with a written paper purporting to be the handwriting of Christopher Poutney, and did fraudulently obtain three ells of dowlas, a remnant of woollen cloth, a handkerchief, buttons and thread to the amount of 17/11d. the property of said Mr.Lawson.

436/10   Information of Richard Leonard Kent who saith on oath that Richard Kible did come to his masters shop, Mr.William Lawson, a linen draper, under a false pretence to obtain certain goods, to wit three ells of doulas, one pocket handkerchief, one pair of hose, three quarters of a yard of woollen cloth, three yards and a quarter of printed cotton and sundry other goods valued 17/11d. and produced a paper purporting to be an undertaking from one Poutney to be answerable for the said goods by means of which false pretences he did obtain from the said William Lawson the aforesaid goods with intent to cheat and defraud him.
Recognisances 436/7 & 8.
Presentment of the jury 436/13. Endorsed 'A true Bill'.

436/11   List and values of items taken by Kibble. Total value 17/-.

436/12   Note presented by Kibble.
'Please to lett the barer hereof to have the things. I will be answerable.
                                                                      J.Poutney'.

436/14   Certificate of Conviction. James Bryant convicted of stealing a dog, the property of Samuel Gold of the Borough, grocer.

436/15   Bill of Clerk of the Peace, Easter Sessions 1791 to Epiphany 1792. Total £6..17..0.

SESSIONS ROLL 437, Midsummer 1792   (19th.July)

437/1   Writ proclaiming Quarter Sessions and Gaol delivery.

437/2   Calendar of prisoners for the Borough Gaol. (No prisoners).

437/3   List of jurors for the Grand and Petty juries.

SESSIONS ROLL 438, Michaelmas 1792   (5th.Oct.)

438/1   Writ proclaiming Quarter Sessions and Gaol Delivery.

438/2   Calendar of prisoners for the Borough Gaol.
William Smith committed. To keep the peace towards Phoebe his wife and whereas he the said William Smith hath refused to find sureties.

438/3   List of jurors for the Grand and Petty juries.

SESSIONS ROLL 439, Epiphany 1793   (18th.Jan.)

439/1   Writ proclaiming Quarter Sessions and Gaol Delivery.

439/2   Calendar of prisoners in the Gaol of the Borough.

439/3   List of jurors for the Grand and Petty juries.

439/4   Information and Complaint of Thomas Piggott of the Parish of St.Alban. 22nd.Oct. Who on oath saith on the 21st.Sept. last This informant lost from his dwelling house a silver pint mug and doth suspect that the mug is concealed in the dwelling house of John Peele blacksmith. This informant therefore prayeth a search warrant.
Recognisances 439/6 & 7.
Presentment of the jury 439/15 concerning a silver pint mug worth 40/-.
Endorsed 'A true Bill'.

439/5   The Examination and Complaint of May the wife of Gazely Munn of the Parish of St.Michael 27th.Oct. Who on oath saith Ann the wife of Thomas Munn did this day assault her.
Recognisances 439/8 & 9.
Presentment of the jury 439/16.   Endorsed ' A true Bill'.

439/12 & 13 Recognisances. Concerning John Oxton appearing to prefer a bill of indictment against Thomas Piggott for an assault.

439/14 Recognisances. Concerning William Day appearing to answer what is objected to him by John Day for breaking the peace.

439/17 The jurors present Thomas Evestaff for assault upon John Wilkes.
Endorsed 'A true Bill'.
Recognisances 439/10 & 11.

SESSIONS ROLL 440 Easter 1793   (12th.April)

440/1   Writ proclaiming Quarter Sessions and Gaol Delivery.

Note on reverse. John Cowper Gent., Thos Smith, George Honor. 'A true Bill'.

440/2 Calendar of prisoners for the Borough Gaol. (No prisoners).

440/3 List of jurors for the Grand and Petty juries.

440/4 Examination of Ann Hicks, 20th.April, who 13 months before gave birth to twin bastard girls, christened by the parish, Ann and Mary, fathered by William Day, who is ordered to pay 40 shillings for the lying-in, the sum of £4..8..0 for their support and weekly 4 shillings for their maintenance as long as both the children are chargeable to the parish, and a weekly sum of 2 shillings when only one is chargeable to the parish. Ann Hicks charged with paying 2 shillings weekly for both the bastards and one shilling when only one is chargeable to the parish. Since 10th.July, no payment has been made of any kind by Wm.Day, (butcher).

440/5 Bill of the Clerk of the Peace. Entries Include:-	s .. d
Fee for one prisoner committed to jail.	6 .. 8
Fee for one prisoner discharged by proclamation.	6 .. 8

440/6 Presentment of the jury concerning an assault by Peter Henry Jones upon Richard Mason. Endorsed 'A true Bill. Pleaded Guilty'. Recognisance 440/9. Recognisance for counter claim 440/8.

440/7 Coroners bill. Entries include:-	£ .. s.. d
Warrant for summoning a jury for the purpose of taking an inquisition on the body of Thos.Humbley.	2.. 6
Inquisition.	6.. 8
Coroners fee.	13.. 4
Jury.	12.. 0
Bailiff.	5.. 0
The like fees for the taking an inquisition on the body of Richd. Hodges, a vagrant, who died in the House of Correction.	2 .. 2.. 0
The like for taking an inquisition on the body of a boy killed in London Colney.	2 .. 2.. 0

SESSIONS ROLL 441, Midsummer 1793 (19th.July)

441/1 Writ proclaiming Quarter Sessions and Gaol Delivery.

441/2 Calendar of prisoners for the Borough Gaol.
John Perriam, committed on the oath of Fredrick William Buller Esq. on suspicion of having violently assaulted him and David Ogilvy Esq., on the highway near Stoney Stratford, with intent to rob them.

441/3 List of Jurors for the Grand and Petty juries.

441/4   The Complaint of Edward Ellis who on his oath saith that William Marston did assault this informant by taking him by the collar and shaking him against the Peace.
Recognisances 441/6 & 7.
Presentment of the jury 441/11. Endorsed 'No true Bill'.

441/5   Examination of Jenny Huggins, widow, delivered of a male bastard on 16th.April, the father being Richard Edgar.
Recognisances 441/8.

441/12   Presentment of the jury concerning 'A violent assault and battery' by Edward Ellis upon William Marston. Endorsed 'No true Bill'.
Recognisances 441/9 & 10.

441/13   Bill of payment to James Deayton gaoler. Entries include:-
To the fees of John Perriam.   13s..4d

SESSIONS ROLL 442.   Michaelmas 1793   (11th.Oct.)

442/1   Writ proclaiming Quarter Sessions and Gaol Delivery.

442/2   Calendar of prisoners in the Gaol of the Borough.
James Gore, committed August 3rd. upon the oath of Wm.Tompson, that he was assaulted.

442/3   List of jurors for the Grand and Petty juries.

442/4 & 5   Recognisances concerning an assault upon William Tompson by James Gore.

442/6   Recognisances concerning Samuel Parrott being required to answer a bill of indictment preferred by William Smith, apprentice, for certain neglects in instructing in his trade, not supplying proper food and necessaries.

442/7   Presentment of the jury concerning John Stevens, hairdresser, now constable. Mary Field was assaulted by Wm.Day, butcher, and a warrant for this was delivered to John Stevens who 'unlawfully and contemptuously did neglect and refuse to execute the said warrant according to law should and ought to have done to the great hindrance of justice to the evil example of all others.......'
Endorsed 'A true Bill'.

442/8   Bill of payment to James Deayton.   s .. d
Two fires for the day.   5 .. 0
Pens, ink and paper.   1 .. 0
To the fees of John Perriam.   13 .. 4
41 days subsistence to

| John Perriam @ 4d.per day. | £1.. 13 .. 8 |
| Removal of John Perriam to Aylesbury. | £1.. 3 .. 0 |

442/9   Bill of payment to J.Boys - King against Stevens.

Taking instruction for a prosecution ag't the defend't	s .. d
for disobeying a warrant of one of the magistrates of	
this Borough.	6 .. 0
To Mr.Aspinasse drawing the indictment.	£1.. 1 .. 0
Attending the sessions when defend't pleaded guilty.	13 .. 0
Paid Clerk of the Peace.	13 .. 0

SESSIONS ROLL 443, Epiphany 1794   (17th.Jan.)

443/1   Writ proclaiming Quarter Sessions and Gaol Delivery.

443/2   Calendar of prisoners for the Borough Gaol. (None)

443/3   List of jurors for the Grand and Petty juries.

443/4   Recognisance requiring that Thomas Clark shall keep the peace and be of good behaviour towards Thomas Lewis, yeoman, for six months.

443/5   Recognisance requiring J.Osborn to answer a bill of indictment preferred by John Ray, for assault.

SESSIONS ROLL 444, Easter 1794   (2nd.May)

444/1   Writ proclaiming Quarter Sessions and Gaol Delivery.

444/2   Calendar of prisoners for the Borough Gaol. (No prisoners).

444/3   List of jurors for the Grand and Petty juries.

444/4   Committed.
Three female vagabonds for 7 days and one for 5 days. Two male paupers committed for one month. *(Names and dates given)*.

444/5   Bill of Clerk of the Peace. Easter 1793 - Epiphany 1794.

444/6   Payment to James Deayton. Entries include:-
| To the fees of James Oddey for horse stealing. | 13..4d |
| To conveying James Oddey to Hertford. | 12..0d |

444/7, 8 & 9   Bills of John Stevens Constable of Middle Ward, James Cole Constable of Holywell Ward and Samuel Parrott Constable of Fishpool Ward.

SESSIONS ROLL 445, Midsummer 1794   (18th.July)

445/1   Writ proclaiming Quarter Sessions and Gaol Delivery.

445/2   Calendar of prisoners for the Borough Gaol. (No prisoners).

445/3   List of jurors for the Grand and Petty juries.

445/4 & 445/5 Recognisances concerning John Bradshaw answering a bill of indictment preferred by John Bush for assault. And John Bush answering a bill of indictment preferred by John Bradshaw for assault.

445/8   Presentment of the jurors concerning Christopher Poutney answering a bill of indictment preferred by William Marston for assault. Endorsed 'No true Bill'.
Recognisances 445/6 & 7.

445/9   Bill of James Deayton. Main entry:-
George Dawson and John Maxwell being two deserters, committed.
20 days subsistence, but not being owned, to be discharged. £1 .. 0 .. 0

SESSIONS ROLL 446, Michaelmas 1794   (10th.Oct.)

446/1   Writ proclaiming Quarter Sessions and Gaol Delivery.

446/2   Calendar of prisoners for the Borough Gaol.
Jane Lloyd, committed on the oath of William Nelson Lucas on suspicion of stealing one linen clout, his property. (Bailed out).
Ann Rodd, committed on the oath of Martha Kilby, for stealing a tablecloth and a Bible of the value of five shillings, the property of Jeremiah Kilby.

446/3   List of jurors for the Grand and Petty juries.

446/4   Sacrament Certificate of John Kentish.

446/8   Presentment of the jury concerning Jane Pales (late Jane Lloyd) wife of William Pales, of the parish of Aldenham, with force and arms in the parish of St.Albans, stealing one piece of linen cloth called a clout, the value of 10 pence-the property of William Nelson Lucas.   Endorsed 'No Bill'.
Recognisances 446/5 (Bail note) & 446/6.

446/9   Presentment of the jury concerning Ann Rodd, wife of Samuel Rodd, with force and arms feloniously stealing one linen tablecloth, value 6 pence, one book called The Bible, value 4 pence, the goods of Jeremiah Kilby.   Endorsed 'A true Bill'.
Recognisances 446/7.

446/10 Bill of Joseph Kilby.
                                            s .. d

	s .. d
Bill of Joseph Kilby.	
Paid the constables for taking Ann Rodd	1 .. 6
Paid in court	2 .. 4
Loss of time	2 .. 6

446/11 Account of Mary Twitchell.
To maintaining two vagrants, being unable to work from July 26th.to Aug.2nd. Being one week at 2/4d pr.week.   4 .. 8d

SESSIONS ROLL 447, Epiphany 1795   (16th.Jan.)

447/1 Writ proclaiming Quarter Sessions and Gaol Delivery.

447/2 Calendar of prisoners for the Borough Gaol.
William Gilbert, committed on the oath of Ann Perkins, with having gotten her with child and hath also refused her security.

447/3 List of jurors for the Grand and Petty juries.

447/4 Bill. To James Deayton. Entries include:-	s .. d
To fires for the day	5 .. 0
To pens, ink, & paper	1 .. 0
To the fees of Ann Rodd	13 .. 4
To eight days subsistence	2 .. 8

SESSIONS ROLL 448, Easter 1795   (17th.April)

448/1 Writ proclaiming Quarter Sessions and Gaol Delivery.

448/2 Calendar of prisoners in the Gaol of the Borough.
John Taylor, committed 21st. February 1795. Charged upon oath by Joseph Beach with having feloniously stolen his silver watch.

448/3 List of jurors for the Grand and Petty juries.

448/6 Presentment of the jury concerning John Taylor stealing one silver watch to the value of 10 shillings. Endorsed 'A true Bill'. Recognisances 448/4 & 5.

448/7 Bill of the constable of Holywell ward - James Denham.

1794	s .. d
Paid for swearing in.	1 .. 0
Conveying Mary King, a vagrant, to St.Michaels.	4
Serving a warrant on Redbourn constable for 10 waggons for the 44th.regiment.	2 .. 6
Paid for oath on the licence day.	1 .. 0
Serving a warrant on Sleep ward constable	

for a waggon for 16th Light Dragoons.	2 .. 6
29th.Oct. Paid for a letter from Deputy Lieutenant.	5$^{1}/_{2}$
Conveying Mary Robinson, Elizabeth Towers & Mary Banbury to Sleep Ward - 3 vagrants.	1 .. 0
Attending the Deputy Lieutenants.	1 .. 0 *
1795.	
Attending the drawing the militia.	1 .. 0 *
Conveying Maria Pugh, a vagrant, to St.Michaels.	4
	11 .. 1$^{1}/_{2}$
(Two shillings deducted)	2 .. 0
Allowed by John Kentish.	9 .. 1$^{1}/_{2}$

* *These entries crossed out.*

448/8   Bill of Clerk of the Peace. Easter 1794 to Epiphany 1795.

448/9, 10 & 11   Bills of S.Parrot, John Stevens and Henry Stevens, respectively the constables of St.Peters Ward, Middle Ward and Fishpool Ward. Similar in content to item 448/7.

448/12 Bill. 17th.April 1795.		s .. d
To Mr.Cowper paid.		2 .. 4
To the constable for going to Smallford, Sleepside, Nast Hide and Beech Farm.		2 .. 6
Expenses for prisoners.		2 .. 6
	Total	7 .. 4

448/13   An account of bricklayers work done by Mr.Benjamin Fowler at
the Sessions House 16th.& 17th.Sept.   s .. d
Bricklayer & labour repairing the brick-work of
underpinning at the back part of the Sessions
House & tiling at Sessions House. One each day.   4 .. 6
To 130 bricks, 7 hods of mortar & half hod of lime
& hair, 20 hard lath, 200 of 4d nails & peck tite pins.   9 .. 6
Bricklayer & labour repairing, tiling & plastering. One day each. 4 .. 6
To 40 plain tiles, 16 bricks, 1.5 hod of lime & hair
& half hod fine stuff, 6 hard lath & 50 4d nails.   4 .. 0
                       Allowed. Percival Lewis.   £1.. 2 .. 6

448/14 Bill of K.Mason. 19th.Sept.1794.	s .. d
19 feet tin pipe at the Borough Gaol.	12 .. 8
2 elbows.	6
3 trons.	1 .. 0
Allowed, Percival Lewis.	14 .. 2

SESSIONS ROLL 449, Midsummer 1795   (17th.July)

449/1   Writ proclaiming Quarter Sessions and Gaol Delivery.

449/2   Calendar of prisoners for the Borough Gaol. (No prisoners).

449/3   List of jurors for the Grand and Petty juries.

449/4 & 5   Return of persons enrolled as volunteers to serve in His Majesty's Navy under an act entitled 'An act for raising a certain number of men, in the several counties in England for the service of His Majesty's Navy'. With sums agreed to be paid as bounty.
For Middle Ward, from Kildare, Ireland, a labourer aged 27.   £20
For Holywell Ward, from Sharfelt, Yorks, a labourer aged 33.   £17..17s
For Fishpool Ward, from Waterfreston Yorks. a labourer aged 33 £10..10s
For St.Peter's Ward, from Killey, Ireland, a labourer aged 18.   £12 12s

449/6   Bill for work done at Borough Gaol. 1794.   £2 .. 19s .. 0¼d

449/7   Bill of James Deayton. Entries include:-   s .. d
To six days subsistence to Mack Addley on suspicion a
deserter from the 'Oxford Blews', & not being owned,
ordered to be discharged.   3 .. 0
To the fees of John Taylor.   13 .. 4

449/8   Bill of Mary Twitchell.
Maintaining a female vagrant and her two children committed for 7 days at 4d per woman & 2d per child. Total 4s..8d.

SESSIONS ROLL 450, Michaelmas. 1795   (9th. Oct.)

450/1   Writ Proclaiming Quarter Sessions and Gaol Delivery.

450/2   Calendar of prisoners for the Borough Gaol.
Philip Gregory committed on an oath of James Willcox with having stolen a watch, a coat, a waistcoat, breeches, a handkerchief & thirteen guineas, the property of the said James Willcox.

450/3   List of jurors for the Grand and Petty juries.

450/4   Rough note
Respecting the rates for the relief of poor of St.Peters & whether the amounts of the overseers of the poor of the said parish for the last & current year, whether such matters are included in ----- of appeal or not be referred to the award & arbitrations of Arthur Palmer.   .... charge of 25 pounds 4 shillings paid for providing a man for the navy for no part of the parish called [*Left blank*] ---- the appellants having paid the charges on them in respect of their own hamlets.

450/5, 6 & 7   Three rough notes concerning the previous item.

451/1   Writ proclaiming Quarter Sessions and Gaol Delivery.

451/2   Calendar of prisoners for the Borough Gaol.
Mary Watson: Committed on suspicion on the oath of Ann Gee in stealing a shift of the value of eight pence the property of Mary Clark.

451/3   List of jurors for the Grand and Petty juries.

451/4   The Examination of Ann, wife of Edward Gee Who on oath saith that last night about 6 o'clock a person whose name she has since been informed is Samuel Gregory came to her house in the Borough aforesaid with a message from her sister at Charlton in Northamptonshire - she asked him to come in - he said he had a woman at the door with him - the said Ann Gee desired him to bring her in - they both came into the house, drank a pint of beer - after a few minutes they went away & the said Ann Gee shut the door after them but did not fasten it. She had occasion to go into another room with a young woman who came in for a cape & going to the said room she observed Mary Watson, the woman who had just before left her house with Samuel Gregory open the door and take a shift from the rails of the stairs which was hanging to dry & had been sent to her by Mrs.Sams (?) of the Kings Head to wash. The said Ann Gee immediately with proper assistance went in pursuit of Mary Watson & found her at the Rose & Crown in Saint Michaels - that she charged Mary Watson with having robbed her and on searching, a bundle which had been taken from her house was found - Samuel Gregory was with her.
Recognisances 451/15.
Presentment of the jury 451/14 concerning theft of a linen shift of the value of 8d.   Endorsed 'A true Bill'.

451/5   Order of Vestry, St.Peters churchwardens & overseers. (note).

451/6   St.Peters parish overseers. 'Appeals regarding overseers account'.(note).

451/7   St.Peters parish chuchwardens & overseers. 'To move to discuss all the appeals depending against the poor rates'.

451/8   St.Peters parish - churchwardens & overseers. 'Motion to make order of vestry'.

451/9   A Bill. St.Peters ward 1795. Entries include:-   s .. d
To a horse & cart to remove vagrants to Hatfield Hall.   4 .. 0
Turnpike.   9
To a horse & cart to remove two vagrants
to Hatfield Hall & turnpike.   4 .. 9

451/10 & 11 Accounts of The Recorder and Jeremy Rogers, similar to previous item. Same destination, but turnpike only 6d. in each case.

451/12 Bill of Ann Gee 15th.Jan. 1796.	s .. d
Three days loss of time	3 .. 6
Paid in court	2 .. 4

451/13 Bill of James Deayton.	s .. d
To the fees of Philip Gregory.	13 .. 4
2 Fires for the day.	5 .. 0
To pens, ink and paper.	1 .. 0
To seven days subsistence to Philip Gregory.	2 .. 4
To removing Philip Gregory to Hertford.	12 .. 0
To the fees of Mary Watson.	13 .. 4
2 Fires for the day.	5 .. 0
To pens, ink and paper.	1 .. 0
Allowed. P.Lewis.	£2 .. 13 .. 0

451/16 & 17 Recognisances concerning appearance of John Levermore at the next Quarter Sessions to prefer a bill of indictment against William Brown for assault.

SESSIONS ROLL 452, Easter 1796   (8th.April)

452/1   Writ proclaiming Quarter Sessions and Gaol Delivery.

452/2   Calendar of prisoners for the Borough Gaol. (No prisoners).

452/3   Lists of jurors for the Grand and Petty juries.

452/4   Bill for glazing work done on Town Hall and Compter. £5..18..0.

452/5   The bill of the Clerk of the Peace for the Borough from Epiphany Sessions 1795 to Epiphany Sessions 1796.   £24..19..11.
Entries include:-
Attending on the Mayor and Mr.Osborn for them to appoint a day for holding a General Sessions under the late Navy Act.   6s..8d
Drawing out a notice thereof and fair copy for the Printer.   10s..0d
Paid for advertising the same in the County Chronicle.   11s..0d
The Magistrates afterwards entertained some doubts whether they were empowered under the Act to hold a General Sessions for the Borough by themselves or whether there should be a General Sessions for the County at large thought it would be proper that I should attend the County Sessions and take the sense of the County Magistrates thereon. Therefore journey to

Hertford for that purpose when the proportion of men to be raised by the Borough was then ascertained and a petty Sessions appointed.

Chaise and expenses. 2s..0d

Attending on the Mayor getting him to appoint a meeting of the Magistrates for putting in execution the late Act of Parliament enabling them to raise under certain regulations able-bodied and idle persons for the service of the Navy. 6s..8d

Drawing out and recording an order for appointing James Deayton Inspector of Weights and Balances and for purchasing weights according to the Standard in the Exchequer. 5s..0d

Drawing out long and special order relative to the scarcity of Bread Corn and the resolutions and recommendation of the Court in consequence thereof.
10s..0d

Drawing out long and special order of Sessions containing the order made at the the last Sessions for prohibiting the Bakers from selling other than Standard Wheaten bread and recording the same. 10s..0d

Drawing out and recording an order for appointing the Mayor and Mr.Kentish visitors of the Gaol and House of Correction. 5s..0d

Fee on the commitment of one prisoner to Gaol. 6s..8d

Drawing out order of Sessions for the removal of Philip Gregory to Hertford to take his trial at the next Assizes and fair copy for the Gaoler. 10s..0d

Journey to London to swear to and deliver the same (Estreat Roll of Fines) at the Exchequer. Coach hire and expenses. £2 .. 2 .. 0

452/6   June 1795. Coroners fee and charges for taking an inquisition on the body of Samuel Smith, a prisoner who died in the Liberty Gaol.

		s .. d
Warrant for summoning a jury to take an inquisition on the body of Samuel Smith deceased.		2 .. 6
Inquisition.		6 .. 8
Coroners fee.		13 .. 4
Ward certificate to bury the body.		2 .. 6
Jury and Bailiff.		17 .. 0
	Allowed	£2 .. 2 .. 0

SESSIONS ROLL 453, Midsummer 1796   (15th.July)

453/1   Writ proclaiming Quarter Sessions and Gaol Delivery.

453/2   Calendar of prisoners for the Borough Gaol.
John Pocock committed on the oath of John Avelin with having broken and entered the dwelling house of Thomas Hill in the night.

453/3   Lists of jurors for the Grand and Petty juries.

453/4   Recognisances concerning William Marston appearing to answer the complaint of Charles Surity for having threatened to do him bodily hurt.

453/9 & 453/10 Recognisances concerning Thomas Hill preferring a bill of indictment against John Pocock for burglary.

453/11 The jurors present William Scourfield, Samuel Giles and John Edwards making an assault upon Joseph Beech. Endorsed 'No true Bill'. Recognisances 453/5, 6, 7 & 8.

SESSIONS ROLL 454, Michaelmas 1796 (7th.Oct.)

454/1 Writ proclaiming Quarter Sessions and Gaol Delivery.

454/2 Calendar of prisoners for the Borough Gaol. (No prisoners).

454/3 List of jurors for the Grand and Petty juries.

454/4 Sacrament Certificate of John Harrison.

454/5 Bill of James Deayton. Expenses £2..11..8.

SESSIONS ROLL 455, Epiphany 1797 (13th.Jan.)

455/1 Writ proclaiming Quarter Sessions and Gaol Delivery.

455/2 Calendar of prisoners for the Borough Gaol.
Murdoc Mackay and John Macnair, committed on the oath of Thomas Dennis with having violently assaulted and beat him and on suspicion of having forcibly and feloniously taken from his person five shillings and six pence.
John Putnam (bailed out) committed on the oath of Lewis Sells on suspicion with having feloniously taken and carried away a pair of breeches the property of Lewis Sells.

455/3 Lists of jurors for the Grand and Petty juries.

455/9 Presentment of the jury concerning Murdoc Mackay and John Macnair for assaulting Thomas Dennis. Endorsed 'Both cut. Fined 6d. each and discharged. A true Bill'.
Recognisances 455/4 & 5.

455/10 Presentment of the jury concerning Murdoc Mackay and John Macnair stealing 5/6 belonging to Thomas Dennis. Endorsed 'A true Bill'.
Recognisances 455/4 & 5.

455/11 Presentment of the jury concerning Joseph Putnam feloniously stealing one pair of breeches value five shillings, the goods of Lewis Sells. Endorsed 'No Bill'.
Recognisances 455/6, 7 & 8.

455/12 Bill of James Deayton. Expenses £2..2..0.

SESSIONS ROLL 456, Easter 1797 (28th.April)

456/1 Writ proclaiming Quarter Sessions and Gaol Delivery.

456/2 Calendar of prisoners for the Borough Gaol.
Abraham Needham, committed as a deserter from the Hertfordshire Militia on his own confession.

456/3 List of jurors for the Grand and Petty juries.

456/4 Notice of vagrants each committed for seven days.
4 males and 1 female. *(Includes names and dates).*

456/5 Bill of the Clerk of the Peace, Easter 1796 to Epiphany 1797.

456/6 The information and complaint of Thomas Clark apprentice to Christopher Poulney, whitesmith, who saith, that he is an apprentice bound by indenture to Christopher Poulney and that he the said Christopher Poulney hath and doth refuse to employ and teach him his said trade and to provide his necessaries according to the terms of his indenture.

456/7 At the General Quarter Sessions of the Peace it is ordered as followeth:- Upon the petition of Thomas Clark, apprentice to Christopher Poulney to be relieved upon certain neglects of the Charter in refusing to employ him and to find him sufficient necessaries according to the terms of his indentures of apprenticeship. And Christopher Poulney the Master having likewise appeared upon his recognisance to answer to the complaint and having proved nothing whereby to clear himself of the complaint, but on the contrary. Thomas Clark having given full proof of the truth of the complaint to the satisfaction of the court, we do pronounce that the apprentice is discharged and freed from his apprenticeship and that Christopher Poulney do return and pay to John Fisher, Thomas Clark's father in law, the sum of five pounds and five shillings being one half part of the apprentice fee which he paid to Christopher Poulney. This to be a final order betwix master and apprentice.
Recognisances 456/10 & 11.

456/8 To wit be it remembered that on the eighth day of April 1797, Tabitha Manniard is convicted for that Tabitha Manniard after the passing of a certain Act of Parliament made and passed in the thirty sixth year of his present Majesty's reign entitled an Act for regulating the Trade or business of Pawn Broker did then and there take and receive from one Richard Warren on redeeming the pawn or pledge hereafter mentioned the sum of two pence of lawful money by way of profit upon two shillings and six pence the same being a sum not exceeding the sum of two shillings and six pence theretofore on the 5th.April 1797 then and there lent and advanced by her upon a certain pawn or pledge that is to say a shirt to the said Richard Warren the said sum of two pence being contrary to the statute and I John Osborn do adjudge Tabitha Manniard to pay and forfeit the sum of five pounds.

456/9   Similar to above.

SESSIONS ROLL 457, Midsummer 1797   (14th.July)

457/1   Writ proclaiming Quarter Sessions and Gaol Delivery.

457/2   Calendar of prisoners in the Borough Gaol. (No prisoners).

457/3   List of jurors for the Grand and Petty juries.

457/4   The Complaint of Thomas Sweatman who on his oath saith : That yesterday in the evening, about the hour of eight, Francis Shaw, coachman, belonging to the Chester Heavy Coach, did violently assault this informant by striking him with his fist near the temple by which he fell down - and at the same time Thomas Bellows - when this informant was recovering from the fall - did assault this informant by striking him and assisting Francis Shaw in the assault against the Peace. He therefore prayeth a warrant against them. (Note of recognisances on reverse).
Recognisances 457/5, 6, 7 & 8.
Presentment of the jury 457/9 concerning assault by Thomas Belles. Endorsed 'A true Bill'.

SESSIONS ROLL 458, Michaelmas 1797   (6th.Oct.)

458/1   Writ proclaiming Quarter Sessions and Gaol Delivery.

458/2   Calendar of prisoners for the Borough Gaol.
Elizabeth Prudden committed on the oath of Ann Taylor with having feloniously taken and carried away a pair of pattens, her property.

458/3   List of jurors for the Grand and Petty juries.

458/4   The Examination of Ann Taylor of the Borough, spinster, 4th.Oct.1797. Who saith that Elizabeth Prudden came to her aunts house, Ann Ashdown at the sign of the Crow in the Borough, yesterday morning about 9 o'clock and asked for a quartern of gin which she drank and paid for. This examinant then went into another room and Elizabeth Prudden wished her a good morning and went away. That this morning this examinant missed a pair of patterns which stood against the kitchen door at the time Elizabeth Prudden was in the house for which reason she did suspect that she had stolen them. Accordingly went in pursuit of her and having found her at a lodging house in the town she charged her with having taken the patterns which she after some hesitation confessed and went with her to the person to whom she had sold them and the patterns were found in the possession of such person.

Recognisances 458/5 & 6.

Presentment of the jury 458/7 concerning a pair of patterns of the value of sixpence. Endorsed 'A true Bill'.

458/8	Prosecutors Bill. Michaelmas Sessions 1797.	
	Ann Taylor against Elizabeth Prudden.	s .. d
	Paid for the indictment.	2 .. 4
	Prosecutors and witnesses loss of time.	5 .. 0
	Allowed, Percival Lewis, Recorder.	7 .. 4

458/9   Bill of Henry Stevens, Constable of Middle Ward.

Attending at the Angel Inn.	£ .. s .. d
Seven times attending with list and appeals. Drawing and attending with list and appeals. Drawing and swearing in at 5/- per time according to the court at Hertford.	1 ..15 .. 0
Returning 100 names at 1/- per 20.	5 .. 0
Serving 5 Warrants on persons balloted at 6d. each.	2 .. 6
	2 .. 2 .. 6

458/10, 11 & 12   Bills of Samuel Suety, Samuel Suety *(sic)* and William Brown, Constables of St.Peters Ward, Holywell Ward and Fishpool Ward. Similar to previous item.

SESSIONS ROLL 459, Epiphany 1798   (12th.Jan.)

459/1   Writ proclaiming Quarter Sessions and Gaol Delivery.

459/2   Calendar of prisoners for the Borough Gaol.

Elizabeth Prudden, convicted of feloniously stealing one pair of pattens. Ordered to be transported for seven years. Remains now in Gaol.

James Wilson committed on the oath of Daniel Rose and others with having feloniously taken a pair of breeches the property of Daniel Rose.

459/3   List of jurors for the Grand and Petty juries.

459/4   Notice of vagrants each committed for seven days.

3 males and 3 females. *(Includes names and dates)*.

459/5   Examination and Complaint of Daniel Rose who on oath saith :-
That on Wednesday night last a pair of leather breeches were feloniously stolen and taken from the top of the bed in which he slept at the Green Man in the Borough aforesaid and that he doth suspect that one James Wilson, a

traveller, who then lodged in the house and slept in the same bed with him did steal and take away the said breeches his property - and this examinant further saith that he so suspects the said James Wilson because he hath heard and verily believes that the breeches were seen in his custody and that he offered them 'to sale' to one Mary Stevens the wife of Henry Stevens .
Recognisances 459/9, 10 & 11.
Presentment of the jury 459/12 concerning theft of breeches of the value of two shillings and six pence. Endorsed 'No Bill'.

459/6 Examination of Mary Stevens, wife of Henry Stevens taken on oath who saith :- That on Wednesday last between four and five in the afternoon a person whose name she has since heard is James Wilson came to her husbands house and offered to sell a pair of leather breeches to her but she refused to purchase them believing them to be soldiers breeches and supposing them not to be his own.

459/7 & 8 Recognisances concerning Charles Flanagan preferring a bill of indictment against John Jones for an assault.

459/13 Expenses of Daniel Rose.	s .. d
Loss of time.	4 .. 0
Mr.Stevens.	2 .. 6
Samuel Avis.	2 .. 6
Paid in court.	2 .. 4
Epiphany Sessions 1798 P.Lewis.	11 .. 4

459/14 Bill of James Deayton. Entries include:-	s .. d
Twenty four days subsistence to Abraham Needham committed for six months being a deserter from the Hertfordshire Militia.	12 .. 0
Four days subsistence to John Ealing charged on the oath of Sarah Lush being the person who broke out of Licester Goal.	2 .. 0
Six days subsistence to Stephen Clemency committed as a deserter from the 57th.Regt. being no deserter, ordered to be discharged.	3 .. 0
To the fees of Elizabeth Prudden.	13 .. 4
One fire for the examination of James Wilson for felony.	1 .. 6
One fire for the examination of a Frenchman.	1 .. 6
Fourteen weeks subsistence to Elizabeth Prudden.	12 .. 0

SESSIONS ROLL 460, Easter 1798   (20th.April)

460/1   Writ proclaiming Quarter Sessions and Gaol Delivery.

460/2   Calendar of prisoners for the Borough Gaol.

Elizabeth Prudden, remains in gaol.
Robert Spencer (bailed out) committed on the oath of Sarah Reed on suspicion of having feloniously taken and carried away a silver watch the property of John Baldwin. (Copy of this calendar 460/3).

460/4   List of jurors for the Grand and Petty juries.

460/5   2nd.Feb. 1798. Thomas Kinder to the Constable of the Goal (sic) in the Borough. To convey and deliver the body of John Spencer - alias Robert, on suspicion of stealing one silver watch the property of John Baldwin of London Colony. And you said keeper are hereby required to receive John Spencer into your custody until tomorrow for further examination.

460/6   The Information and Complaint of Sarah Reed of London Colony, who on her oath saith :- On this morning a man who saith his name is John Spencer, alias Robert, came into the house of John Baldwin of London Colony to sell some herrings which he laid upon a dresser where was a silver watch. This deponent having mislaid half a crown which she could not find therefore could not pay for them. The said John Spencer, alias Robert, took the herrings off the dresser and she verily believes he took the watch up with the herrings as no other person had been in the house but herself and the said John Spencer whom they followed and apprehended in the Borough. This deponent further saith the watch was marked J.B. and was upon the dresser when the said John Spencer came in to sell the herrings.
Recognisances 460/7, 8 & 9. Also note on reverse of 460/6.
Presentment of the jury 460/10 concerning theft of one silver watch of the value of five shillings. Endorsed 'No true Bill'.

460/11   Bill of James Deayton.
To fourteen weeks subsistence to Elizabeth Pudden at two shillings and four pence per week.   £1 .. 12 .. 0.

460/12   Bill of the Clerk of the Peace for the Borough from Easter Sessions 1797 to Epiphany 1798 inclusive.

SESSIONS ROLL 461, Midsummer 1798   (13th.June)

461/1   Writ proclaiming Quarter Sessions and Gaol Delivery.

461/2   Calendar of prisoners for the Borough Gaol.
Elizabeth Prudden, to be transported for seven years. Remains in gaol.
Catherine Steward, committed on the oath of Joseph Coventon and others of felony in stealing a piece of meat about five pounds weight of the value of two shillings the property of William Crawley.
William Fleming, committed on suspicion of stealing one pewter pot from T.Ford, Bull and Gate, Kentish Town.

461/3   List of jurors for the Grand and Petty juries.

461/4   The Information and Complaint of Henry Lines jun. who on his oath saith :- This afternoon William Fleming, labourer, came to the shop of this informant and offered for sale one pewter quart pot with the name of Ford, Bull and Gate, Kentish Town, which he refused to buy having a strong suspicion of him stealing the same.

461/5   The Deposition and Examination of Ann, the wife of William Crawley, butcher, and Joseph Coventon, cordwainer, taken on oath. Who severally say and first the said Joseph Coventon saith that about one o'clock this day he saw a woman go into the shop of William Crawley and that she soon after came out again with a piece of meat which she had put under her cloak. That suspecting she had stolen something, he called out to Mr.Crawley, but not being able to make him hear, he went to Crawleys house and described the woman to him whereupon the wife of William Crawley went in pursuit of the said woman. And the said Ann Crawley for herself saith that she was present when the woman above mentioned, whose name she hath since learned is Catherine, wife of Humphrey Steward, was apprehended and further that a piece of pickled pork about five pounds in weight which is the property of her husband William Crawley was found upon Catherine Steward and that Catherine Steward acknowledged that she had taken the piece of meat from her husbands shop in the Borough and she further saith that she cut the said piece of pork and knows it was in her husbands house this morning.
Recognisances 461/7 & 8.
Presentment of the jury 461/12 concerning the theft of five pounds weight of pickled pork of the value of 10d. Endorsed 'A true Bill'.

461/6   The Examination of Catherine Steward, wife of Humphrey Steward of Hampton in Arden, Warwickshire. Catherine Steward is charged for feloniously taking and carrying away a piece of meat about five pounds weight the property of William Crawley. Saith that she did take the said piece of meat in manner aforesaid and that she hath no other excuse but that she did it through hunger.

461/9 & 10 Recognisances concerning Humphrey Mansell appearing to prefer a bill of indictment against William Marston for assault.

461/11 Recognisances concerning appearance to answer the examination of Ann Webb of St.Albans Parish, singlewoman, who is with child likely to be born a bastard and to be chargeable to the Parish of St.Alban and that Thomas Walker is the father. That he should appear at the next Quarter Sessions concerning bastards begotten and born out of lawful matrimony.

461/13 Bill from the Liberty of St.Albans. To Thomas Lines for prisoners.

461/14   Bill of James Deayton.

SESSIONS ROLL 462, Michaelmas 1798   (5th.Oct.)

462/1   Writ proclaiming Quarter Sessions and Gaol Delivery.

462/2   Calendar of prisoners for the Borough Gaol.
Elizabeth Prudden remains in gaol.
Susanah, Wife of John Wetherby, committed on the oath of Henry Lines
and others with having stolen twenty one yards of cotton, the property of
the said Henry Lines.
Sarah Kelly, committed on the oath of Martha Element and others with
having feloniously taken and carried away a check apron the property of
Martha Element.

462/3   Calendar of prisoners for the House of Correction.
John Vincent for a bastard child.   Aug.9th.- Sept.5th.
John Townsend for ill using his wife.   Aug.20th.- Sept.1st.
Plus two male vagrants for 7 days.

462/4   List of jurors for the Grand and Petty juries.

462/5   Examination of William Hortin, servant to George Hands of
Acres Green, Birmingham, in the County of Warwickshire, common carrier.
Taken on oath 12th.Sept.1798. Who saith that he drives his said masters
waggon from Birmingham to London; that on Sunday night last he took up
a trunk at Weedon in Northamptonshire directed to be left at Solomon Goffs
house at St.Albans, which trunk was locked and tied with cord. That when
he came to St.Albans he took out the said trunk which was still corded but
he observed that the lock had been opened. That on delivering it to the
owner, Mrs.Element, she informed him that it had been opened and that
several of the things which had been put in it had been taken out. And this
deponent further saith that he immediately went back to the wagon and
found all the things which had been taken out of the trunk except one check
apron. And on enquiring it appeared that the said apron had been sold to one
Sarah Cogdell of St.Albans. And this deponent saith he hath reason to
suspect and doth suspect one Sarah Kelly a passenger in his said waggon
whom he took up at Weedon did break open the said trunk and did steal the
said apron.

462/6   The Examination of Martha Element, wife of William Element,
labourer, of Bone End in the Parish of North Church. And also Sarah wife
of Joseph Cogdell of the Borough, labourer. First Martha Element saith that
on Thursday night last she returned from Weedon where she had been to see
her mother and not being able conveniently to take all her things with her
by coach, she left a trunk containing a black gown and apron, two shifts a
silk handkerchief, two white handkerchiefs, two pillow cases, a pair of black
stockings, a check apron and a blue apron, half a dozen cups and saucers,

four tumbler glasses, a cotton gown and a black silk handkerchief, a muslin apron, a childs white frock, a pair of cotton stockings and a few other trifling things to be sent by the waggon direct for her at her Brother-in-laws, Mr.Solomon Geoff at St.Albans. That she locked the said trunk and kept the key and also fastened the said trunk with a cord. That when the same was brought to her at St.Albans, she observed that it had been opened and several of the things which she had put therein, had been taken out. On searching the waggon all the things which had been taken out were there except one check apron which had been taken and sold to Sarah Cogdell of St.Albans by one Sarah Kelly a passenger in the waggon as she hath been informed and believes. And this examinant Sarah Cogdell for herself saith that Sarah Kelly now charged with stealing a check apron did yesterday sell the said check apron to her for the sum of one shilling and four pence.
Recognisances <u>462/13, 14 & 15</u>.
Presentment of the jury <u>462/16</u> concerning the theft by Sarah Kelly of one check apron of the value of sixpence.   Endorsed 'A true Bill'.
Presentment of the jury <u>462/17</u> concerning the theft by Sarah Kelly of two muslin aprons of the value of ten pence.   Endorsed 'A true Bill'.

462/7   Information and Complaint of Henry Lines jun. Who on his oath saith about two months last past, he lost from out of his shop, twenty one yards of cotton. And he has a strong reason to suspect that the whole or part of the same is concealed in the dwelling of Berkshire of Sleepside or Smallford in the Liberty. This informant preyeth a search warrant against the said Berkshire.
Recognisances <u>462/9 & 10</u>.

462/8   The Complaint of Thomas Johnson Who on his oath saith that George Ferdinand Sherman, musician, did last night violently assault and beat him without any just cause or provocation.
Recognisances <u>462/11 & 12</u>. Also note on reverse of 462/7.
Presentment of the jury <u>462/18</u>. Endorsed 'A true Bill'.

462/19 Bill of James Deayton. Oct.5th.1798.	£ .. s .. d
To twelve weeks subsistence to Elizabeth Prudden	
at two shillings and four pence per week.	1 .. 8 .. 0
To four weeks subsistence for Catherine Steward.	9 .. 4
To the fees of Susanah, wife of John Wetherby.	13 .. 4
To the fees of Sarah Kelly.	13 .. 4
To pens, ink and paper.	1 .. 0
To two fires for the day.	5 .. 0
Allowed. John Osborn.	3 .. 10 .. 0

462/20 Expenses of William Hortin and Mary Hawkins. The King	
against Sarah Kelly for felony.	s .. d
Two bills of indictment.	4 .. 8
Paid for two hours of time and hiring another man.	6 .. 0
Expenses and coming up 80 miles.	10 .. 6
The womans expenses 47 miles.	10 .. 6

Four witnesses.
　　　Allowed. J. Osborn.

16 .. 0
£2.. 17 .. 2

SESSIONS ROLL 463, Epiphany 1799　　　(18th.Jan.)

463/1　Writ proclaiming Quarter Sessions and Gaol Delivery.

463/2　Calendar of prisoners for the Borough Gaol.
Elizabeth Prudden remains now in 'goal'.
Thomas Walker, bailed out, ordered at Michaelmas 1798 to be committed until we shall enter into a recognisance with sufficient surety upon condition to appear at the next General Quarter Sessions of the Peace for begetting Ann Webb with child which is likely to be born a bastard and to be chargeable to the Parish of St.Alban.

463/3　List of jurors for the Grand and Petty juries.

463/4　Notice of vagrants each committed for seven days.
A man, wife and child, also a female and her 3 children.

463/5　Recognisances concerning answering an Act relating to bastards, preferred by the Churchwardens and Overseers of the Poor of the Parish of St.Alban, in relation to Ann Webb, singlewoman.

463/6 & 7 Recognisances concerning an assault upon Thomas Deayton by Edward James.

	£ .. s .. d
463/8　Bill of James Deayton.	
To 14 days subsistence to Susanah Weatherley.	4 .. 0
To removing the same to Hertford.	12 .. 0
To 8 weeks subsistence to Sarah Kelly.	18 .. 4
To 3 days subsistence to Barnard Davison a deserter committed, ordered to be discharged.	1 .. 6
To 15 weeks subsistence to Elizabeth Prudden.	1 ..15 .. 0
To two fires.	5 .. 0
To pens, paper and ink.	1 .. 0
Allowed, Percival Lewis, Recorder.	3 ..17 .. 6

SESSIONS ROLL 464, Easter 1799　　　(5th.April)

464/1　Writ proclaiming Quarter Sessions and Gaol Delivery.

464/2　Calendar of prisoners for the Borough Gaol.
John McGwyer, committed on the oath of Elizabeth Nash and others with having feloniously taken and carried away a silk cloak.

464/3   Lists of jurors for the Grand and Petty juries.

464/4   The Examination of Elizabeth the wife of Job Nash, Robert Russell and Susannah Dover, spinster. Who severally say and first : This examinant Elizabeth Nash for herself saith that on Thursday last she was on a visit at a neighbours (Mrs.Dover) who keeps the Blue Boar in the Borough, from about six o'clock till eleven in the evening. That when she went there she had on a black silk cloak which was taken from her and put into one of the rooms of the said house. That when she was about to return home her cloak was missing and not to be found and from the circumstances of a man being seen in the house who was a stranger, whose name is said to be John Mc.Gwyer she verily believes that her said cloak was feloniously stolen.
Susannah Dover saith that she was at the Blue Boar (her mothers house) on Thursday last when a man came into the kitchen and called for a pennyworth of ale which she refused to draw him whereupon he turned from her and was going into the back parlour. She asked him why he went there and he replied "Because I thought you said go into the Tap Room" - she then desired him to leave her house but did not follow him out - but believed that he went away then or soon after - She believes the prisoner John Mc.Gwyer to be the person although she cannot positively say that he is.
Robert Russell saith that on Thursday night last about 10 o'clock he was at the George Inn in the Borough when a man was brought into the house by the guard of the waggons which stop at the last mentioned inn - on suspicion of having some evil intent having attempted to get into a waggon which stood at the said inn gate and this examinant was present when the man was searched and he further saith that a black silk cloak was found upon him concealed under his jacket, which the said cloak was taken from him and hath since been owned as the property of Miss Nash.
Recognisances 464/5 & 6.
Presentment of the jury 464/8 concerning the theft by John McGwyer of one black silk cloak of the value of two shillings and sixpence. Endorsed 'A true Bill'.

464/7   Recognisances concerning Thomas Walker getting Ann Webb with child.

464/9   Sessions, 5th.April 1799.
John Wane and others, Appellants, and The Churchwardens and Overseers of St.Peters, Respondents. To move for leave to enter the appeal against the Overseers Accounts with the Liberty.

464/10 Bill of the Clerk of the Peace from Easter Sessions 1798 to Epiphany 1799.   £17 .. 12 ..8. Entries include:-   s .. d
Drawing out and recording an order for the allowance
of the Treasurers accounts.   10 .. 0
The like for the levy and making 4 fair copies thereof. £1..   10 .. 0
Attending on the Treasurer and Overseers of the Poor
to deliver such copies.   13 .. 4

The like payments of the Gaolers bill.   5 .. 0
The like payments of $^{1}/_{3}$ part of Mrs.Twitchell's bill.   5 .. 0
Fees of one prisoner discharged by proclamation.   6 .. 8
Drawing out the Gaol Calendar and fair copy for the Gaoler.   5 .. 0
Drawing out and recording an order for appointing
visitors of the Gaol and House of Correction.   5 .. 0
The like for payment of one third part of the Gaolers bill
for fires provided by him for the use of the magistrates.   5 .. 0
The like for payment of the Gaolers bill for the fees and
maintenance of the prisoners committed to his custody.   5 .. 0
Fees for one prisoner discharged by proclamation.   6 .. 8
The like for one prisoner committed to Gaol.   6 .. 8
Copy order of Sessions for removing Susanna Weatherley
a prisoner to Hertford Gaol in order to take her trial
at the next Assizes.   5 .. 0
Drawing out and recording an order for the appointment
of Mr.W.Wilson to be High Constable for the Borough in
order to enforce the payment of Levy Money which was
ordered to be raised at the last Easter Sessions.   10 .. 0
Making a copy of an order sentencing Elizabeth Prudden
to transportation to send to the Duke of Portland.   5 .. 0

464/11   Sacrament Certificate of John Boys, Gentleman.

464/12   Bill of James Deayton. Entries include:-   £ .. s .. d
           To ten weeks and one day subsistence to
           Elizabeth Prudden at 2/4d per week.   1 .. 3 .. 8
           To the fees of John McGwyer.   13 .. 4

464/13   April 4th.1799. Borough of St.Alban. Order of John Osborn Esq.
for J.McGwyer.
To Ann Baxter.   s .. d
           To 1pr. Drill breeches.   3 .. 10
           To 1 shirt.   4 .. 10
           To 1pr. stockings.   2 .. 4
                                    11 .. 0

464/14   Bill of Humphrey Mansell, a constable for the Borough.

SESSIONS ROLL 465, Midsummer 1799   (19th.July)

465/1   Writ proclaiming Quarter Sessions and Gaol Delivery.

465/2   Calendar of prisoners for the Borough Gaol.
Thomas Coventon called Brandy Tom. Committed on the oath of John
Hornsey with having feloniously taken a Great-coat the property of John
Goodge of Northampton.

465/3   Lists of jurors for the Grand and Petty juries.

465/4   Notice of vagrants committed. One male for 7 days.

465/5   Examination of Sarah Cook on her oath doth declare that Thomas Archer of Hatfield Woodside did get her with child.
Recognisances 465/7.

465/6   The Information and Complaint of John Hornsey, waggon servant to Charles Fitzhugh of Northampton, carrier. Who saith that on or about 11th.April instant he was with his masters waggon going from Northampton to London when a caddee or person employed as an assistant waggoner in or about St.Albans, called by the name of Brandy Tom, was with him in the Town of Redbourn and proceeded with him to St.Albans. That between Redbourn and St.Albans the said Brandy Tom complained that he was not well and got into the waggon. That he had not any Great-coat on when he got in, but when he came out of it, which was in the Town of St.Albans, he had on a Great-coat with a coloured collar, which this examinant then supposed he had put into the waggon at Redbourn and was his own property, but this examinant hath since been informed that the said coat was the property of John Goodge of Northampton and the said Brandy Tom did steal the same. And lastly he says that he had seen the coat in the waggon before the said Brandy Tom got into the waggon and observed that the coat had a coloured collar, but supposed that it was the property of the said caddee.
Recognisances 465/8.

465/9   A return of penalties under convictions against persons having weights not according to the Standard, seen before John Osborn and Thomas Kinder at the Petty Sessions. Saturday 13th.July 1799.

	No. of weights.	No. of offences.	Penalties.	Cost.
Joseph Walker.	5	1	5s	4s
John Missenden.	3	1	5s	4s
Richard Mason jun.	2	3	15s	4s
James Witney.	1	2	10s	4s
Samuel Wildbore.	4	2	10s	4s
John Day.	1	4	£1	4s
Samuel Fisher.	3	2	10s	4s
Joseph Ansell.	1	2	10s	4s
Joseph Harding.	3	1	5s	4s
John Bacon.	1	1	5s	4s
Edward Eling.	3	3	15s	4s
A. Perrin.	1	1	5s	4s
William Chapman.	1	2	10s	4s
Charles Kentish.	2	2	10s	4s

465/10 A return of penalties levied under statute of George 3rd. against persons having false weights. *Entries here summarised by name & number of false weights.*

William Batten	13	William Brown	1	William Harris	2
John Shephard	4	Mrs.Moore	1	George Wilsher	5
William Thomas	1	Joseph Ansell	1	Elizabeth Oakes	4
Mary Walker	2	James Smith	1	Wittington	4
Samuel Wildbore	4	Michael Mason jun.	3	John Day	4
Daniel Gold	1	Eling	2	James Bennett	4
George Baker	3	Thomas Compere	1	William Harris	2
Jonathan Dover	5	George Louch	2	George Gower	3
William Chapman	2	John Day	4	Edward Eling	2
Samuel Marston	5				

465/11, 12 & 13 Bills of Joseph Cogdill, John Missenden and William Wingrave, Constables of Holywell Ward, Middle Ward and St.Peters Ward.

SESSIONS ROLL 466, Michaelmas 1799   (11th Oct.)

466/1 Writ proclaiming Quarter Sessions and Gaol Delivery.

466/2 List of jurors for the Grand and Petty juries.

466/3 Calendar of prisoners for the Borough Gaol. (No prisoners).

466/4 House of Correction Calendar.
Aug.13th.John Murty for an assault until discharged by due course of law. Discharged Aug.16th.
Aug.22nd.Thomas Wood for leaving his wife chargeable to the Parish of St.Alban. Discharged. Sept. --.
Vagrants committed for seven days:- 1 male, 4 females and 2 children.

466/5 Notice concerning arbitration in the matter rates, between John Wane and other appellants. The late Overseers of the Poor of the Parish of St.Peter in the Borough and Liberty of St.Alban respondents.

466/6 Account of James Deayton.	s.. d
To the fees of Thomas Coventon.	13.. 4
To pens, ink & paper.	1.. 0
To 5 days subsistence to George Bayly committed on suspicion as a deserter from His Majesty's Navy.	2.. 6
To 6 days subsistence to John Stroud and Thomas Laws, committed on suspicion as a deserter from His Majesty's Navy.	6.. 0
To 2 fires.	5.. 0
To Pens, Ink & paper.	1.. 0
Allowed, Thomas Baker, Mayor. Total	£1 .. 8..10

467/1   Writ proclaiming Quarter Sessions and Gaol Delivery.

467/2   List of jurors for the Grand and Petty juries.

467/3   Calendar of prisoners for the Borough Gaol.
Thomas Bullcock committed on the oath of John Page with having feloniously taken and led away one gelding of the value of ten pounds the property of the said John Page.

467/4   House of Correction Calendar. Vagrants committed between 28th.Oct and 11th.Dec. for seven days.
10 males, 7 females (one very ill) and three children.

467/5   The Examination of John Slade a Private in the Queens Bays now quartered at St.Albans & Sarah Standbridge of the Borough Servant to Martha Ellis. First this examinant Sarah Standbridge for herself saith that on Saturday night last about 7 o'clock a person who says her name is Elizabeth Saten came to the house of her mistress Martha Ellis at the Bell Inn at St.Albans as being the wife of the Trumpeter belonging to the 28th.Regiment then quartered at the said house - That the said Elizabeth Saten soon after she had eaten her supper went to bed and kept her room all the next day being Sunday. That about 8 o'clock this morning the said Elizabeth Saten came downstairs and asked for her husband meaning the Trumpeter who not being there she went away - As soon as the said Elizabeth Saten had left the house this examinant Sarah Standbridge went up stairs, having some mistrust, and immediately missed one of the sheets belonging to the bed where the said Elizabeth Saten had slept.
And this examinant John Slade for himself saith that he was desired to pursue the said Elizabeth Saten and overtook her near Mr.Avis's in the Borough whereupon he requested her to go back with him for that there was a suspicion that she had stolen a sheet - she acknowledged that she had the sheet and said that she had taken it thro' distress and want, she then pulled the sheet off her it being wound about her under her petticoat and delivered it to this examinant John Slade. This examinant then took the sheet to the Bell and delivered it to the care of Sarah Standbridge And this examinant John Slade said that some other things being missed out of the house the said Elizabeth Saten was again pursued and overtaken a short distance from the turnpike and upon being searched by the said John Slade in the presence of a young lad (John Smith the son of Henry Smith of St.Peters, blacksmith) a blanket - the property of Martha Ellis a handkerchief, the property of Thos.Dennis were found upon her which it afterwards *(a sentence erased by crossing out)*...and further that the said Elizabeth Saten was soon after taken into custody by a constable who this informant is informed found upon her a waistcoat also the property of Thomas Dennis.
Endorsed with note of recognisances.
Recognisances <u>467/7 & 8</u> concerning the theft of a linen sheet and a blanket.

467/6 Recognisances concerning John Page appearing to prefer a bill of indictment against Thomas Bulcock for feloniously taking one gelding the property of John Page.

467/9 'Nessasarie supplys' by order of Thos.Baker MD Mayor.
For Elizabeth Saten died in Goal   £3..12..0.

467/10 Bill concerning woman deceas'd at the Upper Gaol. Thomas Warren, Surgeon. 15 entries for various date in November and January totalling £1..7..0. Supplies include:- The Powder (1/-), The Pills for night (1/-). The Mixture (2/6), Alternative pills (1/6), The Draught (1/-) and Hartshorn (6d).

467/11 Bill of Sarah Mannard.
1799 Dec.28th. for Elizabeth Saten.

	s .. d
1 gown.	3 .. 0
2 petticoats.	4 ..10
Stays.	2 .. 0
Cap.	0 .. 8
Blanket.	2 .. 6
Apron.	1 .. 0
Total.	14 .. 0

467/12 Bill of Ann Batten
1799 Dec.24th. for Elizabeth Saten.

	s .. d
2 shifts at 4/-.	8 .. 0
1 handkerchief.	1 .. 6
Pr.stockings.	1 .. 8
Total.	11 .. 2

467/13 Bill of William Nicholl.
To a coffin for a woman that died in the Borough Gaol Jan.8th.   11s..6d

467/14 1800 Jan.10th. The burial of Elizabeth Saten at the Abbey Church of St.Alban

	s .. d
To the Minister.	2 .. 0
To the Clerk.	1 .. 4
Total	3 .. 4

467/15 The Sexton burial fees of Elizabeth Saten at the Abbey Church of St.Alban. Jan.10th.1800.   4s..0d

467/16 Bill of Ann Twitchell.
Jan.9th.1800. To wool for a person that died at Mr.Deacons. 1s.. 0d

467/17 Bill of Thos.Boys, Coroner. 28th.Jan.1799.
Coroners fee for inquisition taken on the body of
Thomas Wheeler found dead near Holywell.   £1.. 0 .. 0
Paid Jury and Baliff   17 .. 0

The like charge for inquisition taken on the body of
James Seabrook found dead in the Buildings.   £1..17 .. 0.
The like for inquisition taken on body of Elizabeth Saten. £1..17 .. 0
              Total £5..11 .. 0

467/18 Late High Constable Allowance.
Appointment of a new High Constable and annual allowance to him for the execution of his office.
Allowance to James Deayton as inspector of weights and balances.

467/19 Sacrament Certificate of John Parlar, Officer of Excise.

467/20 Bill of James Deayton.		s .. d
Fees for Elizabeth Saten.		13 .. 4
Fees for Thomas Bullock, alias Palmer, alias Brown.		13 .. 4
Necessaries provided by order of doctor for Elizabeth Saten.		8 .. 4
To laying her out & putting her in coffin.		1 .. 0
To paying 4 bearers for going to church.		4 .. 0
To two fires.		5 .. 0
To pens, ink and paper.		1 .. 0
	Total.	£2.. 6 .. 0

SESSIONS ROLL 468, Easter 1800   (25th.April)

468/1 Writ proclaiming Quarter Sessions and Gaol Delivery.

468/2 Calendar of prisoners for the Borough Gaol.
James Kentish & William Johnson committed on the oath of John Price with having feloniously taken and carried away a quantity of hay and corn the property of Elizabeth Shaw.
William White committed upon the oath of John Price for receiving a quantity of corn & hay the property of Elizabeth Shaw knowing the same to be stolen.
John Saunders committed on the oath of John Clark for suspicion of felony in receiving a quantity of straw of the value of six shillings the property of John Clark Esq. knowing the same to be stolen . Bailed out.
James Woodward committed on the oath of William Costin & others with having feloniously taken a piece of pork his property.
Samuel Golding & Charles Huggins committed on the oath of Lucy Hawes & others with having wilfully & maliciously assaulted her in a public street with an intent to burn her 'cloathes' and with having so burnt her 'cloathes'.
Seth Weedon committed on the oath of William Brandon and others with having unlawfully obtained from William Brandon five shillings with intent to cheat and defraud him.

(On reverse) Borough of St.Alban. House of Correction Calendar.

Notice of vagrants each committed for seven days.
12 males, 6 females and 3 children.
Also Thomas Langham for getting drunk, for 1 month, committed March
10th. but discharged March 17th.

468/3 List of jurors for the Grand and Petty juries.

468/4 The Examination and Complaint of William Brandon, shopman
to Miss Blows of the Borough, widow, taken & made this fifth day of April
1800 who on his oath saith that on Saturday last about but after 7 o'clock in
the morning one Seth Weedon of London Colney came to his mistress's
shop in the Borough and told him that Miss Gower of Colney had sent him
to borrow five shillings for that she had made a purchase in the market &
had not enough money with her to pay and further that Miss Gower would
call in an hours time to pay the money back again - whereupon this
examinant did advance & hand to Miss Gower as he supposed on behalf of
his mistress the sum of five shillings which Seth Weedon went away with
and did not return And this examinant further saith that he soon afterwards
saw his mistress's niece to whom he related what he had done when she
informed him that Seth Weedon was a cheat & had defrauded her aunt
Mrs.Whittington in the same way & finding on enquiry that Mrs.Gower had
not been at market, this Examinant is convinced in his own mind that Seth
Weedon did knowingly & falsely pretended to him that he was sent by
Mrs.Gower who had been a customer of Mistress Blows in her business &
way of trade of a broker whereby Seth Weedon defrauded this examinant of
the sum of five shillings which he at first advanced on account of his
mistress but after discovering the fraud did not think proper to charge to her
account & whereof he hath sustained loss himself & Seth Weedon hath
never since offered to return the said sum.

468/5 Examination of Elizabeth the wife of Joseph Gower of London
Colney who saith that she knows Seth Weedon named in the examination
herewith arrested & that she did not authorise him to ask for or borrow any
sum of money on the day mentioned nor at any other time nor was she at
St.Albans on the 29th.day of March last nor did she know of the
circumstances therein mentioned in respect to Seth Weedons having obtained
the sum of five shillings of William Brandon but positively saith that the
same was so obtained without her knowledge or consent.
Recognisances 468/29 & 30.
Presentment of the jury 468/14 concerning Seth Weedon defrauding
Elizabeth Blows and William Brandon. Endorsed 'A true Bill. Guilty on the
first count'.
See also 468/16 for sentence.

468/6 Examination of John Price, servant of Mrs Elizabeth Shaw of
Hatchcliff in the County of Bedford, labourer, who saith That he is
employed by his mistress to look after her horses belonging to different
coaches which she contracts to run from Hockcliff to St.Albans at the Angel
Inn & other purposes And this examinant further saith that on Thursday the

30th.day of January last about 7 o'clock at night he was in the stables belonging to the Angel Inn together with James Kentish & William Johnson two other persons in the employment of Mrs. Shaw in the care of the horses when William Johnson desired this examinant to go up into the hay loft & fetch down some hay for the horses - And having some suspicion that James Kentish & William Johnson were about something improper he stood behind the left door & watched them & he further saith that William Johnson opened the corn bin where his mistress's horse corn is kept & he saw William Johnson take out about a gallon of beans & oats mixed together & put it into a bag which James Kentish held in his hand & they also took about three parts of a truss of hay & tied it up with straw bands - and they then carried both the corn and hay out of the stable into the street and as this examinant believes sold it to some person in the town of St.Albans - and he further saith that one Wight of the Borough was with James Kentish & William Johnson & he believes assisted in taking the corn & hay and was the receiver thereof knowing it to be stolen.
Note of recognisances on reverse.
Recognisances 468/19, 20 & 21.
Presentment of the jury 468/12 concerning theft to the total value of 1/8d.
Endorsed 'A true Bill'.
See also 468/16. All acquitted.

468/7 Information of John Clark of Sandridgebury in the Parish of Sandridge and Henry Cherry of the Borough, ostler. First this examinant John Clark for himself saith that by agreement with Mrs.Ann Marks of the Peahen Inn at St.Albans he hath for sometime past and now does serve the said inn with straw for the use of the stables and when the same is converted into dung the same is taken away by him for the use of his farm at Sandridge as his own property the straw being not sold but merely sent there for the purpose of being converted into dung for his use That on the first day of February this examinant was informed that two trusses of his straw were clandestinely and feloniously taken from out of the stables or outhouses belonging to the inn and were carried to the house of John Saunders in the Borough by some person or persons unknown.
And this examinant Henry Cherry for himself said that on Thursday night between six and seven o'clock in the evening he missed two trusses of straw the one being wheat and the other barley straw which had been furnished by Mrs.Clark for the use of the inn and that he traced the same by the little ---- ---- ---- to the alley near Mr.Kinder in the Borough and upon enquiry he was informed by Joseph Walker that he saw two soldiers take some straw to the house of John Saunders And this examinant further saith that he went to John Saunders house and there observed some clean wheat straw that had been lately littered down in his pigsty and from the whole of the circumstances this examinant hath reason to suspect and does suspect that John Saunders did receive the straw knowing the same to be stolen.
Recognisances 468/22 & 23.
See also 468/16. Saunders discharged for want of prosecution.

468/8   The Examination of William Costin of the Parish of St.Stephen in the Liberty of St.Alban, higgler, and John Latchford of St.Albans, son of William Latchford of St.Albans, labourer. Who severally say   And first William Costin for himself saith that he attended the St.Albans market yesterday where he purchased a quantity of pork for sale and that the same was hung up at the door of Augustin Brooks until about seven o'clock in the evening where being at a small distance from his stall he was informed a piece of meat called a butt piece had been feloniously taken away by a man who had been some time standing near the stall   That this examinant went immediately in pursuit of the aforesaid man and soon after apprehended him and also that the piece of meat was found dropped in the track in which the man had been pursued.

This examinant John Latchford saith that last night he was employed by William Costin to take care of his meat at the stall when he observed the prisoner who says his name is James Woodward after some considerable time loitering about the stall take a piece of pork meat from the hook where it hung and conceal it inside his frock and run away with it whereupon this examinant went and informed Mr. Costin and the prisoner was pursued and taken.

Recognisances 468/24 & 25.

Presentment of the jury 468/13 concerning theft of 8lb of pork valued at 2/-. Endorsed 'A true Bill'.

See also 468/16 for sentence.

468/9   The Examination of Thomas Higbid, son of William Higbid of the Borough. Who saith that on the 26th. he was in the town of St.Albans on his masters business between the hours of eight and nine in the evening when he met with Samuel Golding who went into Mr.Evans shop and asked him to wait until he came out for he was going to buy some spirits of vitriol but he did not then tell this examinant for what purpose he was going to buy it.   After he came out of Mr.Evans shop Samuel Golding followed this examinant and overtook him near the end of the Market House Samuel Golding then asked him if he had seen Hawes daughter   This examinant answered that he had seen Mr.Hawes daughter just before but did not then know where she was   Samuel Golding told him that the vitriol was to throw on Lucy Hawes for that she had told stories of him to his master   Golding then gave him the bottle containing the vitriol   desired him to throw it upon her but he refused and returned him the bottle   Charles Huggins was coming by at the time on his return home   Golding gave him the bottle with the vitriol and asked him to throw it   Charles Huggins asked what it was   Golding answered that it was snuff   Charles Huggins looked at the bottle and seeing it a liquid said it could not be snuff   At this time Lucy Hawes was coming by with another young woman   Samuel Golding showed him Lucy Hawes and desired him to go and throw it upon her which he immediately did   Charles Huggins came back with the bottle and returned the same to Samuel Golding and said that it had burned his fingers   Golding made answer that well it might for it was spirits of vitriol and soon after went to Mr.Evans and returned the bottle.

468/10 The Examination and Complaint of Lucy Hawes, the daughter of Edward Hawes of the Borough, currier. Who saith that last night the 26th.March being in the highway or public street called St.Peters Street she was assaulted by some person or persons wilfully and maliciously with an intent as she believes to burn her 'cloaths' and that a cotton gown and a dimity petticoat which she had then worn and had on her was burned and spoilt by a quantity of oil of vitriol being thrown thereon And she further saith that she hath reason to believe that Samuel Golding Thomas Higbid and Charles Huggins were the persons who so assaulted her.
Recognisances 468/26, 27 & 28.
Presentment of the jury 468/15 concerning an assault with intent to damage garments of total value 10/-. Endorsed 'A true Bill'.
See also 468/16. Acquitted.

468/11 The Complaint of Thomas Lewis, collector of the Land Tax within the Borough. Who saith that by virtue of his office he had occasion to distrain the goods and chattels of one William Agglinton of the Borough, bricklayer, for the sum of three pounds and upwards being an arrears of Land Tax due for the messuage or tenement wherein William Agglinton resides That William Agglinton came to the house of this complainant about ten o'clock last night and on this complainants going to the door William Agglinton immediately struck him with great violence The same time knocked the candle out of this complainants hand and endeavoured to enter the house That William Agglinton with many horrid oaths and imprecations said that this complainant had got his goods and he would beat him within an inch of his life or words to that effect That with much difficulty this complainant pushed him from the door and fastened it upon which Agglinton made several attempts to break it down by running against it and trying to break the panels with his feet and the said William Agglinton threatened that he would do the complainant injury to the amount of ten times the value of his goods by way of revenging himself for having his goods taken away and many other such threats.
Recognisances 468/18.
Articles of the Peace 468/17 exhibited by Thomas Lewis against William Agglington through fear of receiving some bodily harm.

468/16 Thomas Kentish and William Johnson indicted for feloniously stealing one pottle of horse beans value of 6d. One pottle of oats to the value of 2d & 30lbs weight of hay the value of 1s. The property of Elizabeth Shaw, widow. Acquitted.
William White indicted for feloniously receiving the above mentioned goods knowing the same to be stolen. Acquitted.
John Saunders discharged for want of prosecution.
James Woodward convicted of feloniously stealing 8 lbs weight of pork of the value of 2s. the property of William Costin ordered to be imprisoned 2 months and to be publicly whipped at the Market Cross on Saturday the 3rd. May next between the hours of 12 noon and one in the afternoon.
Samuel Golding and Charles Huggins indicted for wilfully maliciously and

feloniously making an assault on one Lucy Hawes, spinster, with an intent to spoil burn and deface her clothes & garments & feloniously spoiling burning & defacing one cotton gown of the value of 5s and one cotton dimity petticoat of the value of 5s the goods and chattels of the said Lucy Hawes.   Acquitted.

Seth Weedon convicted of obtaining 5s the money of Elizabeth Blows under false pretences. Ordered to be imprisoned one week & at the expiration thereof to be passed to his legal settlement.

468/31 King against James Woodward.		s .. d
Expenses of apprehending & keeping him in custody.		4 .. 0
Indictment.		2 .. 0
3 witnesses.		10 .. 0
Constable.		5 .. 0
	Total	£1.. 0 .. 0

468/32 The King against Seth Weedon.		s .. d
Paid for Bill of Indictment.		10 .. 0
2 witnesses attending at that Sessions and expenses.		15 .. 0
	Total	£1.. 5 .. 0

468/33 The King against Samuel Golding and Charles Huggins.		
Three witnesses & sundry other expenses.		£1 ..13 .. 0
Constable.		5 .. 0
Bill of Indictment.		5 .. 0
	Total	£2 .. 3 .. 0

468/34 Bill of the Clerk of the Peace. 48 entries of which one was crossed out. Final total £21..0..10d. Entries include mention of:-
Attending on the Treasurer and High Constable. Reference to payment of one third the bills of Mrs.Twitchell, Mr.Boys, John Hale & James Deayton. Drawing out and recording an order for appointing James Deayton Chief Constable in room of William Wilson. Removal of Thomas Bullcock, alias Palmer alias Brown, to Hertford to take trial at the Assizes. Benefit Society held at the Crow Public House. Recording an order for the Overseers of St.Peter's to reimburse the Treasurer monies paid for the families of Militia men.

468/35 Constables Bill. Henry Lines, St.Peter's Ward.
Entries largely concern conveyance of vagrants and pressing waggons for the military.

468/36, 37 & 38 Bills of ------ Russell, ------ Evans and Edward Evans, constables of Middle Ward, Holywell Ward and Fishpool Ward. Similar to the last item.

468/39 Bill of James Deayton. The main entries being:
Seven days subsistence Thomas Bullock (2s..4d). Removing same to Hertford (12s..0d). Fees for seven prisoners (13s..4d each).

SESSIONS ROLL 469, Midsummer 1800   (18th.July)

469/1   Writ proclaiming Quarter Sessions and Gaol Delivery.

469/2   Calendar of prisoners for the Borough Gaol. (No prisoners).

469/3   List of jurors for the Grand and Petty juries.

469/4   Calendar of prisoners for the House of Correction.
May 1st. James Norman for 1 month for ill behaving in St.Peters Workhouse. Discharged May 29th.
Vagrants committed for seven days. 5 males, 5 females and 2 children. (Two females ill and one male very ill).

469/5 & 6   Recognisances concerning Charles Green appearing to prefer a Bill of Indictment against James Field, Thomas Dawson and Joseph Coventon for making riot and assaulting him.

469/9 & 10 Sacrament Certificates of Jeremiah Lowe & Daniel Adey Esq.

469/11 Bill of James Deayton.	s..d
To 8 days subsistence to Seth Weedon.	2..8
To the public whipping of James Woodwards.	10..0
To 8 weeks subsistence to James Woodwards.	18..8
Total	£1.. 11..4

469/12 Bill James Deayton. For fires for Magistrates on Saturdays Sept.1799 to May 1800.
41 at 1/6d each and Pens, ink and paper at 1/-d. Total £3..2..6.
£2..1..8 to the Liberty, £1..0..10. to the Borough.

SESSIONS ROLL 470, Michaelmas 1800   (10th.Oct.)

470/1   Writ proclaiming Quarter Sessions and Gaol Delivery.

470/2   Calendar of prisoners for the Borough Gaol.
James Harding committed 16th.Sept. charged on the oath of Philip Parsons on suspicion of having feloniously stolen and taken away 7 silver tablespoons, 12 silver teaspoons, a plated fishspoon and a great-coat his property.

470/3   List of jurors for the Grand and Petty juries.

470/4   Vagrants Committed for 7 days between July 7th.& Sept.27th.
10 males, 4 females and 3 children. (Names and dates included).

470/5   The Information of Philip Parsons of the Borough, surgeon, who on his oath saith that on Friday night last or early on Saturday morning seven silver tablespoons twelve silver teaspoons a plated fishspoon and a great-coat the property of him the said Philip Parsons were feloniously stolen and taken away from out of his dwelling house situated in the Borough of St.Albans and that the said Philip Parsons hath reason to suspect and does suspect that James Harding his servant did steal and take the same.

470/6 The Examination and Confession of James Harding, servant of Philip Parsons. That he did not feloniously take the said several things above mentioned but that his masters house having been broken open and robbed he did a few days afterwards find a great-coat and a pair of breeches belonging to his master in the dung-heap in the yard and that soon after he asked his masters leave to go to Uxbridge and went to London and took with him the great-coat and breeches which he so found and there sold them to a person in Monmouth Street for eight shillings.
Recognisances 470/8 & 9.
Presentment of the jury 470/14 concerning theft by James Harding. Endorsed: 'A true Bill'.

470/10 Recognisances concerning Thomas Clark and James Clark, higglers, for an assault upon William Latham, an infant.

470/12 Recognisances concerning Robert Beaumont appearing to answer such matters as shall be objected against him for a misdemeanour.

470/13 Presentment of the jury concerning an assault upon James Putnam, gardener, by William Prudden, yeoman.
Recognisances 470/7 & 11.

470/15 Draft Order. John Boys, Treasurer, hath laid before this court an account of monies paid by him for the relief of the families of William Jefferies, James Strong and James Sharp, substitutes serving in the militia for the Parish of St.Peter, the sum of £17..3..6. (That is to say) for the relief of the child of William Jefferies from 27th.July 1797 to 29th.Dec.1798, the sum of £5..11..0. For the relief of the wife and child of James Strong 1st.Apr.1798 to 16th.Mar.1799, the sum of £7..10..0. For the relief of the wife of James Sharp 7th.Apr.1798 to 11th.May 1799, the sum of £4..2..6, Pursuant to an Act .... The Overseers of the Poor of the said Parish are ordered to reimburse John Boys the respective sums of money out of the Poor Rate of the parish.

470/16 Bill of Benjamin Fowler for bricklayers and plasterers work done at the Town Hall. Mention made to the walls of the front prison, cleaning hall staircase, whitewashing kitchen and front rooms ceilings. Total £3..12..11.

470/17 Bill of James Deayton.	s .. d
The fees of George Herbert committed for rioting.	13 .. 4

The fees of Robert Beaumont.	13 .. 4
The fees of James Harding.	13 .. 4
2 fires, pens, ink & paper.	6 .. 0
Total	£2.. 6 .. 0

470/18 A Bill.   To fixing a new bell with 2 pulls & 2 ivory handles at the Town Hall.   £1..13..6.

SESSIONS ROLL 471, Epiphany 1801   (16th. Jan.)

471/1   Writ proclaiming Quarter Sessions and Gaol Delivery.

471/2   List of jurors for the Grand and Petty juries.

471/3   Calendar of prisoners for the Borough, in the House of Correction. William Grubb committed charged on the oath of Rebecca Swain with having gotten her with child which said child is likely to be born a bastard and become chargeable to the Parish of St.Alban.

471/4   Calendar of prisoners for the Borough Gaol.
James Harding convicted at Michaelmas Sessions 1800 of petty larceny ordered to be transported for seven years. Remains in 'goal'.
Thomas Messenger committed for suspicion of felony in stealing a quantity of wheat about one bushel and $^1/_2$ of the value of 15/- the property of Edward Shirley of Shenley in the county of Hertford, farmer, on the oath of Th.Shirley and others.

471/5   Calendar of prisoners committed to the House of Correction.
Vagrants committed between Oct.& Jan. *(names & dates included).*
10 males, 12 females and four children committed for 7 days.
1 male and 1 child for one day.
Also committed Dec.20th. William Grubb for a bastard child. Sent to Quarter Sessions.

471/6   Examination of Job Nash of the Borough, stationer, who on his oath saith that about two years ago Thomas Dearman then of the Parish of Sandridge in the Liberty of St.Alban, but now of the Parish of Abbots Langley, husbandman, came to his shop in the Borough and bought $^1/_2$ quire of letter paper for which he offered a counterfeit $^1/_2$ guinea which the wife of this examinant took as she did not at that time observe that it was counterfeit - That on the Saturday following or the Saturday week following, Thomas Dearman having heard that application had been made to a magistrate respecting the same, came to this examinant and changed it to a good $^1/_2$ guinea and took the counterfeit away with him. And this examinant further saith that on Saturday last Thomas Dearman came to his shop just before candlelight and asked for a day book of the price of 5/6 and other articles, together about 9, which he bought and that in payment for the same

he again tendered a counterfeit $^1/_2$ guinea which this examinant did not then observe was a counterfeit as it was in the dusk of the evening and the said Thomas Dearman threw it down on a book or some paper whereby it made no sound, but yesterday he discovered that the said $^1/_2$ guinea was counterfeit and from the circumstances above mentioned he hath reason to suspect and does suspect that Thomas Dearman knew the same to be counterfeit at the time he paid and believe that it is the same counterfeit piece of money which was taken in payment as first above mentioned.
Recognisances 471/8 & 9.
Presentment of the jury 471/13 concerning the misdemeanour of uttering counterfeit coin. Endorsed 'No true Bill'.

471/7   Examinations of Thomas Shirley of Shenley in the County of Hertford, farmer, Samuel Deayton of the Borough of St.Alban and Henry Norris of the Parish of St.Stephen in the Liberty of St.Alban, miller. Thomas Shirley for himself saith that his father Edward Shirley, farmer, hath for these last 6 weeks or thereabouts employed one Thomas Messenger, a labourer, resident at South Mimms, to thresh for him a quantity of wheat at his farm in the Parish of Shenley. That Thomas Messenger in threshing the wheat for the first fortnight produced one load or 5 bushels per day by his threshing, but for the last 9 days he produced by his threshing produced only 5 loads and a $^1/_2$ without there being any cause for such deficiency, from which circumstances this examinant and his father had reason to suspect that Thomas Messenger had stolen some of the wheat. And the examinant further saith that Thomas Messenger quitted his fathers service on Saturday last. And Henry Norris for himself saith that last Monday sennight Thomas Messenger about six o'clock in the morning came to his mill called Sopwell Mill in the Parish of St.Stephen and offered him for sale 1 bushel and $^1/_2$ of wheat as gleanings wheat. That this examinant looked at the wheat and being convinced that the same was not gleaned but strongly suspected that it had been stolen, refused to purchase it. And this examinant Samuel Deayton for himself saith that on Sunday last Thomas Messenger came to his house in the Borough and offered for sale a quantity of wheat in a bag about a bushel and $^1/_2$. That he asked 14/- per bushel for it but this examinant suspecting that the same was stolen, took Thomas Messenger before a magistrate. And lastly, Thomas Shirley for himself saith that he had compared the wheat found in the custody of Thomas Messenger with part of the wheat belonging to his father as threshed by Thomas Messenger and that the same correspond in the sample. And that he hereby believes that the wheat so found in the custody of Thomas Messenger is his father's property and was feloniously taken away by Thomas Messenger.
Recognisances 471/10 & 11.
Presentment of the jury 471/12 concerning the felonious theft of one bushel of wheat of the value of 5/-. Endorsed 'No true Bill'.

471/14   Account of James Deayton 28th.Oct.1800.   s .. d
4 days subsistence straw for John Aslin, committed
by Thomas Kinder on suspicion of felony.   3 .. 0

5 days subsistence straw for John Darben, committed by Richard Brabant, deserter, discharged.	3 .. 6
5 days subsistence straw for Robert Pett, deserter from the Royal Navy.	3 .. 6
Fees for Thomas Messenger.	13 .. 4
1 shirt for above ordered by Richard Brabant.	5 .. 0
14 weeks subsistence for James Harding at 2s 7½d	£1 ..16 .. 9½
2 fires.	5 .. 0
Pens, ink and paper.	2 .. 0

471/15 Coroner's Inquest Fees.	£ .. s .. d
On body of Mary Smith, pauper who died in the workhouse under suspicious circumstances.	1 .. 0 .. 0
Paid Sgt at Mace and jury	17 .. 0
On the body of ------- Parsons who poisoned himself.	1 ..17 .. 0
	3 ..14 .. 0

SESSIONS ROLL 472, Easter 1801 (17th.April)

472/1 Writ proclaiming Quarter Sessions and Gaol Delivery.

472/2 List of jurors for the Grand and Petty juries.

472/3 Calendar of prisoners in the Borough Gaol. (No prisoners).

472/4 Calendar of prisoners committed to the House of Correction. Dec.12th.William Grubb for a bastard child. Discharged Jan.28 Vagrants committed for seven days between Dec.12th.& Apr.10th. 6 males, 10 females and 15 children. *(Names & dates included).*

472/5 An account of penalties on convictions of persons having in their possession false weights at a Petty Sessions held the 5th.July 1800.

Names of persons.	No. of wts.	Offences.	Penalties.	Costs.
Charles Kentish	1	3	£1..0..0	4s
George Wilshere	1	2	5..0	4s
Edward Eling	3	6	£1..0..0	4s
Henry Jefferies	1	1	5..0	4s
John Saunders	1	1	5..0	4s
George Irons	1	1	5..0	4s
William Howes	3	1	5..0	4s
			£3..5..0	£1.. 8..0
Paid the Constable			7..6	
			£2..17..6	

472/6 An account of false weights and convictions 23rd.Jan.1801. Similar to last item. Persons convicted:- Saml.Wildbore, Joseph Edey, Wm.Brown, Wm.Lintot, Jonathan Brewers, Jonathan Shepherd, Jonathan

Twinace, Wm.Harris, Ann Deayton, Ann Batten, Jonathan Whittington & Elizabeth Moore.

472/7 Recognisances concerning William Joscelin being prosecuted for regrating.

472/8 Note. Easter Sessions 1801.
The King on the prosecution of Henry Norris against Wm.Josceline for a misdemeanour. W.Watson to move - Court to plead & traverse indictment to next Sessions on putting in good & sufficient bail.

472/9 Constables appointed at the Quarter Sessions, Easter 1801.

John Wright	St.Peters Ward	Sworn.
Edward Eling	Middle Ward	
James Farley	Holywell Ward	Sworn.
Joseph Parsons	Fishpool Ward	Sworn.

Jeremiah Rogers in the room of Edward Eling by leave of the Court. Sworn.

472/10 The Constables Bill for St.Peters Ward. *(Spelling as in original).*

1800		s .. d
April 25th.	The Oath.	1 .. 0
May 30th.	Pasing Seth weeden.	0 .. 4
June 9th.	A warnt to Colney Street 4 miles.	2 .. 0
10th.	To ditto.	2 .. 0
Sept.8th.	To sumonsing the Landlords.	1 .. 0
13th.	Attending at the Hall.	1 .. 0
Nov.17th.	To pasing Ann Brown.	0 .. 4
1801		
Jan.7th.	To sumonsing the over Seers.	1 .. 0
10th.	Attending at the Hall.	1 .. 0
23rd.& 24th.	Searching the Login Houses.	2 .. 6
	Attending the 4 Quarter Seshons.	6 .. 0
	J.Rogers Constable.	18 .. 2

Easter Sessions   Allowed   Rd.Brabant, Mayor.

472/11 Constables bill. Joseph Eady Constable for the Middle Ward.

1800		s .. d
April 25th.	For being sworn in Constable.	1 .. 0
July 26th.	To a horse and cart for conveying the body of Sarah Territ to Colney Street.	4 .. 0 X
Sept.8th.	To summoning the Publicans for taking out their Licenses.	1 .. 0
13th.	To attending the Justices at the Town Hall.	1 .. 0
1801		
Jan.7th.	To summoning the Overseers to the Town Hall.	1 .. 0
13th.	For a horse and cart to convey the body of Mary Lee to London Colney.	4 .. 0 X

17th.	For a horse and cart to convey the body		
	of Sarah Cooper to London Colney.	4 .. 0 X	
	For attending the 4 Quarter Sessions.	6 .. 0	
23 & 24th.	To searching the Lodging Houses thro		
	the Borough.	2 .. 6	
		£1 .. 3 .. 6	
	Deduct	12 .. 0	
Easter Sessions Allowed Rd.Brabant, Mayor.		11 .. 6	

472/12 Constables Bill. Similar to above, but includes the following items. Total £1 .. 18 .. 6.

1800	'The Constabells Bill for Holewell Ward.'	s .. d
June 10th.	'For pressing 3 Waggons for the 55 Rigt.of feet.'	2 ..0
29th.	'One Waggon 1 Cart for the Bucks Militia.'	1 .. 6
Sept.4th.	'For Pressing 2 waggons for the first	
	Dragon Gards.'	1 .. 6
6th.	'For Pressing 3 waggons for the feet Gards.'	2 .. 0
Oct. 17th.	'For Pressing a waggon & Cart for the	
	Rumney fenseabells.'	1 .. 6

Also mentions: the 5 Dragon Gards, the 12 Draggons, the 14 Draggons, the 55 Rigt. of feet and the Atilerey. 'H.Mansell Constabell.'

472/13 Constables Bill. '1800 Constable Bill fishpole Word', similar to items 10 & 11, but includes 28 entries with names, presumably vagrants, under an order for 'having men and women out of the town by order of the Justices'. For example:

'For having Elbth.Cordmen 4d '
Joseph Hulks, Constable.

472/14 Bill of James Deayton. s .. d

Feb.9th.1801.	To 25 days subsistence to James Harding at 4½ d	
	per day. Was under sentence of Transportation.	9 .. 4½
	'To Removing the Same on baard the Ulks at	
	Woolwich'	£2 .. 2 .. 0
April 17th.	To pens, ink & paper	2 .. 0
	To two fires	5 .. 0
	Easter Sessions 1801.	£2 ..18 .. 4½

472/15 Bill of the Clerk of the Peace from Easter Sessions 1800 to Epiphany Sessions 1801 inclusive. Itemised bill totalling £24..14..10 and containing 56 entries including :-

	£ .. s .. d
The King against Weedon. The like for payment of the prosecutors expenses.	5 .. 0
The King against Golding.	5 .. 0
The King against Woodward	5 .. 0
Fees of six prisoners discharged by Proclamation.	2 .. 0 .. 0
Fees of two prisoners committed to Gaol.	13.. 4

Writing circular letters to all the acting magistrates by

the Marquis of Salisbury's desire, recommending the
prompt suppression of all kinds of riot and tumult and
to the encouragement of the free supply of the Markets.   13.. 4
Journey to London and attending the Exchequer to swear
to and deliver the Estreat Roll of Fines. (out two days).   2 .. 2 .. 0
Coach hire and expenses.   2 .. 2 .. 0
Making a copy of the Marquis of Salisbury's circular letter
to the acting magistrates and of His Majesty's Proclamation
recommending certain measures for diminishing the
consumption of Bread Corn, to get printed.   5 .. 0
Writing letter of instruction to the Constables for
carrying into execution the Population Act.   3 .. 6
Drawing out and recording an order for adjourning the
Sessions to the 17th.inst. to receive the report of the
magistrates under the late Act of Parliament for making
better provision for the maintenance of the poor
by directing the manner of applying Parish Relief.   5 .. 0

SESSIONS ROLL 473, Midsummer 1801   (17th.July)

473/1   Writ proclaiming Quarter Sessions and Gaol Delivery.

473/2   List of jurors for the Grand and Petty juries.

473/3   Calendar of prisoners for the Borough Gaol. (No prisoners).

473/4   Calendar of prisoners in the House of Correction.
James Cummings committed the 25th.June charged with assaulting Ann
House widow and refusing to find sufficient surety for his personal
appearance at the General Quarter Sessions.
Lawrence Aspinal committed July 6th. charged with assaulting Mr.George
Sherman in his dwelling house and breaking his window.

473/5   Vagrants committed between Apr.16th.& Jun.13th.
8 males, 8 females and 14 children committed for 7 days and 1 woman and 2
children for 3 days. *(Names & dates included).* Also
May 12th. John Rigby for leaving his family. Discharged May 26th.
June 25th.James Cummings for an assault, for the Sessions.
July 6th. Lawrence Aspinal for assaulting George Sherman, for the
Sessions.

473/6   Rex v.Hatcher & Dudley (R)
Examination and complaint of John Peacock labourer Who saith that one
John Hatcher of the Borough, labourer together with divers other persons did
on Monday last the 28th. May make a great noise riot & disturbance in the
Kings highway and in and about the house of one William Dudley known
by the sign of the Cock to the disturbance of His Majesty's peaceable
subjects by carrying about two effigies with a large pair of horns and

collecting together men women and children to the number of 50 or more and shouting and encouraging those others to shout and halloo continuing for the space of 4 hours and that John Hatcher by way of keeping up and continuing the riot and disturbance did collect from the bystanders and passengers money to be spent at the house of William Dudley and there did keep the effigies which were to represent the wife of this complainant and some other person and that William Dudley was also present and was going to fight and offered to fight because some person wishing to put an end to the disturbance had knocked down the effigies and John Hatcher did otherwise misbehave himself.
Recognisances 473/8 & 9.

473/7 Examination of Ann House against James Cummings (R). Ann House saith that James Cummings has ill-used her by making use of various threats and striking her with his fist on the head last night saying "Damne you old bitch won't you die" and she further saith that she is fearful from the threats he hath made that he will so her some bodily mischief and he threatened to murder her whereupon she prays articles of the peace against him.

473/10 Bill of James Deayton. Total £3. $^2/_3$ to the Liberty & $^1/_3$ to the Borough.

473/11 Bill of James Deayton 1801.   s .. d
To 4 days subsistence & straw to Nathaniel Marsh
ordered into custody by Richard Brabant Esq.Mayor,
as a rogue & vagabond.   3 .. 0
To 20 days ditto to Edward Liggins ordered into custody
by Daniel Adey Esq. as a deserter.   11 .. 0
To 6 days ditto to Thomas Chandler ordered into custody
as a deserter from the Glatton Kings Ships.   4 .. 0
To 8 days ditto to Thos.Jones ordered into custody by
Daniel Adey Esq. on suspicion of being a deserter.   4 .. 0
Pens, ink and paper.   2 .. 0
                                    Total   £1 .. 4 .. 0

473/12 Names of persons passed from 'Holewell' Ward. 1800-1801
Humphrey Mansell, Constable.   s .. d
For conveying Mary Davis to Colney 3 miles.   2 .. 0
For a cart and horse to convey Thomas Williams to
Watford 8 miles..   6 .. 0
For my own time and expenses.   2 .. 0
For conveying John Sansbury to Colney Street 4 miles.   2 .. 6
For my own time and expenses.   1 .. 0
For a cart and horse to convey Elizabeth Seayer to
Rickmansworth, 12 miles.   7 .. 0
For bed and reliefs.   7
For my own time and expenses.   2 .. 6
        Total   £1 .. 3 .. 7

473/13 1800 December 16th. Joseph Hulks, Constable. (Similar to 473/11 & 12). Includes one female to Hatfield.

473/14 1800 July. Joseph Eady's bill for passing vagrants. (Similar to 473/11 & 12). Includes three females to London Colney.

473/15 J.Rogers bill for passing vagrants to Hatfield etc. (Similar to 473/11 & 12). 7 vagrants to Hatfield

473/16 Bill of John Cowper.
For the fees as Clerk of the Peace of 3 returns made by Overseers under the population Act at 1s each.   Total: 3s 0d.

473/17 Bill of Mr.Boys. (similar to 473/16).

SESSIONS ROLL 474, Michaelmas 1801   (9th.Oct.)

474/1 Writ proclaiming Quarter Sessions and Gaol Delivery.

474/2 List of jurors for the Grand and Petty juries.

474/3 Calendar of prisoners for the Borough Gaol.
William Lucas committed 29th.July on the oath of Elizabeth Cook and on his own confession with having feloniously taken from and out of the dwelling house of John Cook one silver tablespoon.
Thomas Hopkins and William Birch committed 22nd.August who are charged on the oath of Elizabeth Day and others with having uttered and tendered in payment counterfeit money knowing the same to be counterfeit.
                                                        'James Deayton, Goaler'.

474/4 Vagrants committed for seven days between July 10th.& Sept.30th. 4 males and 12 females committed for 7 days (4 sick) plus one female for 14 days. (Names & dates included).

474/5 Presentment of the jury concerning Thomas Hopkins late of the parish of St.Albans, labourer, and William Birch of the same place, labourer, uttering a piece of counterfeit coin in the similitude of a gold coin of this realm called a 7 shilling piece and uttering one other similar false coin to Elizabeth Day, widow.
Further, concerning Thomas Hopkins and William Birch uttering one piece of false coin in the similitude of a gold coin of this realm called a 7 shilling piece to one Mary Moss. Endorsed 'A true Bill'.
Recognisances 474/8, 9 & 10.

474/6 Examination of Elizabeth Cook, spinster, who saith that William Lucas late of Kingsthorpe in the county of Northampton, labourer, did this day feloniously take one silver table spoon marked with the letters EC being

the property of her father John Cook from and out of the dwelling house of John Cook.
Endorsed with note of recognisances.

474/7 Examination of William Lucas charged with feloniously taking and carrying away one silver table spoon marked EC the property of John Cook of the Borough, yeoman. Doth acknowledge and confess that he did feloniously take the same.
Recognisances 474/11 & 12.

474/13 Sacrament Certificate of Michael Price.

474/14	Bill of James Deayton 9th.Oct.1801.	£ .. s .. d
	To the fees of William Lucas.	13 .. 4
	To the fees of Thomas Hopkins & William Birch.	1 .. 6 .. 8
	To two fires.	5 .. 0
	To pens, ink and paper.	2 .. 0
	Allowed J.Searanke	2 .. 7 ..0

474/15 Fees of Isaac Piggott & Job Nash, late Overseers of the Parish of St.Albans, for taking an account of the population of the Parish in the month of March 1801 pursuant to the late Act of Parliament. Out 3 days each and for making out the Book to deliver over to the Churchwardens. £2..10..0. Number of persons returned 1900.

474/16 Fees of Richard Bradshaw late Overseer of the Parish of St.Michaels in the Borough of St.Albans. For taking the population in March last, out one day 12/6 Number of persons returned 287.

474/17 Fees of Mr.Joshua Kentish late Overseer of the Parish of St.Peters in the Borough of St.Albans. For taking the population in March last, out two days £1..5..0 Number of persons returned 840.

SESSIONS ROLL 475, Epiphany 1802 (15th.Jan.)

475/1 Writ proclaiming Quarter Sessions and Gaol Delivery.

475/2 List of jurors for the Grand and Petty juries.

475/3 Calendar of prisoners for the House of Correction.
Thomas Groom committed on the oath of Mary Nash of the Parish of St.Alban with having gotten her with child which is likely to become chargeable to the Parish.

475/4 Calendar of prisoners for the Borough Gaol.
Thomas Hopkins and William Birch convicted for uttering false and counterfeit money. Remain in gaol.

475/5   Calendar of prisoners committed to the House of Correction.
Vagrants committed for seven days between Oct.14th.&Jan.12th.
7 males, 3 females and 1 child. *(Names & dates included).*
Also James Hannel for a bastard child. Oct.17th.to 18th.

475/6   Bill of James Deayton.   £ ..s ..d
To 56 days subsistence to William Lucas from
Oct.9th.to Dec.4th. at 4 $\frac{1}{2}$d per day.   1 ..1 ..0
To 90 days subsistence to Thomas Hopkins & William
Birch from Oct.9th. to Jan. 15th. 1802 at 4 $\frac{1}{2}$d per day.   3..13..6
Paid Thomas Howse for a second hand coat for William Lucas   5..0
To Ink and Paper.   2..0
To 2 fires.   5..0
        Allowed. F.C.Searancke, Mayor   Total   £ 5 ..6..6

SESSIONS ROLL 476, Easter 1802   (30th.April)

476/1   Writ proclaiming Quarter Sessions and Gaol Delivery.

476/2   List of jurors for the Grand and Petty juries.

476/3   Calendar of prisoners for the Borough Gaol.
Thomas Hopkins & William Birch. Convicted for uttering fake and counterfeit money.
John Peel committed on 30th.March, charged on the oath of James Farley blacksmith, with having feloniously stolen six copper screws and one buttress the property of James Farley.   'Goaler'.

476/4   Calendar of prisoners committed to the House of Correction.
Vagrants committed between Jan.12th.& Apr.17th.
5 males 4 females and a number of children committed for 7 days.
2 males for 2 days and 1 male, 1 female and a number of children for 12 days.
Also Jan 15th. Thomas Hannoway for a bastard child. Discharged Jan.20th.
And April 29th. Andrew Oliver committed by the Mayor.

476/5   The Examination of James Farly blacksmith of the Borough who saith that on the 30th.March he found in the shop of John Peele one buttress which was stolen from him and that he believed John Peele did steal the buttress.
Endorsed with note of recognisances.

476/6   The Examination of James Farly Who saith that he lost several copper screws amounting to six and hath sufficient reason to suspect that John Peele, smith of the Borough, has got the screws in his possession either in his dwelling house or shop or some other part of the premises of the said John Peele.

476/7 The Examination of Thomas Peele who saith that he saw some copper screws lying in the dwelling house of John Peele blacksmith about five weeks ago.
Recognisances 476/8.
Presentment of the jury 476/9 concerning the felonious theft of one iron buttress to the value of one shilling and six copper screws of the value of six pence, the property of James Farly. Endorsed 'A true Bill'.

476/10 The Bill of the Clerk of the Peace for the Borough of St.Albans, from Easter Sessions 1801 to Epiphany 1802 inclusive.
Itemised bill totalling £20..12..6. and containing 44 entries including :-
Appointing Visitors of the Gaol and House of Correction.   5s..0d
Drawing out and recording an order for increasing the allowance to persons providing carriages for soldiers baggage.   10s..0d

476/11 James Farley's bill of expenses as prosecutor in the King against John Peele for felony.

Paid for subpoena for James Bates to give evidence, for serving same and Conduct Money.	9..6
Paid for indictment.	2..0
For loss of time of the prosecutor and witness in attending Quarter Sessions.	12..0

476/12 Borough of St.Albans to James Deayton.   £..s..d

Jan.26th.1802 Paid Mr.Samuel Giles for a pair of stout blankets for the use of the Borough Gaol by order of Francis Carter Searanke Esq. Mayor.	17..6
April 30th.To 105 days subsistence to Thomas Hopkins at 4 $\frac{1}{2}$d per day.	1..19..4 $\frac{1}{2}$
To do to William Birch	1..19..4 $\frac{1}{2}$
To the fees of John Peele.	13..4
To two fires.	5..0
Pens, Ink and Paper.	2..0
Allowed F.C.Searanke.	£5 .. 16..7

476/13 26th.Jan.1802. By the Order of Francis Searanke Esq., Mayor.
Bt. of Samuel Giles, 1pr. stout blankets.   17s..6d
For Mr.Giles.   T.Bruton.

476/14 Bill of J.Rogers, Constable Middle Ward, from Easter 1801 to Easter 1802. Itemised bill totalling £7..12..6 and containing 48 entries including :-   s..d

Date	Entry	s..d
April 17th.	The oath when sworn inn.	1..0
April 25th.	Pressing a cart.	1..0
May 12th.	Pressing 3 waggons.	3..0
July 7th.	A warrant to the Constable of 'St.Mickel'.	1..0
July 22nd.	'Floggin' Thos.Mackline.	2..6
Aug.28th.	Taking Thos.Hopkins & Willm.Birch.	7..6
Sept.6th.	Summoning the 'Land Lords attendin' Licence Day.	2..6

Oct.18th.   A horse & cart & passing Mary Spencer to Colney.   4..6
1802
Jan.28th.   Do & do   passing John Anderson to   do.   4..6
April 18th.   3 nights making a general search.   7..6
             Attending the 4 Quarter 'Seshons'.   6..0
             13 Sundays stopping the wagons.   £1..12..6
             Setting down the Militia, attending the day
             of appeal and at the Angel   10..0
(To pressing 51 wagons & 4 carts & 7 warrants to Constables at 1/- each.
various dates).

476/15   Bill of James Farley, Constable Holywell Ward. Entries
include:-   s..d
April 17th.   Being sworn in constable.   1..0
April 2nd.   Passing Joab Loins a vagrant with horse and cart to
             Windridge Ward and relief.   6..4
May 16th.   Do. Thos.Harris to Do.   6..4
May 22nd.   Do. Eliz.Hammond & son with cart & relief to
             Windridge Ward.   6..8
July 28th   Do. Mary Gibbs & her two Children Do. Do.   7..0
July 22nd.   Flogging Thos.Macklan.   2..6
Aug.2nd.   Lodging & relief for Mary Gibbs & her two children.   1..6
Aug.3rd.   Passing Mary Gibbs & children & relief & horse &
             cart to Windridge Ward.   7..0
Sept.5th.   Summoning the Landlords & attending
             Licence day.   2..6
Apr.25th.   To 3 nights Privy Search.   7..6
             Attending the 4 Quarter Sessions.   6..0
             Setting down the Militia & attending the day of
             appeal and at the Angel.   10..0
             To 13 Sundays attending on
             waggons & Stre.   £1.. 12..0

476/16   Bill of John Wright, Constable St.Peters Ward. Entries
include:-   s..d
             Being sworn in Constable.   1..0
July 3rd.   Going to Sleepside to summon Mr.Briton.   2..0
July 21st.   Taking Thos.Grove & paying assistance.   2..0
July 22nd.   Whipping Thos.McLane a vagrant.   2..6
July 28th.   Passing Mary Gibbs & two children with relief.   2..0
Aug.16th.   Passing Isaac Tyerel to Colney with horse & cart. 4..6
Oct.8th.   Do. Mary Hollingsworth to Sleepside   Do.   4..6
Oct.24th.   Do. Hannah Bridges & child to Sandridge Do.   3..6
Jan.10th.   Do. Mary Mills to Sleepside   Do.   4..6
March 20th.Do. Alexander Potts & wife to Do.   Do.   4..6
Various dates. Vagrants : 6 males, 4 females & 1 child at 4d each. *(Names
given)*.
Summoning the Landlords & Attending the Licence Day.   2..6
Setting down the Militia, attending the Lieutenants.   10..0

| Three Privy Search nights. | 7..6 |
| To attending four Quarter Sessions. | 6..0 |

476/17 Bill of J.Hulks, Constable Fishpool Ward. Entries include:-

		s..d
Apr.17th.	The oath when sworn in.	1..0
July 22nd.	Flogging Thos.Mackline.	2..6
Sept.5th.	Summoning the Landlords & attending the Licence Day.	2..6
	3 nights making a general search.	7..6
	Attending the four Quarter Sessions	6..0
	13 Sundays stopping the waggons.	£1.. 12..6
	Setting down the Militia attending the Day of Appeal at the Angel.	10..0
	Passing 45 vagrants to the Constable of St.'Mickel' at 4d each.	15..0

SESSIONS ROLL 477, Midsummer 1802 (16th.July)

477/1 Writ proclaiming Quarter Sessions and Gaol Delivery.

477/2 List of jurors for the Grand and Petty juries.

477/3 Calendar of prisoners for the Borough Gaol.
Thomas Hopkins and William Birch, committed for uttering counterfeit money. Remain in gaol.
Mary Bill bailed out. Committed on the 22nd.June 1802 on the oath of Mary Howel of St.Michael in the Borough that Mary Bill has repeatedly ill treated her whereby she is in bodily fear and hath prayed Sureties of the Peace against Mary Bill.

477/4 The Complaint of Thomas Peacock of the Borough, bricklayer, who saith that as he was standing at the door of the house where he lodges in the said Borough at about half after 12 o'clock at noon, he observed a great number of persons coming through Lamb Alley going round the bounds of the Parish of St.Albans when one Charles Green, Joseph Baker and two other persons laid hold of this complainant and with force and violence against his consent hit his body several times against a post near the Red House whereby he was considerably hurt and otherwise illtreated him.
Recognisances 477/5, 6 &7.

477/8 Sacrament Certificate of John Bacon of Frying Barnet from the Parish Church of East Barnet.

477/9 Bill of James Deayton. 1802 July 16th.
	£ .. s .. d
To 77 days subsistence to Thomas Hopkins at 4½ per day	1 .. 8 ..10½

To 77 days subsistence to William Birch at 4$^1/_2$ per day   1 .. 8 ..10$^1/_2$
Pens, ink and paper   <u>2 .. 0</u>
         Allowed, Percival Lewis, Recorder.   2 ..19 .. 9

SESSIONS ROLL 478, Michaelmas 1802   (8th.Oct.)

478/1   Writ proclaiming Quarter Sessions and Gaol Delivery.

478/2   List of jurors for the Grand and Petty juries.

478/3   Calendar of prisoners for the Borough Gaol.
Thomas Hopkins and William Birch, convicted for uttering false and counterfeit money.

478/5   Presentment of the jury concerning George Irons, victualler, for an assault upon Jeremiah Harris. Endorsed 'A true Bill'.
Recognisances <u>478/4</u>.

478/6   Bill of James Deayton. October 8th. 1802.
Main entries concern 85 days subsistence each for Thos.Hopkins and William Birch at 4 $^1/_2$d per day.

SESSIONS ROLL 479, Epiphany 1803   (14th.Jan.)

479/1   Writ proclaiming Quarter Sessions and Gaol Delivery.

479/2   List of jurors for the Grand and Petty juries.

479/3   Calendar of prisoners in the Gaol of the Borough.
Patrick Scully and Michael Allen committed Jan.5th. who are charged on the oath of James Ivory and Thomas Durrant with having violently assaulted them in the dwelling house of the said James Ivory within the Borough
Vagrants committed for seven days. 7 males (one sick), 1 female and an illegible entry. Also one disorderly person for four days.

479/4   Information and Complaint of James Ivory, victualler, Who saith that he keeps a public house in Sopwell Lane called the White Lion. That one Patrick Scully a corporal in the 7th. Regiment of Dragoon Guards and Michael Allen a Private soldier in the same regiment were quartered at his house yesterday. That he had retired to rest and had just gone to sleep he was awakened by a great noise. That he discovered the above two soldiers and one Thomas Durrant a lodger in his house fighting and scuffling together and that his bedroom door had been forced open. That after those persons had been scuffling together about five minutes the candle which was in the room was put out in the scuffle and one of the soldiers coming to his bedside said "Now you old bugger I have done for one and I will do for you", upon which he pulled him out of bed upon the floor and began to beat him very violently. That immediately afterwards the soldier who calls himself Michael Allen came into the room with a lighted candle in his hand and this complainant then discovered that it was the corporal Patrick Scully who had beat and ill treated him. That being on the floor with Scully the corporal laying under him the other soldier Michael Allen began to beat this complainant with a stick which he had in his hand and bruised him very much over his loins and thighs. That his wife having opened the the window of the room and called murder a number of persons who lived in the neighbourhood and were alarmed with her cries came into this complainants bedroom when the said two soldiers Scully and Allen both ran into their own sleeping room and having both carbines swore they would shoot the first man that stepped a step towards them and that after the space of an hour or thereabouts they were both secured.

Presentment of the jury 479/12 concerning Patrick Scully late of the Parish of St.Alban, labourer, and Michael Allen late of the same place, labourer, assaulting James Ivory. Endorsed 'Pleaded guilty. Verdict guilty'. Recognisances 479/9.

479/5 The Information and Complaint of Thomas Durrant of the Borough, labourer, Who saith that he has lodged for several years past in the house of James Ivory called the White Lion Public House. That last night about 12 o'clock he had retired to rest in the same room where two soldiers belonging to the 7th.Regiment of Dragoon Guards who were quartered at the above house were to sleep. That when this complainant went upstairs one of the soldiers whose name appears to be Patrick Scully and a corporal in the above regiment accompanied him into his bedroom. That he appeared to be rather intoxicated with liquor. That when they entered the bedroom together the other soldier whose name is Michael Allen appeared to be asleep. That about half an hour after this complainant had laid down in his bed Patrick Scully loaded his carbine and coming to this complainants bedside insisted upon this complainant getting out of his bed or otherwise worse should follow. That he immediately got out of bed and was proceeding downstairs when he met Patrick Scully who had been below to light a candle upon the stairs. That he immediately struck this complainant a violent blow on the face and repeated his blows several times. That this complainant made the least resistance he could and whilst he and Scully were scuffling together they both fell against the door of Mr.Ivory's bedroom and the door burst open. That the other soldier Michael Allen then came into Mr.Ivory's bedroom and assisted his companion Scully in beating and bruising this complainant until the candle which was in Mr.Ivory's room went out when he extricated himself and ran downstairs to let the people in who had collected together at the street door in consequence of Mrs.Ivory (the landlady) opening the window and calling out murder.

Presentment of the jury 479/13 concerning Patrick Scully late of the Parish of St.Alban, labourer, and Michael Allen late of the same place, labourer, assaulting Thomas Durrant. Endorsed 'Verdict guilty'. Recognisances 479/7.

479/11 To the Churchwardens and Overseers of the Poor of the Parish of St.Alban in the Borough and the Churchwardens and Overseers of the Poor of the Parish of Elstree in the Liberty of St.Alban. Whereas complaint has been made unto us being two of His Majesty's Justices of the Peace in and for the Borough by the Churchwardens and Overseers of the Poor of the Parish of St.Alban. That Mary Marshall, widow, lately introduced and came into the said Parish of St.Alban and is actually become chargeable to the same. ....and do also adjudge the place of the last settlement of the said Mary to be in the Parish of Elstree in the Liberty of St.Alban.

.... do require you, the Churchwardens and Overseers of the Poor of the Parish of St.Alban on sight hereof to remove and convey the said Mary from and out of your Parish of St.Alban to the Parish of Elstree ....

We the magistrates do hereby consent and agree that the within written order for the removal of the within named Mary Marshall, widow, from the Parish of St.Alban to the Parish of Elstree shall be quashed at the next Quarter Sessions of the Peace for the Borough of St.Albans at the expense of the said Parish of Elstree and that the expense of maintenance shall be given up by each parish and the undersigned William Hart doth hereby undertake to move the court accordingly.

479/14 Presentment of the jury concerning John Powell late of the Parish of St.Alban, yeoman, assaulting Walter Jones. Endorsed 'Plea of not guilty withdrawn at Easter Sessions and guilty pleaded'.
Recognisances 479/6.

479/15 Bill of James Deayton.
Main entries: Fees of Patrick Scully and Michael Allen. 13/4d each.

SESSIONS ROLL 480, Easter 1803   (22nd.April)

480/1   Writ proclaiming Quarter Sessions and Gaol Delivery.

480/2   List of jurors for the Grand and Petty juries.

480/3   Calendar of prisoners for the Borough Gaol.
Patrick Scully & Michael Allen convicted for assaulting James Ivory and Thomas Durrant. Ordered to be severally imprisoned in the Common Gaol of the Borough for the space of three months for assaulting James Ivory and for the further term of three months for assaulting Thomas Durrant. Remains in Gaol.

480/4   Vagrants committed to the House of Correction.
Seven males, five females and three children for 7 days.

480/9 to 14 Recognisances concerning William Birch and Thomas Hopkins being bound to be of good behaviour for two years.

480/15 The jurors present Anthony Dwyr late of the Parish of St.Albans for an Assault made upon Charles Griffin on 22nd.January.
Endorsed 'A true Bill'.
Recognisances 480/5, 6, 7 & 8.

480/16 Bill of the Clerk of the Peace. Easter Sessions 1802 to Epiphany Sessions 1803 inclusive. Bill totalling £23..15..8. containing 44 entries including :-

	s.. d
Fees of one prisoner discharged by proclamation.	6.. 8
Paid for parchment.	5.. 0
Fees of 2 prisoners committed to Gaol.	13.. 4
Attending at my printers in London to get copies printed of an Order of Council respecting the Apprehension by the Magistrates & Deputy Lieutenants of straggling seafaring men which was transmitted to me by the Marquis of Salisbury & for my trouble in conveying such copies to the Magistrates & writing letters with the same.	6.. 8
For my time & trouble in assorting the several Public General Statutes transmitted to me for the use of the Magistrates to the present Session & attending to deliver the same.	£1.. 1.. 0

480/17 Bill of James Deayton. April 22nd.1803.   £.. s.. d

To ninety eight days subsistence to Patrick Scully & Michael Allen at 4 $\frac{1}{2}$ d per day each.	3..13..6
To eleven days subsistence & straw to George Tans ordered into custody on suspicion of being a deserter from H.M.'s Navy.	6.. 6
To six days subsistence & straw to David Ogleby ordered into custody on suspicion as above.	4.. 0
To five days subsistence & straw to James Walker ordered into custody on suspicion as above.	3.. 6
To two fires.	5.. 0
To pens, ink & paper.	2.. 0
Easter Sessions 1803. Allowed Rd.Brabant, Mayor.	£4.. 14.. 6

480/18 30th.April. The Borough of St.Albans to William Deavill, Constable of Middle Ward. Total £3..17..8. Entries include:-

	s..d
The oath.	1..0
Delivering two vagrants to St.Michaels.	8
To watching the waggons 4 'Saboth' days.	10..0
To 'prising' 1 waggon.	1..0
To sending 1 warrant to the Windridge Ward.	2..6
To setting down Militia	10..0
Attending 6 days on Militia at the Angel.	£1..10..0
To 'prissing' 1 cart.	1..0
Attending 4 nights at the two 'fares'.	6..0

480/19, 20 & 21   Bills of William Roson, J.Rogers and Henry Jeffries,

Constables for St.Peters Ward, Fishpool Ward & Holywell Ward. Similar to item 480/18.

SESSIONS ROLL 481, Midsummer 1803 (15th.July)

481/1 Writ proclaiming Quarter Sessions and Gaol Delivery.

481/2 List of jurors for the Grand and Petty juries.

481/3 Calendar of prisoners for the Borough Gaol.
Thomas Wilson committed 29th.day of June on oath of Robert Caustin for suspicion of felony in stealing a silver spoon of the value of five shillings the property of Joseph Ray, victualler, of Aylesbury.

481/4 Vagrants committed each for 7 days. April 20th.to July 8th. Names of 8 males and 2 females with committal and discharge dates.

481/5 Bill of James Deayton.

To 3 days subsistence & straw to Jno.Maloney a	s..d
seafaring man ordered into custody.	2..6
To 2 days subsistence & straw to James Jude and Robert	
Hares seafaring men ordered into custody as above.	4..0
To the fees of Thomas Day committed for an assault	
by Richard Brabant Esq.Mayor. Ordered to be discharged.	13..4
To 2 days subsistence & straw to James Ward &	
Philip Oneigley ordered into custody by Thomas	
Kinder Esq. on suspicion of horse stealing.	4..0
To the fees of Thomas Wilson .	13..4
To 83 days subsistence to Patrick Scully and	
Michael Allen at 4 d per day each.	£3.. 2..3
To pens, ink & paper.	2..0
Total	£5.. 1..5

SESSIONS ROLL 482, Michaelmas 1803 (7th.Oct.)

482/1 Writ proclaiming Quarter Sessions and Gaol Delivery.

482/2 List of jurors for the Grand and Petty juries of the Borough.

482/3 Calendar of prisoners for the Borough Gaol. (No prisoners).

482/4 Vagrants committed each for 7 days. July 30th.to Oct.1st. Names of 7 vagrants (1 sick plus two children) with committal and discharge dates.

482/8 Presentment of the jury concerning an assault by Ann Munn upon Thomas Conisby.
Recognisances 482/5, 6 & 7.

SESSIONS ROLL 483, Epiphany 1804   (13th.Jan.)

483/1   Writ proclaiming Quarter Sessions and Gaol Delivery.

483/2   List of jurors for the Grand and Petty juries of the Borough.

483/3   Calendar of prisoners for the Borough Gaol. (No prisoners).

483/4   Vagrants committed each for 7 days. Oct.8th.to Dec.19th. Names of 7 male vagrants with committal and discharge dates.

483/5   Bill of James Deayton for fires, pens, ink etc. Total 14/-.

SESSIONS ROLL 484, Easter 1804   (13th.April)

484/1   Writ proclaiming Quarter Sessions and Gaol Delivery.

484/2   List of jurors for the Grand and Petty juries of the Borough.

484/3   Calendar of prisoners for the Borough Gaol.
William Hall committed the 10th.March charged on the oath of George Wilsher with having tendered in payment counterfeit money knowing the same to be so.   James Deayton, 'Goaler'.

484/4   Calendar of prisoners in the House of Correction.
Thomas Hall committed charged on the oath of George Wilsher with offering counterfeit money knowing it to be counterfeit.

484/5   Vagrants committed each for 7 days. Feb.6th.to Mar.30th. Names of 2 male and 1 female vagrant with dates.
Also
Feb.26th. William James & John Jennings as deserters. Discharged March 1st.
March 10th.Thomas Abell for offering counterfeit money, till discharged by law.

484/13 Presentment of the jury concerning Thomas Abell and William Hall uttering a counterfeit coin in the similitude of a shilling to one George Dell. Misdemeanour. Endorsed 'A true Bill. Guilty'.
Recognisances 484/6, 7, 8 & 9.

484/14 Presentment of the jury concerning William Fensam the elder, late of the Parish of St.Alban, assaulting Joseph Tarbox, then a constable of Flamstead. And further concerning John Wittington for an assault upon Joseph Tarbox. Endorsed 'A true Bill'.
Recognisances 484/10, 11 & 12.

484/15 Bill of the Clerk of the Peace. Easter Sessions 1803 to Epiphany Sessions 1804 inclusive. 35 entries totalling £16..14..6, including :-

	s .. d
Drawing out Gaol Calendar.	5 .. 0
Fees for one prisoner committed to gaol.	6 .. 8
Fees for one prisoner discharged by proclamation.	6 .. 8
Paid for printing copies of HM proclamation respecting Aliens and letters to the Magistrates with the same.	13 .. 4
Drawing out and recording an order for payment of Ann Twitchell's Bill.	5 .. 0
Paid for horse to send a person after Lord Grimston to attend Sessions as no magistrate besides the Mayor could be met with.	5 .. 0

484/16 Bill of John Boys Gent. Coroner of the Borough.

		s .. d
Taking an Inquisition on the body of Philip Parkins run over by a cart.	£1..	0 .. 0
Paid the Sergeant at Mace summoning the jury.		4 .. 0
Paid the jury.		13 .. 0
Total	£1..	17 .. 0

484/17 Bill of James Deayton. April 13th.1804.
Including:- To fees of William Hale.   13s.. 4d

484/18 Bill relating to Militia. June to October, 1803. An itemised bill of 27 entries totalling £2..7..6 and including :-

	s .. d
To pressing a cart for Mr.Thos.Kinder for the Bucks. Supplementary Militia.	1 .. 0
For a waggon from Mr.Biggs of Burston for the Supplementary Leicester Militia.	2 .. 6
To a cart from Mr.Harris Warwick Supplementary.	1 .. 0
To warning the Constables of Windridge Ward to press a waggon for Northants Supplementary.	2 .. 6
Mr.Spicer for the Darby Militia.	1 .. 0
To Mr.Spicer from Mr.Steaben Knebworth Militia.	1 .. 0
For providing a storehouse for the Depot of Arms for the Lancashire Militia.	1 .. 0
To warning Constables of Windridge Ward to pressing 4 waggons 7 Regt.Dragoon Guard.	2 .. 6
To ditto on Saundridge Constable for two waggons for 69 Regt. First Division.	2 .. 6
To warning on Redbourne Constable to impress 7 waggons for the Guards to convey French Prisoners to Stilton.	2 .. 6

484/19 Constables Bill for Middle Ward. John Brewer. Itemised bill of 28 entries including:

	s .. d
To Letter by Post.	0 .. $^3\!/_2$(sic)
Giving Notice to Publicans to Renew Licences.	1 .. 6
'To filling upp shedule for the Militia, delivering	

out & getting inn.'	8 .. 6
'Attending the appeales.'	2 .. 6
To making list of all poor persons from the ages	
18 to 45 & families.	2 .. 6

484/20, 21 & 22   Bill of John Short, Thomas Carter and an unnamed person, Constables for Fishpool Ward, 'Holeywell' Ward and St.Peters Ward. Similar to item 484/19.

SESSIONS ROLL 485, Midsummer 1804   (13th.April)

485/1   Writ proclaiming Quarter Sessions and Gaol Delivery.

485/2   List of jurors for the Grand and Petty juries of the Borough.

485/3   Calendar of prisoners for the Borough Gaol.
Thomas Abell and William Hall convicted at Easter Sessions for uttering false and counterfeit money knowing the same to be fake. Ordered to be imprisoned one year in the common gaol and until they shall enter into a recognisance in £20 each and two sureties in £10 for their good behaviour for the further space of two years.
A list of prisoners committed to the House of Correction, from Lady Day Sessions to Midsummer Sessions. July 12th.1804.
Thomas Copeland for an assault.
William A-------- for one month for misbehaving in service.
Lucy Seagrave for one month for misbehaving in service.
William Squire for 14 days for misbehaving in service.
John Butler for one month for misbehaving in service.
Ann Durant, a pauper, for 7 days for misbehaving.
Thomas Abell and William Hall convicted for uttering counterfeit money.

485/4   Sacrament Certificate of the Rev.William Mogg Bowen.

485/5   We the Grand Jury or jurors returned to enquire for our Sovereign Lord the King for the body of the Borough do present a certain Public Nuisance to exist by persons exposing themselves naked in a field adjoining to the public highway or turnpike road leading from the Town of St.Albans to Watford which field is the property of the Countess Dowager Spencer and adjoining to the river called Holywell River for the purpose of bathing or washing. Whereby persons particularly female passing and repassing upon such public highway or turnpike road are continually annoyed.

485/6   Borough of St.Alban.
Notice is hereby given that in pursuance of a Presentment made by the Grand Jury at the last General Quarter Sessions, Bills and Indictments will be preferred against all persons who shall assemble together on the banks of the Holywell River and after stripping themselves naked, bathing in the said river.

485/7   Bill of James Deayton concerning subsistence etc.

SESSIONS ROLL 486, Michaelmas 1804   (5th.Oct.)

486/1   Writ proclaiming Quarter Sessions and Gaol Delivery.

486/2   List of jurors for the Grand and Petty juries of the Borough.

486/3   Calendar of prisoners for the Borough Gaol.
Thomas Abell and William Hall convicted at Easter Sessions etc. *(As for 485/3).*
Owen Grogham committed charged on the oath of John Furness with having tendered in his shop in pay for some meat false or counterfeit money.

486/4   List of vagrants variously committed for seven days.
3 males and 4 females. Names and dates included.

486/6   The Information on oath of John Furness, butcher, who saith that Owen Grogham went into his shop on 29th.July and purchased three pound and a quarter of meat and tendered in payment two bad shillings which the deponent refused as bad. Owen Grogham then tendered one or two more shillings of the same sort which were also refused with the observation that they were equally bad. Mr.John Mason at the instant entered into the shop and said Owen Grogham had tendered bad money to his father for the purchase of a 'syckle' upon which John Furness sent for the constable who found upon Owen Grogham seventeen pieces of the same sort of coin.
Recognisances 486/7.
Presentment of the jury 486/5 concerning uttering false coin to one John Furness, and for the second count of uttering false coin to one Richard Mason. Misdemeanours.

486/8   Bill of James Deayton for 84 days subsistence for Thomas Abell and William Hall at $4\frac{1}{2}$d a day, and 13..4d for the fees of Owen Grogham

SESSIONS ROLL 487, Epiphany 1805   (18th.Jan.)

487/1   Writ proclaiming Quarter Sessions and Gaol Delivery.

487/2   List of jurors for the Grand and Petty juries of the Borough.

487/3   Calendar of prisoners for the Borough Gaol.
Thomas Abell and William Hall convicted for uttering false money.
Owen Grogham convicted at Michaelmas Sessions for uttering false money.
Ordered to be imprisoned in the Gaol for one year and until he shall find sureties for his good behaviour for a further two years.

487/4 Committed

Oct.22nd. Sarah Osborn a common cheat to be kept for the Sessions.
Dec.11th. Joseph Gladman & James Ellis for stealing of wood for one month, but discharged paying the penalty Dec.13th.
Also 3 vagrants.

487/5 Calendar of prisoners for the House of Correction.
Sarah Osborn committed 22nd.Oct.1804 on the oath of Thomas Kent one of the Overseers of the parish of St.Alban with extorting money from him under false pretences.

487/6 The examination of Thomas Kent of the Parish of St.Alban who states on oath that Sarah Osborn came to him this day and extracted money from him under the pretence of her being so far advanced in pregnancy as to expect to be taken in immediate labour and unfit to travel which declaration is found after examination to be totally untrue.

487/7 Sarah Osborn has been examined by me from a suspicion of her being with child. I cannot say she is not, but I can assert that she is not far advanced in her pregnancy if she is in that state. I have detected her in a most palpable lie and I have strong grounds to think her an imposter.

                                          Thomas Parsons, Surgeon.
Recognisances 487/8.
Presentment of the jury 487/9 concerning obtaining money by false pretences by pretending an advanced state of pregnancy. Endorsed 'Guilty'.

487/10 Bill of James Deayton chiefly for prisoners subsistence. 105 days for each of Thomas Abell, William Hall and Owen Grogan.

487/11 Bill for maintaining prisoners.	£ .. s .. d
To maintaining Sarah Osborn committed as a common cheat at 4d per day.	1 .. 9 .. 0
To maintaining Mary Jordan committed as a vagrant for seven days.	2 .. 4
To maintaining Joseph Gladman & James Ellis committed for stealing wood for two days at 4d per day.	1 .. 4
To maintaining Mary Adams a vagrant for 7 days.	2 .. 4
Appeal brought for Sarah Osborn by order of Justices.	12 .. 6
Total	2 .. 7 .. 6

487/12 Bill of Thomas Parsons, surgeon.
Relating to medicines for the Gaol. Mainly for February and August.
1 entry for 'Venerial' (10/6), 2 for Febrifuge, 2 for Laxative, 11 for Mixture, 2 for Emetic, 3 for Draughts, 2 for Stomach mixture & 1 for Cathartic Powder. Total £2 .. 6 .. 0.

487/13 Short account relating to court business.

SESSIONS ROLL 488, Easter 1805   (26th.April)

488/1   Writ proclaiming Quarter Sessions and Gaol Delivery.

488/2   List of jurors for the Grand and Petty juries of the Borough.

488/3   Vagrants, 2 male and 4 female, committed for seven days and James Cunisbee as a disorderly person for one month (but discharged after 7 days).

488/4 & 5   Sacrament Certificates of Rev.Carpenter Gape & Thomas Kinder Esq.

488/6   Bill of the Clerk of the Peace. Easter Sessions 1804 to Epiphany 1805. A bill of 49 entries totalling £21..18..10. Including:

Drawing out and recording an order re Persons bathing in Holywell River.	5/-
Drawing out notices in consequence thereof and six copies to affix in different parts of the town.	13/6
Making copies of Lord Hawkesbury's circular letter on the subject of persons uttering counterfeit money and writing letters therewith to the magistrates.	13/4

488/7   Coroners bill.
Aug.14th. Taking an inquisition on the body of Kepple Fox a deserter who hung himself.   £1..0..0.

488/8, 9, 10 & 11   Bills for the Constable for Middle Ward and James Grove, Henry Compton and John Aveling, Constables for Fishpool, St.Peters and Holywell Wards. Entries include:- Sundry attendances at Quarter Sessions, markets and fairs. Six passes to the Constable of St.Michaels, (2/-). Passing Hannah Rigby to Hatfield horse & cart & self to Hatfield on her road to Glasgow, (6/6).

488/12   Bill of James Deayton. 26th.April 1805.

85 days subsistence Thomas Abell & Wm.Hall at 4½d per day each.	£3 .. 3 .. 9
98 days subsistence Owen Croghan at 4½d per day.	£1 ..16 .. 9
Fires etc.	8 .. 0
Total	£5 .. 8 .. 6

SESSIONS ROLL 488A, Midsummer 1805   (19th.July)

488A/1 Writ proclaiming Quarter Sessions and Gaol Delivery.

488A/2 List of jurors for the Grand and Petty juries of the Borough.

488A/3 Calendar of prisoners for the Borough Gaol.

George Homer and Wm.Houndslow committed 25th.May charged on the oath of Ann Green, Amelia Coleman and Mary Latham on suspicion of feloniously taking several quantities of straw plait the property of Ann Green etc.

Owen Craghan convicted of uttering false money.

488A/4 Calendar of prisoners in the House of Correction.
Robert Stevens committed June 22nd. on the oath of George Wilshire with breaking of windows & behaving in a riotous manner on June 13th. Bailed out for Sessions.

488A/5 Vagrants etc. variously committed.
Mary Conyers a disorderly person for 4 days.
James Dixon Jeffery a disorderly person for 3 days.
Robert Stevens for disorderly behaviour for 7 days
Also six vagrants for 7 days and two for 5 days.

488A/6 The Examination & Complaint of Amelia the wife of Wm.Coleman of the parish of St.Michael in the Borough, gardener, 25th.May who saith that having offered a quantity of straw plait for sale in the market, a person of the name of George Homer bargained for the same at the price of 12/6d. That one Ann Markee a person who was with her delivered the plait to George Homer upon his understanding to meet her at the Red Lion and to pay her within about an hour and a half it being about 7 in the morning when the bargain was made. That George Homer soon after absconded with the plait and was apprehended with the same in his possession at Shenley and that at the same time as he was so apprehended as she has been informed he had in his possession plait to a very considerable amount all which he obtained from different persons without paying anything & that she Verily believed that George Homer together with his companion whose name is William Houndslow did obtain & get into his possession plait so belonging to Amelia Coleman & several other persons with an intent feloniously to carry away the same.
Endorsed with note of recognisances.

488A/7 The Complaint of Ann the wife of John Green of Bedmond in the parish of Abbots Langley, labourer, who saith she this morning offered for sale in the market a quantity of straw plait of the value of £2..7..6 to a person of the name of Wm.Geo.Homer who absconded with the same as she has heard & believes forthwith intent to defraud her of the same & she believes that he took the said plait with a felonious intent.
The complaint of Mary Latham of the Borough. *(similar to above, but value of plait £1..10..4).*
Recognisances 488A/23, 24, 25 & 26.
Presentment of the jury 488A/20 concerning the theft by George Homer and William Houndslow labourers of the Borough of 40yds. of plaited straw valued 10 pence the goods and chattels of Mary Latham.
Endorsed on reverse: 'Geo.Homer guilty, 6 weeks in House of Correction.

William Houndslow not guilty'.

Presentment of the jury 488A/21 concerning the theft by George Homer and William Houndslow labourers of the Borough of 20yds. of plaited straw valued 10 pence the goods and chattels of William Coleman.

Endorsed on reverse: 'Geo.Homer pleaded guilty, 6 weeks in House of Correction. William Houndslow not guilty'.

488A/8 The Complaint of William Jackson one of the Constables of the Borough taken on oath 13th.May 1805. Who saith that having been lately chosen into the office of one of the constables and knowing that many persons inhabiting the Borough had for some time past exercised their calling on a Sabbath day he did on Sunday last call on several persons for the purpose of cautioning them to desist from such practices & that being so in the performance of his duty as constable he was ill used by several persons who followed him hooting & calling him names & particularly Thomas Wilkins the younger & his brother Edward Wilkins were there present & made use of many oaths & encouraged the mob there assembled to make a noise rout & disturbance against the Kings Peace.

Recognisances 488A/30.

488A/9 Ann Thomas of the Parish of St.Alban in the Borough, single woman, appeared voluntarily saith on oath that she is now with child which is likely to be born a bastard and chargeable to the Parish. That Thomas Brown of the parish now living in the service of Mr.Philip Parsons, surgeon, is the father of the child.

Endorsed with note of recognisances.

Recognisances 488A/32 & 33.

488A/10 Recognisances concerning the executors named in the last Will of John Cowper prosecuting an appeal against a certain Notice of Requisition. By which notice John Cowper is required at his own cost and within seven days to remove the iron rail or palisades from his dwelling house in the Borough.

488A/11, 12, 13 & 14 Similar to previous item. Requiring James Carpenter Gape, Matthew Kentish Gent. and William Kentish Gent., Thomas Baker Dr.of Physic and Ann Kinder, widow, to remove the rails from the front of their houses in the Borough.

488A/15 to 19 Five notices of appeal concerning the removal of rails mentioned in items 488A/10 to 14. Story's objection citing the fact that when the roads were made up previously, the Commissioners allowed the railings etc. as they are in the present time.

488A/22 Notice of application to the court will be made for an equal assessment to be made not exceeding nine pence in the pound upon all and every occupier of lands tenements titles and heriditaments within this parish for the use and benefit of the highways.

Geo.Wilsher & Mathew Newson Surveyors. 14th.July.

488A/27, 28 & 29. Recognisances concerning an indictment by George Wilsher and George Mead against Robert Stevens for an assault and breach of the peace.

488A/31 Recognisances concerning William Wheeler keeping the peace and being of good behaviour for six months, especially towards Martha, wife of George Groam.

488A/34 & 35 Recognisances concerning Rebecca Hunt preferring a bill of indictment against William Cook concerning her child.

488A/36 Bill of the Clerk of the Peace. Fifteen entries totalling £5..1..10.

488A/37 Bill of James Deayton for providing fires on Saturdays. 33 at 1/6d each.

488A/38 Bill of James Deayton.	£ .. s .. d
84 days subsistence for Owen Groghan at $4\frac{1}{2}$ per day.	1 ..11 .. 6
4 days subsistence and straw for William Whitmore ordered into custody on suspicion of being a deserter, but not being owned, ordered to be discharged.	3 .. 0
2 days Gabriel Jones as above.	2 .. 0
To fees of G.Homer and W.Houndslow	1.. 6 .. 8
Pens, ink and paper.	2 .. 0
Paid to E.Blows for a deal box by order of the magistrate to keep the straw plait in safety.	7 .. 6
	£3 ..12 .. 8

488A/39 Bill of William Carpenter and Thomas Philips.
For bringing George Holmer and William 'Howlinsaw' from Shenley Hill to St.Albans (£2). For attending Sessions July 19th. (£2). Total £4, only £2 allowed.

488A/40 to 43 inclusive. Expenses of sundry witnesses.

488A/44   19th.July
1805. Gaol Visitors Report.
The undersigned JPs for the Liberty appointed at the last Quarter Sessions to visit and inspect the Gaol belonging to the Liberty, report that they have found the said gaol in good conditions and prisoners healthy and well taken care of by the Gaoler of whose conduct they are perfectly satisfied. Stephen Pellet *(?)* and W.P.Nicholson.

SESSIONS ROLL 489, Michaelmas 1805   (11th.Oct.)

489/1 Writ proclaiming Quarter Sessions and Gaol Delivery.

489/2   List of jurors for the Grand and Petty juries of the Borough.

489/3   Calendar of prisoners for the Borough Gaol.
Henry Newton committed 22nd.Sept. on the oath of John Bell that he was last 'knight' knocked down by Henry Newton a Sergeant in the Regiment of Guards and it further appearing to me as well as by the oath of John Bell as also of Francis Kingston, surgeon, that John Bell is dangerously wounded so that his life is in great danger.

489/4   List of prisoners committed to the House of Correction from Midsummer Sessions to Michaelmas Sessions 1805. *(names and dates given)*. Committed for seven days.   8 males, 18 females and 2 children.
        Committed for one day.   2 males and 4 females.

489/5   22nd.Sept.1805. The examination of Francis Kingston of the Borough, surgeon, taken on oath, who saith that he was this morning sent for to attend a man at the Kings Head in his profession as a surgeon. That he found a young man whose name this deponent is informed is John Bell had been wounded by some sharp instrument on the left side on the lower ribs. That the cut was in an oblique direction about one inch and a half in length and had punctured to the ribs and as this deponent believes is of a very dangerous nature and that his life is in great danger.

489/6   22nd.Sept.1805. The examination of John Bell late of Colney in the Parish of St.Peter who on oath saith that he came into the town of St.Albans between three and four o'clock yesterday in the afternoon - went to the Kings Arms and was in perfect health. That he went to the Town Hall being the Mayors Feast and got into company with Michael Sears the younger. That in coming from the Town Hall he met with a Sergeant in the 1st.Regiment of Guards whose name he is informed is Henry Newton who wanted him to go to a Public House and have a pot or two of beer. That this examinant refused to go with him and words ensued and he - this examinant - was knocked down by Henry Newton. That he soon after found himself much hurt by a cut made as this examinant believes with some sharp instrument on his left side but how it was done or by whom this examinant knows not being at the time very much in liquor.
Recognisances 489/9.
Presentment of the jury 489/8 concerning an assault upon John Bell by Henry Newton. Endorsed 'A true Bill. Verdict - Not guilty.'

489/7   27th.July 1805. The complaint of Ann - the wife of George Wilshire of the Borough, baker, taken on oath, who saith that in consequence of a message sent to this complainant a few days ago by Mrs.Hayes that he wished this complainant to call on her and receive a debt which she owed to this complainants husband for bread furnished to Mrs.Hayes and her family she went yesterday morning about ten o'clock to Mrs.Hayes lodgings for that purpose intending at the same time to procure the signature of her son Lieutenant Hayes of the Lancashire Regiment of

Militia who lodges in the same house to certain accounts or returns of bread furnished by this complainants husband to the soldiers belonging to the detachment stationed at St.Albans which it was necessary to procure before the money for such bread could be received - That this complainant found Lieutenant Hayes and his mother at home and that before this complainant could have an opportunity of explaining the nature of her business to them Lieutenant Hayes gave orders to two men who officiate as his servants and were present in the room to take this complainant out of the room but they not attempting to do so and after some altercation had taken place between Lt.Hayes and this complainant he in a furious and violent manner assaulted her and laid hold of this complainant and endeavoured to force her down the stairs which he would have done had not this complainant caught hold of the banisters by the side of the stairs and which he endeavoured afterwards to do wherefore she prays that justice may be done.
Recognisances 489/10.

489/12 Bill of James Deayton. Entries mention 78 days subsistence to Owen Craghan @ 4¹/₂d per day. The fees of Henry Weston and subsistence for two deserters who, 'not being owned', were discharged.

489/13 Bill of Ann Twitchell for maintaining George Homer in the House of Correction for six weeks at 2/6d per week. Total £3..10..0

489/14 Bill of John Granger, Constable of Shenley and William Ewington charged to assist John Granger to bring George Homer and William Houghton to St.Albans prison, attending Sessions. Two days each £2 and two horses and carts, two days hire £1.10..0.
        Allowed £1..15..0.   Signed Thomas Kinder, Mayor.

489/15 Bill of William Jackson, constable of the Borough, for keeping hold of the body of Robert Stevens. 16/-. Allowed.

SESSIONS ROLL 490, Epiphany 1806   (17th.Jan.)

490/1   Writ proclaiming Quarter Sessions and Gaol Delivery.

490/2   List of jurors for the Grand and Petty juries of the Borough.
Also, Calendar of prisoners in the Gaol of the Borough. (No prisoners).

490/3	Bill of Thomas Parsons, Surgery.		s..d
1805.	Apr.6th.	Stomachic Mixture. Pauper	2..0
	Apr.8th.	do	2..0
	Apr.8th.	Cathartic powder	6
			4..6

490/4	To convey Thos.Berry a deserter to the Tender.	s..d
Sept.4th.	To horse and cart.	15..0
	Turnpike.	1..0

To a day to London and back. Two constables	10..0	
To maintenance as a deserter.	12..0	
	£1.. 18..0	
Jan.17th. Deduct	9..0	
Allowed.	£1.. 9..0	

490/5 Gaol Visitors Report. *Similar to 488A/44.*

SESSIONS ROLL 491, Easter 1806 (18th.April)

491/1 Writ proclaiming Quarter Sessions and Gaol Delivery.

491/2 List of jurors for the Grand and Petty juries of the Borough.

491/3 Calendar of prisoners for the Borough Gaol.
John Bockett of the 17th.Regt. of Light Horse, Bailed Out. Committed the 12th.March. stands charged on the oath of Wm.Whitbread, *(sic)* labourer, with having between the hours of 8 & 9 of the morning of 12th.March without any just cause or provocation so violently beaten and assaulted him as to endanger his life.

491/4 Calendar of prisoners in the House of Correction.
Elizabeth Taylor. Committed March 26th.1806. Charged with behaving herself in a loose and disorderly manner.
Floriana Brown. Committed April 5th.1806. Charged with committing an act of vagrancy within the said Borough.

491/5 Calendar of prisoners committed to the House of Correction.
Ten persons committed for 7 days for vagrancy. Four for 14 days.

491/6 The Information and Complaint of James Whitby, labourer, Who saith that between 8 & 9 o'clock last night he went to the Crow public house for the purpose of getting a lodging there having been for some time past out of place. That he procured a bed there, slept in the same room with a Sergeant of the 17th.Regt.Dragoons. That he awoke about 7 o'clock he heard the Sergeant say to his wife who slept with him in the same room "Take this handkerchief" she answered "If I do we shall be sure to be found out". The Sergeant said "No you will not for we are going off with the baggage directly". Upon which the Informant drew his curtain on one side and said "that is my handkerchief don't take it away" whereupon the Sergeant struck this Informant several violent blows on the head and face while he was in bed and said "that he had a good mind to murder him" that this Informant soon after got up and went down into the kitchen and the Sergeant seeing him go followed him and insisted on his going out of the house which this Informant refused to do. The Sergeant then struck him again several times and beat him finally with his doubled fist pushed him between the wall and the screen with such violence as for some time to entirely to deprive him of breath. That this Informant is now very ill and has been

informed by a medical gentleman who attended him in great danger of his life and lastly he has heard and believes that the Sergeant's name is John Bocket.
Endorsed with a note of recognisances.
Recognisances <u>491/16 & 17</u>.
Presentment of the jury <u>491/7</u> concerning an assault by John Bocket upon James Whitby. Endorsed 'A true Bill. Pleads Guilty'.

491/8 Warrant to Constables to convey Jemima Jones to the House of Correction and there keep her to Hard Labour for 14 days, having been committed for wandering abroad and otherways out in an idle and disorderly manner
Recognisances <u>491/12</u>.

491/9 Warrant to Constables concerning Ann Marlen, otherwise Mullins. *(As for previous item)*.
Recognisances <u>491/13 & 14</u>.

491/10 & 491/11 Sacrament Certificates of Thomas Shearman and Charles Curwood.

491/15 Recognisances concerning John Dilley accused of being the father of a bastard child upon Sarah Brewer.

491/18 & 19 Recognisances concerning an assault by John Green, victualler, upon William Jackson, Constable.

491/20 Bill of the Clerk of the Peace. Midsummer 1805 to Epiphany 1806 inclusive. 47 entries totalling £20..17..10d. Entries include:-

	s .. d
Exhibiting & recording orders & regulations of a Society of Good Fellowship held at the Fleur de Luce.	10 .. 0
One third of Mr.Savage's bill for a book to enter the proceedings of the Sessions.	11 ..10
Similar Mr.Hale for a box to deposit the records of the Court.	14 .. 8

491/21 Bill of Benjamin Fowler for repairs at the Town Hall & Gaol. Totalling £13..2..6. Nov.19th.1805 - Mar.31st.1806. 26 entries including:

	s .. d
To 35 oak lathes, 200 3" nails, 9 hods of lime & hair, 1 hod fine stuff & 2 pails of white wash.	11 .. 5
To repairing tiling & fixing chimney pot to Jury Room chimney. Bricklayer & labourer one day.	5 .. 6
To whitewashing & sizing inside front and back cells, 2 bricklayers & 1 labourer for 1 day.	8 .. 8
To repairing lathing & plastering of Debtors Cell & whitewashing & sizing, 2 bricklayers & 1 labourer 1 day.	5 .. 6

491/22 Bill of James Deayton. Entries include:- Paid for cleaning & repairing the Corporations Regulating Scales. £1..11..6.

491/23 Bills of John Cockington, William Jackson, William Bigg and John Stevens, Constables of 'Holewell', St.Peter's, Fishpool and Middle Wards.

SESSIONS ROLL 492, Midsummer 1806 (18th.July)

492/1 Writ proclaiming Quarter Sessions and Gaol Delivery.

492/2 List of jurors for the Grand and Petty juries of the Borough.

492/3 Calendar of prisoners for the Borough Gaol.
William Howe, bailed out, required to find find sureties and in the meantime to keep the Peace especially towards his wife Mary.

492/4 Calendar of prisoners in the House of Correction.
Mary Barber committed charged with stealing a loaf of bread the property of John Missenden. John Palmer, Hundreder.

492/5 Be it remembered that William Clarke came before me and informed me that George Harrison, carrier, did unlawfully suffer a waggon having the sole or bottom of the fellies of the wheels of the breadth of 9 inches to pass on a certain turnpike road with 9 horses contrary to the Statute. Convicted and fined £5. *(Considerably edited).*
Recognisances 492/8 concerning appeal against conviction.

492/6 The information and complaint of Mary the lawful wife of William Howe, labourer, concerning his threat to do her some bodily mischief and requiring sureties. Endorsed with note of recognisances.
Recognisances 492/7.

492/10 The complaint of Joseph Gladman, labourer, concerning Thomas Hale who did violently assault, strike and beat him on the face with his fist without any just cause.
Recognisances 492/9.

492/11 Presentment of the jury concerning Mary Barber, spinster, feloniously stealing a wheaten loaf of bread to the value of 10d. the property of John Missenden. Endorsed 'A true Bill. Guilty'.

492/12 Bill of James Deayton. Including:
To the fees of Mary Holt committed for stealing a
large quantity of straw plait. 13s..4d
To the fees of Joseph Lacey committed for stealing a
quantity of blankets. 13s..4d

492/13 Bill of James Deayton.
Fires, 33 at 1/6d each. $^1/_3$ to the Borough, $^2/_3$ to the Liberty.

492/14 Bill of John Cook, Gaoler.
To straw for 23 Recruits that rioted.   7s..0d

492/15 Bill of Samuel Deayton.
To going to the War Office with a packet.   £1..1..0

492/16 Gaol Visitors Report. (Similar to 488A/44 &490/5, but including:- '.... excepting that the Gaol has been injured by certain deserters in breaking down the 'plaistering' on the walls ......').

SESSIONS ROLL 493, Michaelmas 1806   (10th.Oct.)

493/1   Writ proclaiming Quarter Sessions and Gaol Delivery.

493/2   List of jurors for the Grand and Petty juries of the Borough.

493/3   Calendar of prisoners for the Borough Gaol.
Mary Barber convicted of feloniously stealing one loaf of wheaten bread. ordered to be imprisoned three calendar months and during that time to be once privately whipped.

493/4   Bill of Samuel Deayton.
Beer, liquor etc. found and provided for the constables who apprehended *(blank)* for committing an assault on *(blank)*.   9s..0d.

SESSIONS ROLL 494, Epiphany 1807   (16th.Jan.)

494/1   Writ proclaiming Quarter Sessions and Gaol Delivery.

494/2   List of jurors for the Grand and Petty juries of the Borough.

494/3   Calendar of prisoners for the Borough Gaol.
Susanah Roberts. Committed charged on the oath of Ezekiel Blake & others with the felonious removal of a quantity of straw plait.

494/4   The examination of Sarah the wife of Joseph Puddephatt of the parish of Abbots Langley, labourer, Ezekiel Blake of Hemelhempsted, dealer in straw plait and Elizabeth Willis, wife of William Willis of the 30th.Regiment of Foot and James Messenger of Beds. plait dealer severally taken on oath.
And first this examinant Sarah Puddephat saith that this morning she sold about three score yards of plait to Ezekeil Blake for 10/6d for which she received the money. That the plait was tied with two pieces of linen that she might know her own plait. - And Ezeikeil Blake saith that having purchased the plait he took it into the parlour at the Flower de Luce, being the house which he frequents on market days, and laid it down on a bread tray on the mantelpiece. That Sarah Puddephatt soon after came in for her money and

on looking for the plait which she had sold observed that it was not there amongst the other parcels which had been bought by Ezekiel Blake - whereupon Elizabeth Willis told this examinant that she had seen a woman in the parlour with a quantity of plait answering the description of the parcel missing. - And Elizabeth Willis saith that she saw the woman whose name she believes is Susannah Roberts take the same plait and has heard that she sold the same to James Messenger. - James Messenger saith that he bought a quantity of plait answering the description from Susannah Roberts which he believed to be her own.
Endorsed with note of recognisances and: 'the ors *(others?)* are married wmn, & cd. not be bound in Recogce.'
Recognisances 494/5 & 6.
Presentment of the jury 494/8 concerning theft of plait to the value of ten pence. Endorsed 'A true Bill'.

494/7 Penalties for false weights.
Lists number of false weights, penalty and persons convicted: Evan Evans, Michael Mason, William Harris, Thomas Compere, Joseph Gower and John Ewington.

494/9 Bill. The King against Roberts. Expenses.

494/10 Bill of Ann Twitchell.
To maintaining John White 10 days for leaving his service, at 4d. per day. 3s..4d.

494/11 Bill of James Deayton. Eight entries totalling £4..7..2.
Including: 92 days subsistence Mary Barber   £1.. 14..6
                To whipping Mary Barber.   10..0
                To fees of Susannah Roberts.   13..4

494/12 Bill of the Clerk of the Peace. Easter to Epiphany inclusive.
41 entries totalling £21..13..0, including:-Exhibiting and recording the rules, orders and regulations of a Society of Good Fellowship established at the Kings Head.   10s..0d.

SESSIONS ROLL 495, Easter 1807   (10th.April)

495/1 Writ proclaiming Quarter Sessions and Gaol Delivery.

495/2 List of jurors for the Grand and Petty juries of the Borough.

495/3 Calendar of prisoners for the Borough Gaol.
Susannah Roberts convicted for feloniously stealing 20yds.of straw value 10d. ordered to be imprisoned 3 months. Remains in Gaol.

495/4   Recognisances concerning an assault upon Richard Banks by James Dover, labourer.

495/6   The Complaint of Isaac Piggott, gentleman, and the Examination of William Day, dealer. And first Isaac Piggott saith that William Nicholls, carpenter, hath at various times as this informant believes made use of threats towards the complainant. viz. that he would do this complainant bodily harm wherefore he prays sureties of the peace.   And this examinant William Day for himself saith that he hath at several times heard William Nicholls threaten that he would do Isaac Piggott bodily hurt and that about 10 weeks ago as he and William Nicholls were going together on the turnpike road towards London Colney William Nicholls observed a person coming along the road whom he thought was Isaac Piggott when he made use of the following words "Damn my blood if there isn't Piggott I will be damned if I do not fall to work with him directly I will beat him over the legs with my stick he cannot stand that I know and when he is down I will beat him." That this examinant answered "Let mercy be your guide." fearing that he would put his threat into execution. This examinant ran away and afterwards found upon making towards and coming up to the person who had been supposed to be Mr.Piggott that it was not. And this examinant hath heard William Nicholls at several other times threaten that he would beat Isaac Piggott.
Recognisances 495/5.

495/7   To the letter to the Justices swearing in 45 Special Constables at the election.   £2..5..0.

SESSIONS ROLL 496, Midsummer 1807   (17th.July)

496/1   Writ proclaiming Quarter Sessions and Gaol Delivery.

496/2   List of jurors for the Grand and Petty juries of the Borough.

496/3   Calendar of prisoners for the Borough Gaol. (No prisoners).

496/4, 5 & 6 Recognisances concerning William Latham, William Jeffs and William Townsend appearing to answer an indictment for riot and Affray preferred by Charles Woolham.

496/7 Bill of James Deayton.	£ .. s .. d
To 90 days subsistence to Susanah Roberts at 4½d. per day.	1 ..13 .. 9
To two fires, pens ink and paper.	8 .. 0
To fees board & attendance to John Bowden ordered into custody on suspicious circumstances.	13 .. 4
Paid Thomas Mansell for mending the windows 'broke' by Thomas (sic) Bowden.	1 .. 4
To pens, ink and paper.	3 .. 0
	2 ..19 .. 5

496/8   Paid to Thomas Mansell for 2 in lead.   1s..2d.

496/9   The King on the prosecution of John Brewer against Charles Bliss for Horse stealing. An account of the prosecutors expenses in endeavouring to apprehend the offender who was tried at the last Hertfordshire Assizes. 1806 August 7th.& 8th.

Expenses of the Prosecutors journey with John Drayton as an assistant to attend Smithfield Market & search the different slaughtering houses.	£3 .. 0 .. 0
Horse and cart out, 2 days.	£2 ..10 .. 0
Expenses of the Prosecutors 2nd.journey to London for the same purpose.	8 .. 0
Horse and cart out, 2 days.	12 .. 0
Left by Charles Bliss.	19 .. 0
Expenses of the Prosecutors journey to Wisbech in Cambridgeshire on being informed that his is left	£1 ..19 .. 0
at the White Hart Inn at that place in order to give information	£2 ..10 .. 0
to the magistrates & identify the horse to be his property.	
Expenses 2 days.	18 .. 0
	£12 ..16 .. 0

Allowed £5 on account of the within Bill.

SESSIONS ROLL 497, Michaelmas 1807   (9th.Oct.)

497/1   Writ proclaiming Quarter Sessions and Gaol Delivery.

497/2   List of jurors for the Grand and Petty juries.

497/3   Calendar of prisoners for the Borough Gaol.
Philip Jones committed Oct.9th.1807, on the oath of Edward Atkins on suspicion of stealing one smock frock, one shirt, one knife his property.

497/4   Calendar of Prisoners. House of Correction.
Felix Cain committed, charged on the oath of John Lovett, butcher, with violently assaulting & beating him.

497/9   Information & complaint of John Lovett, cow butcher, who herewith saith that on Saturday evening last as he was returning from the Goat Inn to his own house between 9 & 10 o'clock in the evening he was violently assaulted & beaten near Holywell Hill by Felix Cain, a Private in the 23rd. Royal Welch Fusiliers whereby the said John Lovett prays that justice may be done him.
Recognisances 497/7 & 8.
Presentment of the jury 497/12 concerning the assault by Felix Cain upon John Lovett. Endorsed 'A true Bill. Plea - Not guilty. Verdict - Guilty.'

497/10 Information & Complaint of Edward Atkins of the said Boro', victualler, who on oath saith that on Sat.5th. two privates belonging to the

100

50th.Regt.Foot were quartered at his house called the Fighting Cocks & that in the evening a linen press which stood in this examinants room was broken open & one smock frock, one shirt & one knife his property were stolen which several articles were found upon one of the said privates,whose name he believes is Philip Jones.
Recognisances 497/5&6.
Presentment of the jury 497/11 concerning Philip Jones stealing one smock the value of 2d, one linen shirt the value of 2d, one knife the value of 1d, the goods & chattels of Edward Atkins. Endorsed 'A true Bill. Guilty.'

497/13 The King on the Prosecution of John Lovett against Felix Cain.

	s .. d
Indictment.	3 .. 6
Entering & recording appearance.	4 .. 8
Venire.	2 .. 6
Issue.	2 .. 0
Recording conviction.	8 .. 8
Discharging 2 recognisances @ 3..6 ea.	7 .. 0
Bailiff.	4 .. 0
Jury.	6 .. 0
Examining 2 witnesses.	2 .. 0
	£2..0 .. 4

497/14 Bill of Ann Twitchell. House of Correction.

To maintaining of Benjamin Bishop committed for	s .. d
misbehaviour. Kept 4 days 4d a day.	1 .. 4
To maintaining George Kirk comm'd as a disorderly	
person. Kept 1 month @ 2..6d. a week.	10 .. 0
	11 .. 4

497/15 Bill of James Deayton. Borough Gaol.

Fees of Peter Peacock ordered into custody on suspicion	s .. d
of stealing a 'sickel' from Rich'd Mason senior, ordered	
to be discharged.	13 .. 4
To straw for Felix Cain,Henry Cain & John Daley	
ordered into custody.	2 .. 0
To fees of Philip Jones.	13 .. 4
2 fires.	5 .. 0
Pens, ink & paper.	3 .. 0
	£1.. 16 .. 8

497/16 Bill of the Clerk of the Peace.

Edward Atkins pd. to Clerk of the Peace.	s .. d
	2 .. 0
Attending examination of prisoner & attendance	
on day of trial myself, witness & constable.	10 .. 6
	12 .. 6

497/17 Letter. Admiralty Office. 10th.July.

Sir, I have received & laid before my Lord's Commissioners of the Admiralty your letter of the 8th. representing that you had committed Charles Cooper to St.Albans Gaol as a deserter from H.M. ship L'Aimable & I have their Lordships Command to acquaint you that on sending him on board the Enterprise off the Tower the person having him in charge will be allowed the usual reward & conduct money.

I am, Sir, your very humble servant, John Barrow.

(*On Reverse*) This is to certify that I have received Charles Cooper (boy) deserter from L'Aimable & that I have granted a certificate thereof to the Constable for £1 reward & 6d.a mile conduct money (22 miles)

July.13th.1807.	General Rendezvous Office,Tower Hill
Paid Two Shillings.	F.Richbell, Regt.Captain.

	s .. d
By order of the Magistrates.	
The above prisoner conducted from St.Albans Gaol to the	
Tender by John Stevens, Constable, expenses &	
coach hire St.Albans to the Tender.	11 .. 6
Lodging & supper in London.	2 .. 0
Expenses from London to St.Albans.	5 .. 0
Two days lost time @ 5s a day	10 .. 0
Paid to the clerk in London.	1 .. 0
	£1.. 9 .. 6
Received 11s..0d	18 .. 6
Allowed by me 18s..6d.Grimston, Mayor.	

497/18 to 21 Bills of J.Rogers, Thomas Main, John Wright and an unnamed person, Constables of Middle, Fishpool, Holywell and St.Peters Wards. Long bills with many entries disallowed. Entries mention:- Warrants, searches, attending markets. A number of entries for 'pressing carts'. Also:-

	s .. d
To writing out precepts & delivering to every house	
& making out of list & attending Lieutenants for	
the levying en mass.	10 .. 6
Taking & securing 28 Irishmen.	2 .. 6
4 search nights.	10 .. 0

Deleted entries mostly impressing carriages & carts for Stafford Militia, 3rd.Divn. 58 Regt. of Foot & other Military.

497/22 Gaol Visitors Report. Mentions having ordered some repairs.

SESSIONS ROLL 498, Epiphany 1808 (15th.Jan.)

498/1 Writ proclaiming Quarter Sessions and Gaol Delivery.

498/2 List of jurors for the Grand and Petty juries of the Borough.

498/3 Calendar of prisoners for the Borough Gaol.
Felix Cane convicted for assaulting John Lovet ordered to be imprisoned 3 calendar months and to pay a fine of 40/-. Remains in gaol for not paying the fine.   James Deayton, 'Goaler'.

498/4 Calendar of prisoners in the House of Correction.
John Knowles committed charged on the oath of John Hair one of the Overseers, with running away and leaving his wife chargeable to the Parish of St.Peter.

498/5 & 6 Recognisances concerning James Deayton, victualler, appearing to prefer a Bill of Indictment against Thomas Knight for an assault and misdemeanour.

498/7 Bill of James Deayton. Main entries are:-		s .. d
90 days subsistence to Felix Cane at 4¹/₂ per day.	£1..	16 .. 9
To the fees of Felix Cane.		13 .. 4

498/8 Bill of Ann Twitchell.	s .. d
To Maintaining John Knowles, 8 weeks 3 days at 4d per day.	19 .. 8
To maintaining of Ann Barber for behaving ill in the Workhouse, 5 days.	1 .. 8

498/9 The Complaint and Information of John Hair, hosier, one of the Overseers of the Poor for the Parish of St.Peter, who saith that John Knowles did about three months past run away from his wife by which she became chargeable to the Parish and that she hath ever since been paid a weekly allowance of 1/6d. He the complainant therefore prayeth that justice may be done to him.

498/10 Account of the penalties received on conviction for false weights at the Petty Sessions held at the Town Hall.
Lists 17 names, with numbers of false weights and fine imposed.

498/11 Be it remembered that 1st.Oct. John Webber Sergeant of H.M.Royal Marines informed me upon oath that Jeremiah Rogers did refuse to grant billets to him and recruits under his command whereupon Jeremiah Rogers appeared before me, one of the Justices of the Peace, at my dwelling house. He said that he was not guilty but the case being fully proved upon the oath of Lt.Patrick Lottrell of the Royal Marines a credible witness ......Jeremiah Rogers hath forfeited the sum of £3 lawful money for the offence.

498/12 The voluntary examination of Elizabeth Goodman, single woman, who saith that she is now with child likely to be born a bastard chargeable to the Parish of St.Alban and that William Howe of North Mimms, labourer, is the father of the child.

498/13 Bill of the Clerk of the Peace. Epiphany to Michaelmas inclusive.
15 entries totalling £27..9..6. Entries include: s .. d
Recording Presentment of the Grand Jury that suffering
dogs to be about the streets is a public nuisance. 5 .. 0
Drawing & recording order on such presentment
for the destruction of dogs wandering about the streets
of the Borough. 5 .. 0
Making two fair copies thereof & instructing Constables
to affix the same in conspicuous places in the Borough. 8 .. 4
Exhibiting ...Rules ..... of a Society of Good Fellowship
held at Flower de Luce. 10 .. 0
Do. at Blue Boar. 10 .. 0

SESSIONS ROLL 499, Easter 1808. (29th.April)

499/1 Writ proclaiming Quarter Sessions and Gaol Delivery.

499/2 List of jurors for the Grand and Petty juries of the Borough.

499/3 Calendar of prisoners for the Borough 'Goal'.
Ann Brown committed 30th.Jan. on the oath of Wm.Field on suspicion of
feloniously taking two pieces of Beef the property of John Field. Bailed
Out.
Thomas Grover committed 24th.March on the oath of Charles Hurrell with
a felony. Bailed Out.

499/4 The Examination of William Field of the Borough, butcher,
30th.January, who saith that two pieces of Beef were this day feloniously
taken from out of his Fathers shop and that he hath reason to suspect &
doth suspect that Ann the wife of Thomas Brown of Ellen Brook in the
Parish of St.Peter in the Liberty of St.Albans, Labourer, did take the same -
- & this Examinant further saith that soon after the pieces of Beef were
missed he followed Ann Brown who had been seen near the shop & found
the pieces of meat upon her.
Endorsed with note of recognisances.
Recognisances 499/5, 6, 7 & 8.
Presentment of the jury 499/14 concerning Ann Brown stealing two pounds
weight of Beef of the value of ten pence the goods of John Field. Endorsed
'A True Bill. Plea, Not Guilty. Verdict, Guilty'.

499/9 & 10 Recognisances concerning Joseph Gower to prefer a bill of
indictment against George Sherman for assault.

499/12 The Examination & Complaint of Charles Hurrell of the
Borough, coachman, 24th.March.Who saith that about fifteen pounds
weight of cod fish packed & directed for Mr.Evan Evans, grocer, and sent by
the St.Alban Coach of which this Examinant is the driver was feloniously

104

taken away last night by the person of the name of Thomas Grover who rode on the outside the coach near where the basket containing the fish was fastened & this Examinant further saith that he hath since seen Thomas Grover who hath ackn'd & confessed that he took the same.

Endorsed with note of recognisances.

Recognisance 499/11.

Presentment of the jury 499/16 concerning Thomas Grover feloniously stealing five pounds weight of codfish of the value of ten pence the goods of Ann Smith. Endorsed 'No True Bill'.

499/13 The complaint of Joseph Gower, shopkeeper, 29th January, Who on oath saith that George Sherman, musician, did on Wednesday night last violently assault & strike him a blow on the face without any just cause or provocation.

Recognisances 499/9/10.

Presentment of the jury 499/15 concerning George Sherman assaulting Joseph Gower. Endorsed 'A True Bill. Plea, Not Guilty. Verdict, Guilty'.

499/17 Coroners Bill.

	£ .. s .. d
Oct.23.1807. Taking an Inquisition on the body of James Aldridge, a vagrant,who fell out of the vagrant cart & was killed.	1 .. 0 .. 0
Pd. the Sergeant at Mace & Jury.	0 ..17 .. 0
April 4 1808 The like on the body of James(?) Omiar(?), a private in the 19th.Lt.Dragoons who shot himself.	1 ..17 .. 0
	3 ..14 .. 0

499/18 Bill of James Deayton by order of Lord,Viscount Grimston.

Jan.30th. A Blanket for the use of the Borough Gaol.   13s..0d

499/19 Bill of James Deayton. Borough Gaol.

	£ .. s .. d
64 days subsistence to Felix Cane @ 4½d pr.day.	1 .. 4 .. 0
To fees of Ann Brown.	13 .. 4
Paid Mr.Simcock for a blanket by the order of the Mayor, James, Viscount Grimston, for the use of the Boro'Gaol.	13 .. 0
To 2 fires.	5 .. 0
Pens Ink & Paper.	3 .. 0
	2..18 .. 4

499/20 Bill. The King against Ann Brown.

Indictment, (2/-). Expenses of witnesses, (10/-).

SESSIONS ROLL 500, Midsummer 1808   (15th.July)

500/1   Writ proclaiming Quarter Sessions and Gaol Delivery.

500/2   List of jurors for the Grand and Petty juries.

500/3 Calendar of prisoners for the Borough Gaol.
Catherine Barry committed 23rd.May upon oath of Rich'd Moss with having feloniously stolen one linen sheet his property.
Likewise charged on the oath of Henry Honnor with feloniously taking & carrying away one linen waistcoat & one piece of calico the property of Henry Honnor being in the dwelling house of Rich'd Moss.

500/8 The Information & Complaint of Henry Honnor, tailor, who saith that between the hours of four & five of the afternoon sundry articles of wearing apparel that is to say a pair of Nankeen Breeches a linen waistcoat and a piece of new calico were stolen from out of his lodgings in the dwelling house and that he hath just reason to suspect the same were feloniously taken away by Catharine Barry as the linen waistcoat & piece of new calico were found upon her person when she was searched by James Basset one of the Constables of the Borough.
Endorsed with note of recognisances.
Recognisances 500/4 & 5
Presentment of the jury 500/10 concerning Catharine Barry, widow, feloniously taking one 'linnen' waistcoat value four pence one yard of calico value six pence the property of Henry Honnor. Endorsed 'A True Bill. Plea, Not Guilty. Verdict, Guilty'.

500/9 The Information & Complaint of Richard Moss, victualler, taken on oath 23rd.May. Who saith that a woman who calls herself Catharine Barry came into his House this afternoon between the hours of four & five and watched ....to slip up stairs into a Sleeping Room from out of which she feloniously took one Linen Sheet property of the complainant.
Endorsed with note of recognisances.
Recognisances 500/6/7.
Presentment of the jury 500/11 concerning Catharine Barry feloniously taking & carry away one 'linnen' sheet value tenpence the property of Richard Moss. Endorsed 'Not a True Bill'.

500/12 Bill of the Clerk of the Peace. Epiphany Sessions to Easter Sessions 1808. Totalling £11..0..2.   28 entries including:-

	s..d
Writing three Several Letters to the Secretary at War by order of the Magistrates representing the case of Felix Cain.	10..6
Several Attendances on the Magistrates and at the War Office laying the answers before the Magistrates at their Petty Sessions.	13..4
Drawing & recording an order for fining William Waller, a Grand Juryman for non attendance.	5..0

500/13 Bill of James Deayton. Borough Gaol. Main entries:-

3 days Subsistence to Ann Brown.	1s..1½d
To the fees of Catherine Barry.	13s..4d

500/14 to 17 Bills of James Barnet, John Field, Jacob Moore and William Scourfield, Constables of Middle St.Peters, Fishpool and Holywell Wards respectively. Numerous entries disallowed. Entries include:-

Parading streets by order of the Magistrates.	5..0
Attendance on drawing Militia 9 days @ 2/- per day.	18..0
To taking a list of the inhabitants at Court Leet.	1..6
For preventing the people Bathing By Order.	2..6

(Most deleted items relate to the Militia).

SESSIONS ROLL 501, Michaelmas 1808   (7th.Oct.)

501/1 Writ proclaiming Quarter Sessions and Gaol Delivery.

501/2 List of jurors for the Grand and Petty juries.

501/3 Calendar of prisoners for the Borough 'Goal'.
John Wallis, James Warrick & John Warrick, committed 30th.Sept. upon oath with having violently assaulted beaten & afflicted a deep wound in the head of Daniel Horton with a club and violently assaulting and beating Jacob Moore one of the Constables of the Boro' in discharge of his duty.

501/4 Calendar of Prisoners. House of Correction.
Phebe Wolfe, committed 12th.Sept. charged with ill behaviour & refusing to find sufficient sureties for the same.
Thomas Shepherd, committed 23rd.Sept. charged with ill using his son & unwilling to find sufficient sureties for the same.

501/12 The Complaint & Information of George Calvert one of the Overseers of the Poor of the Parish of St.Albans, 23rd.Sept.1808 who saith that Thomas Shepherd of the Parish of St.Alban, carpenter, hath for some considerable time now been in the habit of beating with brutal severity his son Francis Shepherd of the age of seven years & that Thomas Shepherd hath been repeatedly admonished by his more decent & respectable neighbours of the inhumanity of his conduct and that if persevered in an appeal must be made to the Laws of the Land. He totally disregarding these admonitions did on Tuesday & Wednesday evening beat with the most wanton cruelty his son Francis & did also declare that he would be the death of his son. The state of Francis Shepherd's back in consequence of the floggings he had received being made known to the Complainant he feels it to be his duty to appear before the Magistrates with a view to not only having Thomas Shepherd punished for his most unnatural conduct but also to protect Francis from his design of being his death & he the Complainant therefore prayeth that the Laws of the Land may be enforced.
Recognisance 501/11.
Presentment of the jury 501/18 concerning Thomas Shepherd assaulting Francis Shepherd Endorsed:-Witnesses Francis Shepherd & George Calvert (not preferred by reason of Francis Calvert *(sic)* not being deemed capable of taking an oath).

501/13 The Information & Complaint of John Wellington one of the Churchwardens of the Parish of St.Michaels in the Boro', gentleman, who saith That John Hews of the Parish of Redbourn, labourer, hath this day between the hours of one & two behaved himself in a very riotous & disorderly manner by stripping himself to fight in the public street of the Parish of St.Michaels in the Boro' by cursing & swearing, by abusive and opprobrious treatment of the Complainant & several other inhabitants of the parish to their great terror & annoyance to the destruction of the public peace & order & contrary to the Statute in such case made & provided. Wherefore the Complainant prayeth that the Law of the Land may be enforced.
Endorsed with note of recognisances.

501/14 The voluntary examination of John Hews of the Parish of Redbourn, labourer, respecting his mode of passing the latter part of yesterday Sunday 21st.Aug. who on oath saith That he left his house in the town of Redbourn for the purpose of coming to St.Albans between the hours of six & seven & that he reached St.Albans about eight o'clock & that he went to the public house in George Street known by the sign of the Kings Arms & that he had two pots of ale. From this house he proceeded between the hours of nine & ten o'clock to the public house known by the sign of the Crow with a companion where they had five pints of beer between them and there they stopped about an hour & he the Examinant was rather intoxicated. From the Crow about 11 o'clock he went to the Royal Oak victualling house with the same person as was with him before at the Crow there they had more ale by which the said Examinant became so very drunk that he cannot exactly tell the quantity of ale they had had and that he slept in the house about an hour and a half.
Recognisance 501/5 & 6 concerning John Hews answering a Bill of Indictment for Breach of the Peace & disorderly behaviour brought by John Wellington.

501/15 The Complaint & Information of Daniel Horton, 'tayler', who saith that in consequence of the riotous & disorderly conduct of some soldiers quartered on the Borough last night between the hours of ten & eleven he was charged by Jacob Moore one of the Constables to aid & assist him in restoring peace & order that upon the Complainant obeying the orders of Jacob Moore he did receive a very violent cut upon the left side of his head which he believed to have been inflicted with a club & that he did also receive several blows upon his body whereby he is much injured & he believes that the wound upon his head was inflicted by John Wallis wherefore he prayeth that in consequence of the Injuries he hath received & that the peace of the town may not hereafter be destroyed that the Laws of the Land may in the present instance be restored.
Endorsed with note of recognisances.

501/16 The Complaint & Information of Jacob Moore one of the constables of the Borough who saith that in consequence of having been informed of the riotous & disorderly conduct of some soldiers who were

quartered in the town last night to the destruction of the Peace & the Order of his Majesty's Liege Subjects he felt it to be his duty attended by James Basset another of the constables to go & admonish them of the impropriety & illegality of their conduct about ten o'clock that upon reaching the public house known by the sign of the Red Lion .... by George Calvert in the Parish of St.Alban who found that the soldiers in question whose names he had ascertained to be John Wallis, James Warwick & John Warwick had in their possession one Samuel Swinnerton & were using him in a very violent & rough manner that upon the Complainant going to rescue Samuel Swinnerton from out of the power of John Wallis, James Warwick & John Warwick although apprised of the complainant being a Civil officer of the Law instructed to repair peaceably to their quarters did most violently assault & beat him with their clenched fists and sticks whereby the complainant hath received great bodily injury & doth believe that had not some of the inhabitants come to his aid his life would have been in great danger wherefore the complainant prayeth that the Laws of the Land be enforced. Endorsed with note of recognisances.
Recognisances 501/7, 8, 9 & 10.
Presentment of the jury 501/17 concerning John Wallis, James Warwick & John Warwick unlawfully riotously & routously assembling together assaulting a constable of the Parish. Endorsed 'A true Bill. Pleas, Not Guilty. Verdict (against all three) Guilty'.

501/19 Bill. The King Against John Wallis, James Warwick & John Warwick.

		s..d
3 indictments @ 3/6 ea.		10..6
Entering & recording appearances & pleas convicted of a riot & assault @ 4/8 ea.		14..0
Venire.		2..6
Issue.		2..0
Recording conviction.		8..8
Discharging 6 Recognisances @ 3/6 ea.	1..	1..0
Examining 6 Witnesses @ 1/- ea.		6..0
Bailiff.		4..0
Jury.		6..0
	£ 3..	14..8

501/20 Bill for Expenses of Henry Honnor for the prosecuting of Catherine Berry for a felony 8th.July 1808.

	s..d
Paid into Court.	3..4
To loss of time.	7..0
	14..4

Allowed eight shillings & 6 pence.

501/21 Bill for expenses of Richard Moss for the prosecution of Catherine Berry for a felony. As for last item. Allowed 8/6d.

| 501/22 Bill of James Deayton. Borough Gaol. | £.. s..d |
| 40 days subsistence for Catherine Berry @ 4¹/₂d per day. | 0..15..9 |

501/22   Bill of James Deayton. Borough Gaol.   £.. s..d
40 days subsistence for Catherine Berry @ 4¹/₂d per day.   0..15..9
To two fires.   0.. 5..0
Pens ink & paper.   0.. 3..0
To the fees of John Willes & James & John Warwick.   2.. 0..0
                                                            £ 3.. 3..9

501/23   Bill of Ann Twitchell. House of Correction.
To maintaining Phebe Wolfe committed for   s..d
ill behaviour. Kept for 25 days @ 4d a day.   8..4
To maintaining Thomas Shepherd committed for
ill using his Son. Kept 13 days @ 4d a day.   4..4
                                                                 12..8

501/24   Bill of the Constables of the Boro' for:-
'Wipin' a vagrant at the Market Cross.   10s.

501/25   Bill of the Coroner.
         Taking an Inquisition on the body of   £.. s ..d
         Andrew Stedman who cut his throat.   1.. 0..0
         Paid Sergeant at Mace & Jury.   17..0
                                                            £ 1..17..0

SESSIONS ROLL 502, Epiphany 1809   (13th.Jan.)

502/1   Writ proclaiming Quarter Sessions and Gaol Delivery.

502/2   List of jurors for the Grand and Petty juries.

502/3   Calendar of prisoners for the Borough Gaol. (No Prisoners).

502/4   Declaration 13th.January 1809.
James Maddams, maltmaker, William Birchmore, maltmaker, and Francis
Carter Searancke, maltster & brewer, severally make oath & say that first
Wm.Birchmore for himself saith that on the 30th.day of November last
seven quarters of malt the property of the Francis Carter Searancke then
being in his malthouse in the Parish of St.Albans perished & was totally
lost burnt & destroyed by fire which then happened & James Maddams for
himself saith that the 7 quarters of malt so lost by the fire was an entire loss
to the said Francis C.Searancke & lastly this Deponent Francis C.
Searancke for himself saith that the 7 quarters of malt was the property of
him Francis Carter Searancke.

502/5   An Account of Monies received on Convictions for False Weights
3rd.Dec. Contains list of 5 names for one offence, fined 5 shillings each and
4 names for second offence fined 10 shillings each.

502/7 Calendar of Prisoners. House of Correction.
Vagrants committed between Michaelmas 1808 & Epiphany 1809.
3 men, 7 women and 10 children for 7 days each. 1 sick woman for 9 days.
2 men for 14 days. 1 sick woman for 17 days.

502/8 Gaol Visitors Report.
We the under signed magistrates hereby certify that we have visited the
Gaol. It is in good repair (except in some trifling repairs which have directly
to be done). Wholesome & clean & that the gaoler is in every way attentive
to his duty.

502/9 Bill of the Clerk of the Peace from Midsummer to Michaelmas &
Adjourned Sessions. 49 entries totalling £22 .. 19 .. 11.

Entries include:-	s..d
Fee for one Prisoner discharged by Proclamation.	6..8
Drawing & recording an order for an additional allowance for Carriage for H.M.Forces & their baggage.	10..0
For Payment of one third of the bill of George Fowler & son for repairing the House of Correction.	5..0
Writing a Letter by order of the Magistrates to Major Jones C.O.6th.Regt.Foot, informing him of Conviction & Sentence of John Wallis, James Warwick & John Warwick.	3..6
Writing another Letter by order of the Court to Major Jones informing him that so much of the sentence of John Wallis, James Warwick & John Warwick ordering them to stand in the 'Pilory' was remitted & that the Rest of the Sentence remained in force & requesting him to send for the Prisoners at the Expiration of their Imprisonment.	3..6

502/11 Bill of John Hale for work done at the Town Hall.
29 entries totalling £23..17..11¼ Entries include:-

	£..s..d
Quartering & 'Firring' Gable end of Town Hall next Mr.Rogersons.	0..3.. 4
'Takeing' up floor & joist in 'Mr.Deacon' sleeping room	0..3..10½
Cleaning away rubbish & 'puting' in ground sills & 'Sliceing' of posts & 'Choping' old quarters & quartering side next Dungeon.	1..7.. 6
Laying Chamber floor & 'Scirting' & 'puting molding' to doorway & hanging door & 'firring' joist & mending floor in other room, kitchen & passage etc.	1..5.. 6
'Puting' down steps & riser to Doorway into yard.	0..1.. 8

SESSIONS ROLL 503, Easter 1809   (14th.April)

503/1 Writ proclaiming Quarter Sessions and Gaol Delivery.

503/2 List of jurors for the Grand and Petty juries of the Borough.

503/3 Calendar of prisoners for the Borough Gaol. (No Prisoners).

503/4 Gaol Visitors Report. We two of the Magistrates hereby certify that the 'Goal' of this Borough is in good repair & the 'Goaler' is attentive to his Business.

503/5 Bill of John Field, Constable of St.Peter's Ward.	s..d
Sept.29th. To parading the streets on Statue (sic) night	2..6
Sept.30th. 'Stoping' a riot taken 3 Irishmen & attending the magistrates.	5..0
Oct.7th. Attending the sessions.	2..6
Oct.11-12. Parading the streets Fair Nights.	5..0
Jan.13th. Attending the sessions.	2..6
Mar. Making out a list for the Militia & attending subdivisions meetings.	10..6
Paid for a post letter.	0..3½
Mar.25-27 Parading the Streets Fair nights.	5..0
April 14th. Attending the sessions.	2..6
To be taken off for attending Sessions 7/6.	£1..15..9½

Allowed £1..8..3½.   F.C.Searancke, Mayor.

503/6 & 7 Bills of William Scourfield & Jacob Moore, Constables of Holywell & Fishpool Wards.

503/8 Bill of J.Barnet,Constable for Middle Ward. Entries include:-
Pressing 2 carts & wagons for the 19 Light
Dragoons & 43 Rgt.Foot.   6s..0d
'Whatever Gent. may object to pay the constable for that in St.Alban, I find by enquiry it is allowed by every parish in England.'
Going round the Ward & making out the List of Names & sticking them on the Church Door who are liable to serve in the Militia.   10s..6d
Allowed for atd. a riot.   5s..0d
'Two days previous to the October Sessions was taken for Irishmen for breaking the Peace in the Boro. Do you think proper he should be paid for the trouble.'

503/9 & 10 Supplementary Bill from a Constable and a further bill from J.Barnet.

503/11 Bill of the Clerk of the Justices.
Jan.25th.1809 Swearing in 37 Special Constables for the purpose of preserving the peace at the time of the Election @ 1/- each.   £1..17..0

503/12 Bill of the Coroner for the Borough.	£ .. s .. d
Taking an Inquisition on the body of Andrew Stedman	1 .. 0 .. 0
Paid Jury & Srgts. at Mace	0 ..17 .. 0
The like on the Inqn. taken on the body of Thos. Gosbell	1 ..17 .. 0

503/13 Bills. *(A number of scraps of paper authorising relief mostly due to Constable of Middle Ward. Includes entries for wives & children of soldiers.)*

SESSIONS ROLL 504, Midsummer 1809 (14th.July)

504/1 Writ proclaiming Quarter Sessions and Gaol Delivery.

504/2 List of jurors for the Grand and Petty juries of the Borough.

504/3 Calendar of prisoners for the Borough Gaol. (No Prisoners).

504/4 Note. To the Clerk of the Peace or his Deputy.
I, Solomon George Shaw of St.Albans, do hereby declare that I have a printing press & types for printing which I propose to use for printing within the Borough & which I require to be entered for that purpose in pursuance of an Act passed in the 39th. Year of the Reign of His Majesty King George the Third entitled "An Act for the more effectual suppression of Societies established for seditious & treasonable Purposes & for better preventing treasonable & seditious Practices." May 1809

504/5 Recognisance concerning John Lines, carpenter, likely to be the father of the bastard child of Elizabeth Puddephatt.

504/6 Recognisance concerning Richard Claxton, labourer, late of Bishops Hatfield, likely to be father of the bastard child of Mary Barber.

504/7 Bill of the Clerk of the Peace totalling £11..2..0. 33 entries including:-

	s..d
Payment of Two Thirds of the bill of Ann Twitchell for the maintenance of vagrants.	5..0
Payment of one third of the bill of Thomas Chambers.	5..0
Payment of one third of the bill of John Boys.	5..0

504/8 Bill of Edwin Greenhill.
1809 May 10th. Replacing Two Pales in the Town Hall 2s..6d

504/9 Note. 'Gentlemen by looking over the papers you will find they agree with the bill'.
(2 columns of small entries-no details-from 4d to 2/8d) Total £4..0..3

504/10 Bill of James Deayton, Borough Gaol, for fires. Total £3..6..0. Allowed two thirds of the above bill.

504/11 Bill of Ann Twitchell, House of Correction.
For maintenance of 13 vagrants committed normally for seven days at 4d. per day, but including Richard Evever kept for nine weeks at 3..6d per week, being sick & two vagrants being publicly whipped by order.

SESSIONS ROLL 505, Michaelmas 1809 (6th.Oct.)

505/1 Writ proclaiming Quarter Sessions and Gaol Delivery.

505/2 List of jurors for the Grand and Petty juries of the Borough.

505/3 Calendar of prisoners in the Borough Gaol. (No Prisoner).

505/4 Calendar of Prisoners. House of Correction. (No Prisoner).

505/5 Gaol Visitors Report. Similar to 503/4.

505/6 Relief of Paupers. £7..19..1

505/7 Bill of the Coroner. Entries include:-
Taking an inquisition on the body of Wm.Fellows who hung himself. (£1).
The like Fee for an Inquisition on the body of John Edlin who died in prison
in the Liberty Gaol.

SESSIONS ROLL 506, Epiphany 1810

506/1 Writ proclaiming Quarter Sessions and Gaol Delivery.

506/2 List of jurors for the Grand and Petty juries of the Borough.

506/3 Calendar of prisoners for the Borough Gaol. (No Prisoners).

506/4 Calendar of Prisoners. House of Correction.
William Lane committed, for behaving in a riotous & disorderly manner.
William Parkins committed, charged with misbehaving in his service (to be
confined 1 calendar month).

506/5 & 6 Sacrament Certificates of William Brown and Rev.James
Carpenter Gape.

506/7 Thomas Jones of St.Albans, Gent, certified by Commissioners
for the affairs of Taxes as an Acting Commissioner.

506/8 Coroners Report. Entries mention:-
Taking an Inquisition on the body of Sarah Silby who died suddenly in
Sopwell Lane. (£1). The like charges for taking an Inquisition on the body
of Thomas Gibbs who cut his throat.

506/9 Bill of James Deayton for fires, pens ink etc.

506/10 Bill of the Clerk of the Peace. Midsummer to Michaelmas
inclusive. 23 entries including:-

Drawing & recording order for additional allowance for Carriages provided for H.M.Forces & for their baggage. Attending receiving the Land Tax Duplicate from the Chief Constable. One third of the Gaol Book.

506/11   Bill Relief of Paupers from Oct. to Jan.12th.   £7..8..6

506/12   Gaol Visitors Report.

SESSIONS ROLL 507, Easter 1810   (4th.May)

507/1   Writ proclaiming Quarter Sessions and Gaol Delivery.

507/2   List of jurors for the Grand and Petty juries.

507/3   Calendar of prisoners for the Borough Gaol. (No Prisoners).

507/4   Calendar of Prisoners. House of Correction. (No Prisoners).

507/5   Paid for the Relief of Paupers.   £8..9.. 3
             What you please for my trouble.   3..3.. 0
                                           J.Barnet.   11..12..3

SESSIONS ROLL 508, Midsummer 1810   (13th.July)

508/1   Writ proclaiming Quarter Sessions and Gaol Delivery.

508/2   List of jurors for the Grand and Petty juries of the Borough.

508/3   Calendar of prisoners for the House of Correction.
Thos.Sheppard, committed July 11th. charged with running away and leaving his family chargeable to the Abbey Parish.
Ann Sayelles committed July 4th. for behaving in a riotous manner in the workhouse belonging to the Abbey Parish-to be confined one month.

508/4   Calendar of prisoners for the Borough Gaol.
Jane Coleman committed 11th.June on the oath of Mary Sprigge that several articles were feloniously stolen out of her chamber and that Jane Coleman is suspected of the felony.
Samuel Fisher committed 25th.June 1810 on the oath of Solomon Gough with having feloniously taken two brass weights.

508/10   Complaint of Mary Spriggs in the parish of St.Michael in the Borough. 11th.June that she lodges in the house of James Dearman in the Borough and that about 14 days back Jane Coleman came to lodge with her in the same house and that she the complainant and Jane Coleman did sleep together in the same room. That on Friday morning last she was robbed of a linen gown, bonnet, two caps, two head handkerchiefs, an apron, 3

handkerchiefs, 1 pr. of cotton stockings with other wearing apparel, which articles were feloniously taken and carried away from the sleeping room, and that the complainant hath reason to suspect that the clothing apparel was feloniously taken by Jane Coleman.
Recognisances 508/7 & 8.
Presentment of the jury 508/13 concerning the theft of 1 linen gown of the value of 6d, 1 silk bonnet of the value of 4d. Endorsed 'A true Bill. Verdict guilty'.

508/11 Complaint and information of Judith Pain of the parish of St.Albans, single woman, 9th.May 1810. Who saith that her master Thos.Herbert did between the hours of 2 and 3 in the afternoon strike her a violent blow with a brush and did also seize her by the throat with great force, and violently shook her, at his dwelling house in the parish of St.Albans, without any just cause or provocation whatever. Wherefore she prayeth that justice may be done to her.
Recognisances 508/5 & 6.

508/12 Complaint and information of Solomon Goff of the parish of St.Albans, labourer, 25th day of June, who saith that he lives with his son-in-law, George Calvert, at the victualling house known by the sign of the Red Lion in the parish of St.Albans, as an assistant and that he is allowed to sell butter for his sole and separate profit, that between the hours of ----- and ten of the evening he missed from out of a back house adjoining and forming a part of the dwelling house, two brass weights with which he had this evening been weighing butter. That is to say one one-pound weight and one one-quarter of a pound weight and that he hath reason to suspect and doth suspect that the two weights were feloniously taken and carried away from out of the back house by Samuel Fisher of the parish of St.Albans.
Recognisances 508/9.
Presentment of the jury 508/14 concerning the theft of 1 brass weight of the value of 2d, 1 brass quarter of a pound weight of the value of 1d. Endorsed 'Not a true Bill'.

508/15 Sacrament Certificate of Joseph Pomfret Vandelmeulen.

508/16 Bill of the Clerk of the Peace from Epiphany to Easter Sessions 1810 inclusive. Contains 35 entries totalling £11..18..10d. Entries include:-

	s .. d
Drawing & recording Order for the appointment of Visitors to the Gaol & House of Correction.	5 .. 0
Exhibiting & recording the Rules orders and Regulations of a Society of Good Fellowship established at the Blue Boar in the Borough.	10 .. 0
The like for Payment of the Bill of James Deayton for Fires etc. provided at the Quarter Sessions.	5 .. 0
The like for Payment of 1/3rd of the Bill of George Fowler & Son for repairing the House of Correction.	5 .. 0
The like for Payment of 1/3rd. of the Bill of Ann Twitchell	

for the maintenance of Vagrants.	5 .. 0
The like for Payment of 1/3rd. of the Bill of J.Rickards for Medicines administered to Vagrants in the House of Correction.	5 .. 0
The like for Payment of 1/3rd. of the Bill of Wm.Downing for repairing the House of Correction.	5 .. 0
The like for the Payment of 1/3rd. of the Bill of Roger Bradley for repairing the House of Correction.	5 .. 0
Fees of 2 prisoners committed to Gaol.	13 .. 4
Fee of 1 prisoner discharged by Proclamation.	6 .. 0
Drawing & recording Order of additional allowances for the conveyance of the Baggage & of the Army.	10 .. 0
The like for Payment of 1/3rd. of the Bill of John Boys Gent. Clerk to the Magistrates.	5 .. 0

508/17 July 12th.1810. Bill to the Estate of Ann Twitchell decd.
For one Quarters Salary for keeping the House of Correction for which said
bill due at Midsummer last past. £1 .. 5 .. 0

508/18 Bill of J.Barnet, Constable of Fishpool Ward.
Contains 28 entries totalling £3..12..4d. from which 2/- was deducted.

Entries include:-	s .. d
Sworn in constable.	1 .. 0
Paid for a letter from Mrs.Grover Hempstead.	0 .. 4
Attending the drawing Local Militia.	2 .. 6
Attending the Town Hall door the day they were sworn in.	2 .. 6
Making a list of names & giving notice to send the weights.	3 .. 0
Attending Licence Day.	2 .. 6
To summoning the Stone Wardens to attend the Vestry.	2 .. 0
Attending the nights of the fairs.	5 .. 0
Statute Night.	2 .. 6
Looking after the lights & fireworks.	2 .. 6
Attdg the door at the Jubilee Ball.	5 .. 0
Attdg the two nights of the Fair.	5 .. 0
Delivering out the papers & picking them up in different parts of the town notice local militia.	2 .. 6
Fetching a woman & child from Bedham (Bedmond?).	3 .. 6
Letter from Hertford.	0 .. 6
Preparing Mr.Page's wagon.	1 .. 0
Preparing Mr.Kinder's wagon.	1 .. 0
Taking a warrant to the Constable Redbourn, to prepare a cart for Mr.Frost.	2 .. 6
Lady Spencer's cart.	1 .. 0
Mr.Woodbridge's cart.	1 .. 0
Mr.Missington's cart.	1 .. 0
Preparing a cart for the Bedford militia.	1 .. 0
2 carts for the Herts militia.	2 .. 0
Preparing a cart for the 27th Bat.Foot.	1 .. 0

Taking a warrant to Park Street to get 8 waggons
for Bedford militia. 2 .. 6
Ditto for 3 wagons. 2 .. 6
Paid for a Horse & Cart to Bedmond to fetch the wife &
child of J.Weatherly. 7 .. 6
Whipping a man at the market house by an order
from Mr.Lowe. 10 .. 0

508/19, 20 & 21   Bills of James Clark, John Stevens and William
Scourfield, Constables of St.Peters, Holywell and Middle Wards. Similar to
previous item, entries include:- s .. d
Summoning the Publicans & a list of the license. 2 .. 6
Summoning the Officers & a list of the Stonewardens
of Vestry. 2 .. 0
Parading the Streets Statute Evening. 2 .. 6
Parading the Streets until midnight. 5 .. 0
Attending all Night Jubilee Ball. 5 .. 0
By order of the Mayor looking after the lights & fireworks. 2 .. 6
Attending the Jubilee till 5 in Morning. 5 .. 0
Parading the Streets till 12 o'clock at night. 5 .. 0
By Order of the Mayor in Search after some 'Foreners'
Luggage taken away by some Post Boys - unknown. 1 .. 6

508/22   Bill of James Deayton including:- s .. d
To the fees of Jane Coleman. 13 .. 4
..   .. Samuel Fisher. 13 .. 4

508/23   Bill to William Catlin Constable for the Parish of Abbots
Langley. s .. d
To aid & assist Mr.Barnard in taking John Weatherly &
fetching his wife from Bedmond. 3 .. 6
Horse & cart to bring witnesses to the Town Hall by
order of the Magistrates. 7 .. 6
My attendance. 5 .. 0

508/24   Bill. Indictment (3s..6d). 3 witnesses (7s..6d)

508/25   Bill of J.Barnet £.. s .. d
Paid for the relief of paupers. 7 .. 3 .. 0
Paid in absence of the magistrate. 1 .. 3
'As advancing the money is attended with a little inconvenience will the
gentleman have the goodness to advance me a little on account'.

508/26   Bill of Charles Burch, Constable, Watford in the Liberty of
St.Albans.
Expenses for going after Jane Coleman on suspicion of a robbery on 10th.
June. Apprehending her 4 miles from Watford. s .. d
My own lost time. 2 .. 6
Keeping her in the cage all night. 6

Bringing her from Watford to St.Albans with a horse & cart.	8 .. 0
My own lost time.	5 .. 0
Turnpike.	3

508/27 Bill	s .. d
Paid for indictment.	3 .. 6
Paid for hire of horse & cart to apprehend the prisoner.	12 .. 0
Lost a week's work in searching for the prisoner and attending to prosecute her.	10 .. 6
Paid witness James Dearman 4 days.	10 .. 0
.. .. Barnet 2 days.	5 .. 0
.. .. Birch 1 day 8 miles.	8 .. 0

SESSIONS ROLL 509, Michaelmas 1810 (5th.Oct.)

509/1   Writ proclaiming Quarter Sessions and Gaol Delivery.

509/2   Calendar of prisoners for the Borough Gaol. (None).

509/3   Prisoner in the House of Correction:- Mary Bell committed for two months for being intoxicated and conducting herself in a riotous and disorderly manner.

509/4   List of jurors for the Grand and Petty juries of the Borough.

509/5 Bill of James Deayton	s .. d
To 29 days' subsistence and straw to Jane Coleman.	12 .. 4$\frac{1}{2}$

Also fires, pen, ink and paper.

509/6   Note signed Perc.Lewis, Recorder.
Paid from last Sessions for the relief of paupers:-   £4..12..10d

509/7   Sacrament Certificate of James Preedy.   .

SESSIONS ROLL 510, Epiphany 1811 (18th.Jan.)

510/1   Writ proclaiming Quarter Sessions and Gaol Delivery.

510/2   Calendar of prisoners for the Borough Gaol. (None).

510/3   List of jurors for the Grand and Petty juries of the Borough.

510/6   Complaint and information of John Collins of the parish of St.Michael in the Borough, Cow Doctor, taken on oath 11th.January 1811. He saith that on Saturday last between the hours of three and four of the afternoon Thomas Adams did violently approach and beat him with his

clenched fist upon several parts of his body at the Great Red Lion Public House by which he is so much injured that he has not been able to follow his ordinary business, and the assault was totally unprovoked on his part the complainant prayeth that Justice may be done to him.
Endorsed with note of recognisances.
Recognisances 510/4 & 5.

510/7 Bill of the Clerk of the Peace from Midsummer to Michaelmas Sessions 1810. Contains 52 entries totalling £23..13..4d. Entries include:-

	s .. d
Drawing and recording Order for additional allowance for Carriages provided for His Majesty's Forces and for their Baggage.	10 .. 0
Fair copy for the High Constable.	5 .. 0
Drawing and recording Order for the appointment of John Deayton to be Keeper of the House of Correction in the room of Ann Twitchell deceased.	5 .. 0
The like for Payment of the Bill of Wm Catlin for apprehending a Prisoner.	5 .. 0
The like for Payment of 1/3rd. of the Bill of the Clerk of the Peace.	5 .. 0
The like for the Payment of 1/3rd. of the Bill of Ann Twitchell late Keeper of the House of Correction for the maintenance of Vagrants.	5 .. 0
Drawing and recording Order for Payment of 1/3rd. of the Bill of James Deayton for fires provided at the Petty Session.	5 .. 0
Fees for 4 prisoners committed to gaol.	£1 .. 6 .. 8
Fees for 2 prisoners discharged by proclamation.	13 .. 6
Exhibiting and recording rules, orders and regulations of a Society of Good Fellowship at the St.Christopher.	10 .. 0
The like for the Female Society under the patronage of the Dowager Lady Spencer.	10 .. 0
Drawing & recording order for payment of 1/3rd. the bill of John Boyde Gent. for making out examinations & orders for relief of the families of men serving in the local Militia.	5 .. 0
The like for payment of 1/3rd.the bill of John Deayton Keeper of the House of Correction for the maintenance of vagrants.	5 .. 0
The like for payment to William Hale of the amount of the estimate for building a Cage.	5 .. 0

510/8, 9 & 10 Bills of James Clark, William Scourfield and John Stevens, Constables of St.Peter's Middle and Holywell Wards.

510/11 Bill for relieving the paupers from Oct.to Jan. £8..11..6

510/12 Bill of John Deayton. House of Correction.	s .. d
To 20 days subsistence to Mary Bill.	7 .. 6
To 5 days subsistence to Charles Wilde.	1 ..10 ½
To straw.	1 .. 6

SESSIONS ROLL 511, Easter 1811   (26th.April)

511/1   Writ proclaiming Quarter Sessions and Gaol Delivery.

511/2   Calendar of prisoners in House of Correction. (None).

511/3   Calendar of prisoners for the Borough Gaol.
Thos.Woodland, Thos Pain and John Cordwell bailed out. Committed for want of sureties to keep the peace, especially towards Wm.Jackson.

511/4   List of jurors for the Grand and Petty juries of the Borough.

511/5   Complaint of William Jackson and also the examination of James Tilcock, Yeoman, taken on oath. Wm. Jackson saith that on Thursday last about the hour of eight in the evening, a number of persons assembled in the street in which this complainant resided and made a great noise and disturbance near the complainant's house with horns, kettles and bells to the great nuisance of all the peaceable inhabitants, and this examinant James Tilcock saith that he was passing along the street at the time of the disturbance and that he saw Wm.Grove, Thos.Woodland the Younger, Thos.Pain Jnr, John Cordwell, all of the Borough, present and that they were most active in making the disturbance.
Endorsed with note of recognisances.
Recognisances 511/6, 7, 8, 9 & 10.
Presentment of the jury 511/11 concerning J.Cordwell, Wm.Grove, Thos.Pain the yngr. together with 50 or more evil disposed persons (to the jurors as yet unknown). Endorsed only with names of witnesses.

511/12   Bill of John Deayton. House of Correction.

511/13   Bill of James Barnet, Constable. Entries mainly concern cost of carts for Derby Militia, Nottingham Militia, 73rd.Regt.of Foot, Hertford Militia, 7th.Dragoons and two deserters.

511/14   Bill of Dr.Boys, Coroner, for taking an inquisition on the body of a woman whose name was unknown found dead in Mr.Brown's barn.

511/15   Bill for two pots of ointment for a young woman with itch held in the Town Gaol. (1/6d each).

SESSIONS ROLL 512, Midsummer 1811   (19th.July)

512/1   Writ proclaiming Quarter Sessions and Gaol Delivery.

512/2   List of jurors for the Grand and Petty juries of the Borough.

512/3   Calendar of prisoners for the Borough Gaol. (None).

512/4   Calendar of Prisoners - House of Correction - (None).

512/5   Voluntary examination of Elizabeth Pegrum of the Borough, taken upon oath 26th.April. This examinant saith that she is now with child likely to be born a bastard, and chargeable to the Parish of St.Alban and Thomas Dimmock, a private soldier in H.M.24th.Regt.Light Dragoons is the father.
Endorsed with note of recognisances.
Recognisances 512/6.

512/7   Sworn by Thomas House, one of the overseers of the poor in the Parish of St.Alban, that Elizabeth Pegrum was delivered last Saturday of a bastard child.

512/8   Sacrament Certificate of George Watlington.

512/9   Bill of John Deayton. House of Correction.
Subsistence for prisoners.   £1..0..9d

512/10 Paid for the Relief of Paupers   £7..11..4d

512/11 Bill of the Clerk of the Peace for the Borough of St.Alban.
Epiphany & Easter. Total expenses being £18..10..6d, which included:-
Drawing and recording order for the appointment of
Visitors of the Gaol and House of Correction.   5s.
Exhibiting & recording orders, Rules and Regulations of
a Society of Good Fellowship established at the Windmill.   10s.
Payments to Constables and the House of Correction.
Payment for surgical aid and medicines to a prisoner. The making out of Orders of Relief of the Families of Militia Men, vagrant paupers and examinations. Fees for prisoners.

SESSIONS ROLL 513, Michaelmas 1811   (11th.Oct.)

513/1   Writ proclaiming Quarter Sessions and Gaol Delivery.

513/2   Calendar of prisoners for the Borough Gaol.
Michael Hester, Timothy Riley, Michael McTag, James Hill, Patrick Molloy, Richard Molloy, Stephen Connor, Committed on the oath of Samuel Deayton in that they did last night commit a riot and affray and did beat and ill-treat several of the inhabitants of the Borough.

513/3   Calendar of prisoners for the House of Correction. (None).

513/4   List of jurors for the Grand and Petty juries of the Borough.

513/7 & 8   Recognisance concerning an assault upon John Bean by William Field.

513/11 The Complaint and Information of John Savage of the Borough, stationer, 2nd.Aug.1811, who saith that for some very considerable time now William Gower, broker, hath behaved to him on the streets and highways of the Borough in a very insolent, abusive and reproachful manner using the most scurrilous language and presenting him as unfit for society - the complainant from the whole of the behaviour of William Gower and more particularly from his conduct on Sunday last and yesterday on the highways in the Borough, hath every reason to think that William Gower will do him some bodily injury until he shall be restrained by the power of law. Wherefore the complainant doth require surety of good behaviour and this not from any private malice, vexation or revenge but of very fear and for the necessary safety of his person.
Recognisances 513/9 & 10.

513/12 The Examination Of Complaint of James Farley, farrier, 6th Sept.1811 who saith that Thos.Mowbray, gentleman, did last night violently assault and strike him without any just cause.
Recognisances 513/6.

513/13 The Information and Complaint of Samuel Deayton 17th Oct.1811. That a party of Irish recruits on their march to join the 86th. Regiment of Foot did last night make a riot and affray in the Borough by marching and beating with bludgeons several of the peaceable inhabitants of the town and without any sort of provocation and this examinant further saith the recruits did violently assault & beat Abraham Pooley and John Tomlin and several other persons and that the names of the principal rioters are Michael Hester, Timothy Riley, Michael McTag, James Hill, Patrick Molloy, and Stephen Connor.
Recognisances 513/5.
Presentment of the jury 513/14 concerning Michael Hestor, Timothy Riley, Michael McTag, James Hill, Patrick Molloy, Richard Molloy & Stephen Connor making an assault upon John Tomlin & beating, wounding & illtreating him so that his life was greatly despaired of & other wrongs to John Tomlin to his great damage. Endorsed 'A true Bill. Plea of the whole, Not Guilty. Verdict of the Whole, Not Guilty'.
Presentment of the jury 513/15 concerning the previous defendants together with divers other evil disposed persons to the number of ten unlawfully, riotously & routously gathering together to disturb the peace and assaulting one Abraham Pooley & wounding & illtreating him so that his life was greatly despaired of & other wrongs to Abraham Pooley. Endorsed, 'Plea of the Whole, Not Guilty. Verdict of the Whole, Not Guilty'.

513/16 Articles of the Peace exhibited by John Savage of the Borough, stationer, against William Gower of the same place, broker. The Exibitant on his oath saith that about two years ago he went to the Blue Boar public house to have a pint of beer and William Gower happened to be there also - that soon after this Exibitant went in, William Gower without any provocation on the part of the Exibitant endeavoured to imitate him and use many expressions which this Exibitant considered treasonable, and which were highly offensive to a loyal man and among other things accused the Exibitant of being employed by the government as a trap to catch up the words of persons, and this Exibitant felt himself bound to obtain, indeed get a constable and caused William Gower to be apprehended and taken before a magistrate. That the Exibitant had scarcely returned home from the Magistrates', when his house was beset by a mob throwing stones at his door, and putting the Exibitant and his family in great danger. That the Exibitant took a pistol and stood at his door and desired the mob to desist, and that he would shoot the first person who attempted to force his house, upon which 5 or 6 rushed upon this Exibitant and he struck down the pistol, which flashed in the pan. The Exibitant was then dragged out of the house and very much ill used, and would have been murdered, had it not been for the interruption of the neighbours - altho' William Gower was not present, yet the Exibitant in his conscience believes that all this was at his instigation and this Exibitant also says that he has not since been able to pass along the streets without being insulted and molested in the grossest manner, all which he believes to be at the instigation or encouragement of William Gower. That on 29th July last the Exibitant was walking quietly along a footpath in the Borough when he was again insulted and called many ill names by two young men and that William Gower who was then lying on the ground began to abuse this Exibitant also in the grossest manner and said that he, this Exibitant, was not fit to keep any company in any society, or even to walk upon the footpath, upon which he stood. This Examinant on his oath saith that by means of the premises aforesaid and by reason of the general demeanour and conduct towards him he is fearful that William Gower will do or cause him to be done some bodily hurt, and he further saith that he doth not make this complaint through any hatred, malice or ill-will which he hath or beareth towards William Gower but for fear and from the necessary safety of his person.

513/17 Payment to Joseph Simcock & Thomas House, Overseers of the Poor for the Parish of St.Alban, for taking the population. 958 males, 1194 females. 3 days at 20/- per day.   £3..0..0.
Allowed £2 of the above charge to be paid by the overseers out of the Poor Rate.

513/18 A Bill. The King on the prosecution of Abraham against Michael McTag & 6 others. £3..5..4
  The King on the prosecution of John Tomlin against same. £1..16..10

513/19 to 22 Bills of John Hebbs, J.Barnet, William Scourfield and John Stevens, Constables of Fishpool, St.Peters, Middle and Holywell Wards.
Entries mention Dispersing a mob at the Red Lion. Making out a list of bakers, butchers and shopkeepers. Taking 4 Irishmen to gaol for knocking down Mrs.Mark and her son.

513/23, 24 & 25 Bills of James Deayton, Borough Gaol, John Deayton and J.Palmer, Clerk of the Peace.

513/26   Gaol Visitors report.

513/27   Allowed Jas.Barnet, Constable, for Relief of Paupers. £8..8..6

SESSIONS ROLL 514, Epiphany 1812 (17th.Jan.)

514/1   Writ proclaiming Quarter Sessions and Gaol Delivery.

514/2   Calendar of prisoners for the Borough Gaol. (None).

514/3   List of jurors for the Grand and Petty juries of the Borough.

514/4   Calendar of prisoners for the House of Correction. (None).

514/5   Bill of John Deayton. House of Correction. Subsistence etc.

514/6   Relief of Paupers. Yearly remuneration. £12..15..11d

514/7   Bill of James Deayton. Borough Gaol. Subsistence etc. £1..6..0

SESSIONS ROLL 515, Easter 1812 (10th.April)

515/1   Writ proclaiming Quarter Sessions and Gaol Delivery.

515/2   Calendar of Prisoners for the Borough Gaol.
Sarah Fletcher committed 8th.Feb. on the oath of William Brown, apprentice to Samuel Giles, with having stolen a piece of printed cotton.
Samuel Keer committed 12th.Feb. on the oath of Thomas Wolley Esq. with having received a quantity of hay and corn his property, knowing the same to be stolen.
James Carr alias Watson and James Brown, committed 20th.March on the oath of Samuel Haseldine and others for uttering forged bank notes knowing them to forged.

515/3   Calendar of Prisoners. House of Correction. (None).

515/4   List of jurors for the Grand and Petty juries of the Borough.

515/11 The Information and Complaint of Thomas Wolley taken 11th. Feb. Who saith that diverse quantities of hay and corn have within six weeks been feloniously taken and carried away from his stables in the Borough, and he hath reason to suspect that part of the property stolen is concealed in the stable or outhouse of Samuel Keer of the Borough, victualler. *Note on reverse* '9th Feb. Sunday afternoon 9 trusses $4^{1}/_{2}$ trusses ['good week in one reaping'] 'Better look at the corn bin.'
Recognisances 515/7 & 8.
Presentment of the jury 515/10 concerning Samuel Keer receiving stolen

goods knowing them to have been stolen. Endorsed 'No true Bill'.

515/12 The Examination of William Brown apprenticed to Samuel Giles of the Borough, linen draper, 7th.Feb. Who saith that Sarah Fletcher of Redbourn this morning came into her master's shop under pretence of buying something - that soon after he was informed that she had stolen a piece of cotton print - that he immediately followed her and found upon her one piece of cotton print which was that morning in his shop - that two other pieces were taken from her by her Master which were also taken from his shop.
Endorsed with note of recognisances.
Recognisances 515/5 & 6.
Presentment of the jury 515/9 concerning Sarah Fletcher the wife of Joseph Fletcher, feloniously stealing six yards of printed cotton of the value of 10d. Endorsed 'A true Bill. Plea, Not Guilty. Verdict, Guilty'.

515/13 The Examination of Francis Brown, a private in the 24th Regt. of Light Dragoons, 12th.Feb. Who saith that he has for some time past been employed to look after the horses and stables of Admiral Wolley of the Borough that about 2 months ago being soon after he was first employed to take care of the horses that Samuel Keer at whose house he was quartered asked him whether he looked after Admiral Wolleys's horse - he said yes he did - Samuel Keer said if you have a little corn hay or straw to part with I will take it off you at any time - he further said that when Kingham had care of the horse - I used to take it off him; he would give 2s. a truss for the hay and 1/6d. for the half bushel of oats - this Examinant consented and did accordingly at various time supply Samuel Keer with hay in the whole about 8 trusses and 2 half bushels of oats and this Examinant had the amount thereof in beer at the house of Samuel Keer.

515/14 Bill of the Clerk of the Peace for the Borough. £22..0..8. of which £14..15..8 was allowed. Entries mention the payment of one third the bill of John Deayton for the maintenance of vagrants, also payment of one third the bill of James Deayton for fires provided for the magistrates at the weekly Petty Sessions held at the Town Hall.

515/15 Bill of John Deayton. House of Correction.Subsistence etc.

515/16 Bill. Dec.3rd.1811.Due to William Corby for work done for the Cage by order of Mr.Brown. £6..13..11d. Entries mention quantities of iron plate, 'nales', a new lock and six keys.

515/17 Bill. Due to William Corby for work done for the 'twone jeale' by order of Mr.Brown, 'Mare'.   'To a new bit to a key.   6s..0d'

515/18 To George Watson, an Overseer of the Poor of the Parish of St.Peter for taking the population of that Parish of St.Peter lying with the Borough of St.Alban and Return thereof.   £1..1.. 0

515/19 Bill of D.Hurst for Sarah Fletcher in the Borough Gaol. Sheets, 4 Napkins and a shift.   14s..0d.

515/20 Bill to the Justices of the Borough of St.Alban. for repair work done to the Borough Gaol.   £1..16..9½

515/21 Bill of James Deayton, Borough Gaol. Prisoners subsistence and fees etc. Mention made of 63 days and fees to Sarah Fletcher, 59 days and fees to Samuel Keer, 24 days and fees to James Carr alias Watson and 24 days and fees to James Brown.

515/22 Bill of W.Thornton. For medicines and treatment for prisoners, including Anodyne Mixture. Opening an Abscess in arm and Embrocation of foot.   £1..0..6

515/23 Bill of John Hale for fence to the Cage. Mention made of 25 ft. 8 in. of 5ft. Oak palisade fence with gate etc.   £12..17..2½d.

515/24 Bill. For medicines & attendance on Sarah Fletcher in the Borough Gaol.   £1..1..0

515/25 Bill.From James Barnett, Constable for bringing Keer from Hertford.   19s..6d

515/26 Bill. 2 pairs of '9/4' Blankets for the Borough Gaol.   £2.. 8..0

SESSIONS ROLL 516, Midsummer 1812   (17th.July)

516/1   Writ proclaiming Quarter Sessions and Gaol Delivery.

516/2   Calendar of Prisoners for the Borough Gaol.
Mary Howe committed 27th.May on the oath of Thomas Westwood with having bought a pair of breeches and a hat, knowing them to be stolen.
John Brookes committed 20 June 1812 on the oath of Francis Emmerson with stealing a quantity of straw for plait.

516/3   List of Jurors for the Grand & Petty juries of the Borough.

516/8   The Examination of Thomas Westwood late of the Parish of Kimpton 27th May, who saith that a pair of breeches and a hat being stolen from him on or about the 14th.April, the same were sold to Mary How who keeps a Rag Shop in Spicer Street, and this examinant further saith that he hath reason to believe that Mary How must have known that the breeches and hat were stolen because the hat being a new one was well worth 14/- and she bought it for 4/-, that the breeches were worth 23/- and that she gave not more than 8/- for them and that they were fit for a man and not a boy. Recognisances 516/4 & 5.

127

516/9 The Information and Complaint of Francis Emmerson 20th June who saith that he this day attended the St.Albans market for the purpose of selling straws for plait - that a bundle containing about 13 dozen bundles of straw plait were left at the Flower de Luce yard and were taken away as he was in the house having a Beaver - that he afterwards found them at the Dog Public House and has been informed that one John Brookes took the straws away - with the felonious intent of taking and carrying the same away. Endorsed with note of recognisances.
Recognisances 516/6 & 7.
Presentment of the jury 515/10 concerning John Brooks stealing & carry away 10 pounds weight of straw to the value of five shillings & 20 bundles of straw plait the value of 2 shillings being the goods & chattels of Francis Emmerson. Endorsed 'No true Bill'.

516/11 Bill of the Clerk of the Peace, Epiphany to Easter £13..5..8.

516/12 Bill of Geo. Fowler & Son. Payment for Raising Cage & underpinning ditto, altering & making good the drain from Mr.Rolfe's Wash House.   £3..15..5$^1/_2$

516/13 Bill of Thomas House for 'Magnesgon'.   6s..0d

516/14 Bill of James Deayton. Borough Gaol. £5..14..7. Entries mention:- subsistence for Jas.Brown alias Jas.Watson, Samuel Fletcher & Mary Howe. To removing Jas.Brown alias Jas.Watson, to Hertford. Fees for Mary Howe & John Brookes.

516/15 Bill of John Deayton House of Correction. 10s..1$^1/_2$d   Entries mention:- subsistence for 5 males and 1 female and her child.

516/16 Paid for the Relieving the Paupers   £11..13..2

516/17 Bill of the Constable of Kimpton. The King against How. Ditto for Westwood. Expenses 16..0d. Paid into Court 3..6d.

516/18 Bill of Fras.Emmerson. The King against Brooks.
Expenses attending Court & 2 days lost and Indictment.   15s..6d.

516/19 Bill of J.Barnet, Constable, for getting assistance to take Brooks for stealing straws & attending at the Hall.   5s..0d

SESSIONS ROLL 517, Michaelmas 1812   (9th.Oct.)

517/1 Writ proclaiming Quarter Sessions and Gaol Delivery.

517/2 List of jurors for the Grand and Petty juries of the Borough.

517/3   Calendar of Prisoners. House of Correction.
William Marshall committed 10th.Sept. this day wandering abroad &
begging from door to door & having done these 14 days now & as it appears
that William Marshall was committed by the Mayor some short time since
for a similar offence.   John Palmer, Hundreder.

517/4   Calendar of Prisoners for the Borough Gaol.
John Woodrof & Richard Etherington committed 13th.August charged upon
the oath of James Wood with having late on Sunday night or early on
Monday morning feloniously stolen from & out of the left pocket of his
waistcoat at the public house known by the sign of the Red Lion &
commonly called the Great Red Lion, eleven One Pound Notes of the Bank
of England.
Thomas Gazeley committed 17th.August charged on the oath of Solomon
George Shaw with having feloniously stolen & carried away 60 penny
pieces of the copper coining of this realm his property.

517/11   The Examination of James Wood lately a private soldier in H.M.
39th Regiment of foot 10th August who saith that he is an out pensioner of
Chelsea Hospital with an allowance of 15 pence per day and that on Friday
last he received his pension up to Christmas next at Chelsea and that he
slept that night at Chelsea, that on Saturday he proceeded to Barnet where he
slept, that on Sunday he came to St.Albans which place he reached about 6
o'clock in the evening and that he went to a public house which he has been
told is known by the sign of the Red Lion and commonly called the Great
Red Lion where he had ------- refreshment and having procured a bed in the
house, he retired to it between eleven and twelve o'clock. This examinant
saith that previous to leaving Chelsea he got a fellow soldier to sew eleven
one pound notes of the Bank of England in the left pocket of his waistcoat
and that he felt them in it on his going upstairs to bed last night. That upon
his pulling his clothes off he placed them at the foot of the bed on which he
slept. That upon his arising this morning between the hours of five and six
he found the bottom of the left pocket of his waistcoat very much torn or
cut and the eleven one pound notes of the Bank of England not in it but
taken away. The examinant having been told that three men of the names of
John Martin, John Woodroof and Richard Etherington slept in the same
room with him hath just reason to suspect that the one pound notes were
feloniously stolen by one some or all of the said men. Therefore he prayeth
that justice may be done to him.
Endorsed with a note of recognisances.
Recognisances 517/8, 9 & 10.
Presentment of the jury 517/14 concerning John Martin, John Woodroff &
Richard Etherington stealing & carrying away ten bank notes Endorsed 'No
True Bill'.

517/12   The Confession of Thomas Gazeley apprentice to Solomon
George Shaw of the parish of St.Alban, printer, made 14th.August 1812
Who saith that this morning between the hours of seven and eight he did
steal, take and carry away from out of the post office in the dwelling house

of Solomon George Shaw a piece of brown paper in which were wrapped sixty penny copper pieces which he paid Ann Wilsher the wife of George Wilsher of the parish of St.Alban for tarts and pies which he had had several hours previous to his taking the sixty penny pieces. Thos.Gazeley also confessed that if he had not been pushed by the Ann Wilsher he would not have stolen the penny copper pieces as he stole solely to enable him to pay what was due to Ann Wilsher.

Thos.Gazeley declareth the said confession to have been voluntarily made and not under the institution of any threat or pressure.

Recognisances 517/5, 6 & 7.

Presentment of the jury 517/13 concerning Thos.Gazeley stealing ten pieces of copper coin the property of Solomon George Shaw. Endorsed 'No true Bill'.

517/15 Bill. The King on the Prosecution of James Wood against John Martin, John Woodroff & Richard Etherington. To the expenses of the prosecutor & John Calverly.   £4..3..6

517/16 Bill of Wm.Scourfield, Constable of Middle Ward.
Contains 27 entries totalling £2..18..0. Entries include:-
'Parrading' the streets till 12 o'clock at the Fair.
Attending streets to prevent fireworks.
Search warrant after disorderly people.
Going the other side of Barnett Heath to disperse camps of 'Gipseys'.
Getting up at 12 o'clock to seek after baggage by order of the Mayor.
Taking 2 men before the Magistrate on suspicion of robbing 2 blind men.

517/17 Bill of John Stevens, Constable of 'Fishbourne' Ward.
Contains 39 entries totalling £4..5..6 with 1s..0d deducted. Entries include:-
Given warning to different landlords to shut up their houses at 11 o'clock of the night. Parading the streets to keep the peace on fair nights. Summoning overseers to 'chuse' new ones. Attending the Illumination by order of the Mayor. The summoning of shopkeepers, publicans & stone wardens & making out list. To pressing 7 waggons from Sandridge for the Flint Militia. To pressing 2 waggons & a cart from Sandridge for French Prisoners. *Various other parishes called on to provide for the Militia.*

517/18 Bill of Charles Robert Seear, Constable of Holywell Ward.
Contains 20 entries totalling £2..2..0. Entries include:-
Search warrants on different lodging houses for disorderly persons. Delivering out the local Militia Bills & giving notice to the men in my Ward. Summoning the Vitualers to renew their license. Attending at the fair to keep the Peace. The issuing of Search Warrants. Taking down the number of horses, chaise waggons and carts in the Borough.

517/19 Bill of James Barnet, Constable of St.Peters Ward.
Contains 28 entries totalling £3..2..0. Entries include:-
Taking a man to the Bridewell. Attending to prevent fireworks. Going round with the weights & weighing the bread etc. Searching the houses & getting

assistance & taking 2 men from the Red Lion on suspicion of robbery. Pressing waggon carts for His Majesty's Forces.

517/20 Bill of John Deayton, House of Correction.
Claiming subsistence & straw for prisoners Wm.Marshall, Sam'l Wildbore & a stranger   4s..5d

517/21 Bill of James Deayton, Borough Gaol.
Claiming subsistence & straw for prisoners Richard Etherington, John Woodroff & Thos.Gazeley. Also for 2 fires.   £6..7..1

517/22 Bill of J.Barnet, Constable of St.Peters Ward. £12..19..7. Allowed £11..13..6.

SESSIONS ROLL 518, Epiphany 1813   (15th.Jan.)

518/1   Writ proclaiming Quarter Sessions and Gaol Delivery.

518/2   Calendar of Prisoners for the Borough Gaol.
Benjamin Gilbert committed 1st.Dec. on the oath of Wm.Lewin, grocer & cheesemonger, with having feloniously stolen one whole cheese from out of his shop.
Martha Mardell committed 26th.Dec. charged on the oath of Sarah White with feloniously taking & carrying away 4 score yards of straw plait, her property.
House of Correction. (No prisoners).

518/3   List of Jurors for the Grand & Petty juries of the Borough.

518/8   The Complaint and Information of William Lewin of the parish of St.Alban, grocer and cheesemonger 1st Dec. Who saith that between the hours of six and seven of this evening Benjamin Gilbert came into his shop forming part of his dwelling house for the purpose of purchasing one penny worth of Vinegar - with that article he was served by Thomas Taylor, one of the shop assistants - and that after quitting the shop Benjamin Gilbert feloniously stole took and carried away with him one whole cheese of the sort commonly called Daventry Cheese. Thomas Taylor suspecting that Benjamin Gilbert had taken something pursued him and caught him in the street near to the shop door, when he saw him drop the cheese and picked it up and ----- ----- ---- the said Benjamin Gilbert wherefore William Lewin prayeth that justice may be done to him.
Endorsed with note of recognisances.
Recognisances 518/6 & 7.
Presentment of the jury 518/11 concerning a charge against Benjamin Gilbert for stealing one cheese to the value of five shillings. Endorsed 'A True Bill. Plea, Not Guilty. Verdict, Guilty'.

518/9 The Examination of Sarah White of Redbourn 26th Dec. Who Saith that a young woman who saith that her name is Martha Mardell did on Sat.14th December come into the Market of St.Albans and under pretence of buying straw plait got into her possession four score yards of plait belonging to this examinant of the value of thirteen shillings and fourpence and absconded therewith and in the same manner got into her possession the straw plait of several other poor persons under the like pretence of buying it viz. Catherine Munt of Wheathamstead of the value of five shillings and one penny and Elizabeth Brown of the parish of St.Peter of the value of seven shillings and six pence, and also absconded therewith, and that she left behind her several parcels of straw plait which she had got into her possession in the same manner but which she returned.
Endorsed with note of recognisances.
Recognisances 518/4 & 5.
Presentment of the jury 518/10 concerning a charge against Martha Mardell for stealing 60 yards of straw plait to the value of five shillings.
Endorsed 'A True Bill. Plea, Not Guilty. Verdict, Guilty'.

518/12 Bill. The King against Mardell. Expenses of prosecution, 3 witnesses & indictment.   £2..3..6

518/13 Bill. The King against Gilbert. Prosecution expenses   8s..6d

518/14 Bill of the Clerk of the Peace from Midsummer to Michaelmas. 50 entries totalling £32..9..0. Entries include:-
Journey to St.Albans for the purpose of holding & adjourning Sessions by reason of the necessary absence of the Mayor & Recorder who attended the Prince Regent on this day to present the address of the Borough on Mr.Perceval's assassination. Horse Hire & expenses.
Further entries mainly concern payments to the Parish Constables.

518/15 Bill of Borough Gaol for 1 large blanket.   12s..0d

518/16 Bill of the Coroner, John Boys. Entries mention:-
Taking an inquisition on the body of Thos.Turner who was killed by a fall from his horse. The like fees being an inquisition on the body of Robert Stevens who cut his throat.

518/17 Bill of James Deayton, totalling £3..10..4. Entries include claims for the subsistence, straw & fees for Benjamin Gilbert and Martha Mardale.

518/18 Bill of John Deayton, House of Correction, totalling £3..0..10 for prisoners subsistence.

518/19 Bill of James Barnet totalling £14..10..3 plus '3 guineas allowed for my trouble'. On the reverse 'Ordered that Five Pounds be allowed to James Barnet for his trouble in relieving paupers for one year. G.Watlington. Recorder'.

519/1   Writ proclaiming Quarter Sessions and Gaol Delivery.

519/2   Calendar of Prisoners for the Borough Gaol.
John Andrews, committed 6th.Feb, for on Sunday last violently assaulting & beating John Brooks. Remains in Gaol for want of sureties.
John Hayes committed 20th.March charged on the oath of Mr.Trelfs Esq. with having knowingly by false pretences obtained from him on or about the 16th.February 1811 the sum of forty five pounds.
Joseph Caldwell committed 27th.March on the oath of Samuel Deayton & others with tendering counterfeit money knowing it to be so.

519/3   Calendar of Prisoners in the House of Correction.
Elizabeth Selby committed 22nd.March 1813 as a rogue & vagabond.

519/4   List of Jurors for the Grand & Petty juries of the Borough.

519/5   An Account of the Number of Vagrants committed from Easter 1812 - Easter 1813. 51 names (men & women) including 3 wives and 9 children.

519/6   Recognisances concerning an assault by John Andrews upon John Brook.

519/8   Bail Order. To wit John Hayes of 42 Basinghall St.London & Barry Farm in the Parish of Sulley in the County of Glamorgan, Grazier, is delivered to Bail for his personal appearance next General Quarter Sessions of the Peace to answer all & singular such matters & things as on His Majesty's behalf shall then & there be objected against him & so from day to day should not depart the court without leave.

519/9   The Examination of Samuel Deayton of the Borough, victualler, 27th March Who saith that a man in the character of a sailor came into his house in the Borough of St.Alban on Thursday last between 6 and 7 in the evening being a Fair Day and asked for a glass of rum and a glass of gin intending as he said to treat Thos.Harding a private in the Marines - that having drunk the gin the above mentioned person offered to this examinant's daughter a shilling, which being observed by this examinant he refused as being counterfeit - that he then offered another which was also bad - that the same evening the said person who says his name is Joseph Caswell was searched and several other counterfeit shillings were found upon him particularly that 14 counterfeit shillings were found concealed in the sleeve of the coat.
Recognisances 519/7.
Presentment of the jury 519/13 concerning Joseph Caswell, labourer, uttering counterfeit money knowing it to be so. Endorsed 'A true Bill. Plea, Not Guilty. Verdict, Guilty'.

519/10 The Examination of John Hayes 12th.March. Says that he was living in London at the time the bill drawn by Mackinnell for which he received the value of Mr.Trelss and did not live in the County of Hertford. That he never did live at Reading in the County of Berks. That he lived at the time of paying the bill to Mr.Trelss in George St. Commercial Road, he believes No.2 and was rated in the parish. That he never represented himself to be a maltster at St.Albans or as living and carrying on any business there.

519/11 The Examination and Complaint of William Trelss of the Borough, banker, 6th.March. Who saith that a person who described himself to be John Hayes did on or about the 16th.February 1811 apply to this examinant at his bank at St.Albans and request him to give cash for a document which he produced purporting to be a draft on Messrs.Birch Chambers & Hobbs of London, bankers, drawn by J.P.Mackennell for £45 payable 10 days after date to Mr.J.Hayes or order dated 4th.February 1811. That this examinant gave the said person his own circulating Bank Notes for the draft, but when the sum was presented for payment to Messrs.Birch Chambers & Hobbs, it appeared that J.P.Mackennell had no cash at the last mentioned banking house and that the draft was so negotiated for the purpose of defrauding this examinant and that the person is now in custody at the town of Aylesbury for the offence on the charge of this examinant.

519/12 The Further Examination and Complaint of William Trelss 20th.March. This examinant saith that John Hayes now in custody on a charge of defrauding this examinant out of the sum of 45 pounds did at the time he so defrauded this examinant falsely represent that he did reside in the neighbourhood of St.Albans.
Presentment of the jury 519/18 concerning a charge against John Hayes that he knowingly by false pretences obtained from Wm.Trelss the sum of forty five pounds. Endorsed 'A true Bill'.

519/14 Relief of Paupers Paid £17..6..3

519/15 Bill. Swearing in 63 Special Constables. £3..3..0

519/16 Bill of John Deayton, House of Correction, totalling £7..2..3. For fees, subsistence and straw for named prisoners. Mentions 62 days for Benjamin Gilbert & 31 days for Martha Mardale, and their fees. Both committed by order of Sessions. Also 40 days for Elizabeth Selby.

519/17 Bill of James Deayton, Borough Gaol, totalling £5..16..9. For fees, subsistence, straw etc. for named prisoners.

SESSIONS ROLL 520, Midsummer 1813   (16th.July)

520/1 Writ proclaiming Quarter Sessions and Gaol Delivery.

520/2 Calendar of prisoners for the Borough Gaol.
Joseph Caswell committed at Easter Sessions. Ordered to be imprisoned six months in the Borough Gaol. Remains in Gaol.
Joseph Bunyan & William Bull, committed 1st.May on the oath of Thos.Kinder Esq. that his Brewhouse was broken open & a quantity of beer stolen.

520/3 Calendar of Prisoners in the House of Correction.
George Hill committed 15th.June 1813 on the oath of Elizabeth Brickland of the Parish of St.Alban with having gotten her with child & hath also refused to indemnify the said Parish.
Ann Smith committed 10th.July as a Vagabond & was found wandering & begging in the Parish of St.Peter.

520/4 List of Jurors for the Grand & Petty juries of the Borough.

520/5 & 6 Recognisances concerning an assault by Joseph Reynolds, yeoman, upon Joseph Tearle, labourer.

520/9 Complaint of Thomas Kinder 1st May who saith that last night his Brewhouse was broken open and a quantity of beer his property was stolen out of the same. And that he has reason to suspect and doth suspect that Joseph Bunyan and William Bull labourers did steal the same.
Recognisances 520/7 & 8.
Presentment of the jury 520/11 concerning Joseph Bunyan & Wm.Bull charged with stealing 2 gallons of ale value 10d from Thomas Kinder.
Endorsed 'A True Bill. Plea, Not Guilty. Verdict, Guilty against both'.

520/10 Warrant.
To All Constables......to require you to take Joseph Bunyan & William Bull & bring them before me to answer the said complaint & further to be dealt with according to the Law.

520/12 Bill of Clerk of the Peace. 45 entries totalling £15..15..6 for the Epiphany & Easter periods. Mention made of :
A Society of Good Fellowship established at the 'George'.
Having received an order from the Secretary of State to making out Gaol Calendars for one whole year from . . . .

520/13 Bill £2..11..5 for shirts, trousers, stockings & shoes. Bought of Thos.House.
Examined & allowed with comment 'This should have been allowed for the Liberty.'

520/14 Bill of John Deayton. House of Correction. 16 entries totalling £4..12..1. Concerned with subsistence and straw for prisoners. Includes 56 days and fees for Mary Berry committed by Sessions.

520/15 Bill of James Deayton. Borough Gaol. 13 entries totalling £8..8..0. Concerned mainly with subsistence, fees and straw. Includes 77 days each for Cashwell, Bunyan and Bull.

520/16 Relief of Paupers. Paid £12..2.8

SESSIONS ROLL 521, Michaelmas 1813 (8th.Oct.)

521/1 Writ proclaiming Quarter Sessions and Gaol Delivery.

521/2 Calendar of Prisoners. House of Correction. (No Prisoners).

521/3 Calendar of prisoners for the Borough Gaol.
Joseph Caswell convicted at Easter Sessions 1813 for offering false & counterfeit money. Ordered to be imprisoned in the Gaol for 6 months & that he do find sureties for his good behaviour for 6 months more.

521/4 List of jurors for the Grand and Petty juries of the Borough.

521/5 Bill of George Oakes, Constable of Holywell Ward. 15 entries totalling £1..11..0.

521/6 Bill of William Scourfield, Constable St.Peters Ward. 25 entries totalling £2..15..6 of which only £2..10..0 was allowed. Mention made of:- 'Going to Shaford to disperse a camp of gipseys . . .' 'Taking a man and woman having bad money found on them.' 'Taking a man up with £1..2..0d all bad silver.' 'Taking 2 saylors up on suspision of fordged papers to receive prize money.' 'Taking the sylor and a woman two diferent ways out of town . . . .'

521/7 Bill of J.Barnet, Constable Fishpool Ward. 12 entries totalling £4..13..0. All relate to pressing waggons for the military.

521/8 Bill of J.Barnet, Constable Fishpool Ward. 17 entries totalling £2..16..0.

521/9 Bill of James Deayton, Borough Gaol. 8 entries totalling £4..15..8½. Includes subsistence for Joseph Bunyan (42 days), convicted, William Bull (42 days), committed, and Joseph Caswell (84 days), convicted.

521/10 Relief of Paupers. Paid £15..12..9

SESSIONS ROLL 522, Epiphany 1814 (15th.Jan.)

522/1 Writ proclaiming Quarter Sessions and Gaol Delivery.

522/2   Calendar of Prisoners. House of Correction. (None).

522/3   Calendar of prisoners for the Borough Gaol.
John Butler committed 5th.Nov. on oath of Ann Gower & Wm.Brown & others with stealing 2 pieces of ribbon.

522/4   List of jurors for the Grand and Petty juries of the Borough.

522/5   Rex v Butler examinations Nov.5th 1813.
Examinations of Ann Gower, linen draper, William Brown, linen draper, Nathaniel Chaplin son/l. to Mr.Cockle of the Marines, and James Barnet, constable before one of His Majesty's Justices for the Liberty. First this examinant Ann Gower saith that between 4 and 5 o'clock in the evening of Tuesday 2nd.November the prisoner John Butler came into her house and asked to buy a piece of ribbon - that she served him with 1 yard of scarlet ribbon 1 yard and $\frac{1}{2}$ of blue ribbon and 1 yard and $\frac{1}{2}$ of pea green. The draws with the whole pieces of the ribbon were on the counter - that at the same time Nathaniel Chaplin came into her shop some time after he had purchased the sevl. articles which made her ask him whether he wanted anything else. Chaplin went out first and then soon after returned and asked her whether she had lost anything and whether she knew the man meaning the prisoner. That on looking into her drawer she missed the piece of pea green ribbon from which she had sold him a small quantity as above mentioned - That she saw the piece which was taken from him and believed it to be her property.
And this examinant Nathaniel Chaplin for himself saith that he observed the prisoner take the above mentioned piece of pea green ribbon from out of the drawer on the counter. That he went out without mentioning it conceiving it might have been done in joke. That he soon after saw the prisoner at Mr.Brown's door and asked him for the piece of ribbon which he had bought of Mrs.Gower - he asked him what he wanted to see it for - this examinant then asked him for the piece he took without paying for. He then said he had none. Examinant replied that he was certain that he saw him take a piece. He said he wd.see - he put his hand in his pocket and pulled out the piece he had purchased - this examinant said that was not it and advised him to give it up before there was any more to do about it. Then the prisoner put his hand in his pocket and pulled out the piece now produced which was not the piece he had taken from Mrs.Gower but another. He said this examnt. was a good fellow and begged that he would go with him and have something to drink - At this time Constable Barnet came up.
James Barnet for himself saith that he searched the prisoner and found upon him a piece of pea green ribbon the property of Mrs.Ann Gower and several pieces of ribbon and several other articles now produced except the piece of pea green ribbon belonging to Mr.Brown.
Wm.Brown for himself saith - that the prisoner came into his shop the same evening under pretence of buying ribbon. That he bought a small quantity which he paid for & also a pocket handkerchief. And at the same time privately stole from the drawer a quantity of pea green ribbon the property of

the Examinant which was afterwards found upon him and which was the same piece which the prisoner had delivered to Chaplin.

Endorsed with a note of recognisances.

Recognisances 522/7, 8, 9 & 10.

Presentment of the jury 522/11 concerning stealing 30 yards Sarsnet Ribbon value 10/- property of Ann Gower. Endorsed 'A true Bill. Verdict, Guilty'.

Presentment of the jury 522/12 concerning stealing 10 yards Sarsnet Ribbon value 3/- property of Wm.Brown. Endorsed 'A true Bill. Pleaded, Not Guilty. Verdict, Not Guilty'.

522/6 Recognisance concerning Joseph Caswell convicted at Easter Sessions 1813. To be of good behaviour.

522/13 'Jail' Visitors Report. 15 January 1814.

522/14 Relief of Paupers. Paid by order £11..12..9

522/15 Bill of Benjamin Fowler totalling £6..8..11. 23 entries for labour and materials for building repairs. Mention made of kitchen.

522/16 Bill of James Deayton, Borough Gaol, 18 entries totalling £12..5..0½. Includes subsistence for John Butler (74 days), committed. Further entries cover expenses paid to James Deayton for apprehending Thos.Williams who escaped from the Borough Gaol £12..12..9. Includes cost of 200 advertisements. Payment for Post Chaise to Brickhill and Stoney Stratford and back. Expenses for taking Thos.Williams to Hertford. A doctor & nurse 12 days and 12 nights.

522/17 Bill of John Deayton, House of Correction. 8 entries totalling 18s..10 ½ d. for subsistence and straw.

522/18 Bill of Sarah Cordwell for attending the Prisoner Thomas Williams 12 days & 12 nights.   £1..10..0

522/19 Bill of Joseph Tearle for attending the Prisoner Thomas Williams at the Town Hall 10 days & 11 nights @ 4 shillings per day & night. £2..2..0

522/20 Bill of William Corby for work 'dun' at the Town Hall. 'To fier pan , to a shovel, to 2 new tops to a grate & biting a poker.'   9s..6d.

522/21 Bill of P.Gutteridge for work done at the Town Hall. £2..12..5

522/22 Bill of the Clerk of the Peace. 39 entries totalling £20..10..8.

SESSIONS ROLL 523, Easter 1814 (7th.April)

523/1   Writ proclaiming Quarter Sessions and Gaol Delivery.

523/2   List of jurors for the Grand and Petty juries of the Borough.

523/3   Calendar of prisoners for the Borough Gaol.
John Butler convicted for felony. Ordered to be imprisoned in the Gaol of the Borough twelve calendar months.

523/4   Calendar of Prisoners. House of Correction. (None).

523/8   12th.Feb.1814. Complaint of Solomon George Shaw, printer, who saith That he this day being the Market day did buy of one William Costin a Higler who frequents the market one fowl for the price of four shillings which had before this same day been bought of another person in the market whereby he William Costin hath been guilty of the offence of regrating and the complainant further saith that William Costin being now present doth admit that he did buy and sell the same again in this market. Recognisances 523/5, 6 & 7.
Presentment of the jury 523/10 concerning William Costain purchasing a fowl for 2/- and selling it for 4/- and afterwards purchasing six fowls at 2/- each and regrating one for 4/-. Endorsed 'A True Bill. Plea, Guilty'.

523/9   Gaol Visitors Report.

523/11   Bill of John Deayton, 3 entries for subsistence and straw.

523/12   Bill of William Brown to Treasurer to the Borough Gaol for one pair of large blankets.   £2..0..0

523/13   Bill of Thomas Rogers, Surgeon. For a prisoner in the upper gaol. Sewing up a large wound in the throat & dressing same for ten days. Plasters, ointment etc. with the other medicines.   £2..2..0

523/14   Relief of Paupers.Paid   £1..13..8

523/15   Bill of James Deayton, Borough Gaol, totalling £2..10..9. Entries include:-For 90 days subsistence for John Butler.

SESSIONS ROLL 524, Midsummer 1814 (15th.July)

524/1   Writ proclaiming Quarter Sessions and Gaol Delivery.

524/2   List of jurors for the Grand and Petty juries of the Borough.

524/3   Calendar of prisoners for the Borough Gaol.
John Butler, Imprisoned for 12 calendar months. Remains in gaol.

524/4   Calendar of Prisoners. House of Correction. (None).

524/5   Recognisance William Costin, Augustin Brooks & William Marsh bound to appear.

524/6   Recognisance of James Green, Sergeant in the 49th. Regiment concerning Sophia Smith of the Parish of St.Alban, single woman, with child likely to be born a bastard.

524/7   Bill of Jn.Bradshaw totalling £4..6..8 for repairing the steps & floor at the Town Hall & other repairs.

524/8   Bill of William Corby totalling 4s..0d for the cleaning & repairing the lock at the Town Hall & a pair of hinges for the gaol window.

524/9   Bill of the Clerk of the Peace Epiphany to Easter 1814. 43 entries totalling £13..10..4. Includes:- Drawing and recording order for exonerating the recognisances of Nathaniel Chaplin in case of felony. The like for .... and expenses in conveying Thomas Williams a prisoner to Hertford.

524/10 Bill of James Deayton, Borough Gaol totalling £2..14..3. Entries include subsistence for John Butler (84 days), extra bread allowed by order of the Mayor at 1/2lb. per day for 84 days & straw.

524/11 Bill of John Deayton. Subsistence for 3 prisoners and straw. 11s..7$\frac{1}{2}$d.

524/12 Gaol Visitors Report.

524/13 Relief of Paupers. Paid 4s..4d

524/14 to 524/17   Notes: to pay bearer 1/6d, 1/-, 1/- & 4d. respectively.

SESSIONS ROLL 525, Michaelmas 1814   (21st.Oct.)

525/1   Writ proclaiming Quarter Sessions and Gaol Delivery.

525/2   Calendar of prisoners for the Borough Gaol.
John Butler, remains in Gaol.
James O'Hara committed 15th.Aug. together with John Conmee & Michael Dyer are charged on the oaths of Thomas Kinder Esq., William Pheby & William Haughter with being guilty of a riot & unlawful assembly to disturb the public peace.

525/3   Calendar of Prisoners. House of Correction
John Conmee, Michael Dyer & James O'Hara committed (as above).
Margaret Carter committed 17th.Sept. on the oath of Margaret Robinson

with having feloniously stolen a 3 shilling Bank Token.

525/4   List of jurors for the Grand and Petty juries of the Borough.

525/5   Rex v Carter. Information 17th.September 1814 .
Complaint of Margaret Robinson wife of William Robinson, a private in the 95th.Regiment of Foot who saith that Margaret Carter slept with her at a lodging house in the Borough last night & that a 3 shilling piece of Bank Token was stolen from her pocket in the night or early this morning & that she has reason to suspect Margaret Carter did steal the same.
Endorsed with note of recognisances.
Recognisances 525/9/10.
Presentment of the jury 525/13 concerning Margaret Carter stealing one piece of silver called a Bank Token to the value of 3 shillings. Endorsed 'A True Bill. Plea, Not Guilty. Verdict, Not Guilty'.

525/6   Information re Jas. O'Hara 7 others. 15th.August 1814.
The information & complaint of Thos.Kinder Esq. Who saith that this informant was coming up the street from St.Michaels Vicarage on his way home about a quarter before 10 o'clock last night & that when he came opposite the Crow Public House he saw several persons assembled at or near the door of the Public House endeavouring in a riotous & forcible manner to force an entrance the whole of which persons he took to be Irishmen. That seeing Mrs.Hilliard standing at her own door nearly opposite he went up to her & asked her what was the matter. When she told him that the persons so assembled had been rioting for some time that her husband John Hilliard was in the Crow Public House & that she wished he was out. That this informant immediately went across the road to the men & endeavoured to persuade them to be quiet & withdraw & told them he was the Mayor. That he then knocked at the door & Wm.Slaughter the Landlord opened it & he found several other Irishmen in the house who were very turbulent & noisy. That he then advised the Landlord to let the men go about their business & that if they ordered him anything to let them depart & put up with the loss otherwise something serious might happen. That this informant continued on the outside of the door upon the step & whilst standing there he discovered Wm.Pheby, the coachman to Mr.Trower who was close by the side of him & whom he was glad to see in such a tumult. That the said Wm.Pheby immediately afterwards received several blows with a stick from one of the Irishmen upon which he turned & seized the man who had so struck him & whose name appears to be James O'Hara. That a scuffle then ensued between the coachman & the said James O'Hara & two other of the Irishmen assisted the said James O'Hara but which of them in particular he cannot identify. That this informant then seized James O'Hara & in doing so tore his coat & that immediately afterwards this informant received a violent blow across the forehead with a stick or some instrument of a hard substance rather inclining towards the right eye but that in consequence of the darkness of the night he was unable to fix upon the man who struck him but he was short in stature. That the wound inflicted upon this informant by the said blow bled very profusely & that on Mr.Webster

the surgeon examining it he found one of the arteries divided. That this informant is positive that James O'Hara was the man who assaulted Wm.Pheby having distinctly seen his person from the glance of light which issued from the candles in the Crow Public House while the door was open. Recognisances 525/11.

525/7 Information & complaint of William Pheby, servant to James Trower of the Parish of St.Michael in the Liberty of St.Albans, 15th.Aug. who saith That about a quarter before 10 o'clock last night as he was going down the street nearly opposite the Crow Public House on his way home to his masters house he discovered several men assembled together in a riotous manner & on making his way towards the door to see what was the matter he saw Thos.Kinder Esq. standing in front of the door next the street. That this informant spoke to the men whom he took to be all Irishmen & endeavoured to persuade them to be quiet & he had not been long there before he received a blow at the back part of his head from one of the men who calls himself James O'Hara & who struck the said blow with his fist. That a scuffle ensued & this informant succeeded in throwing James O'Hara down & in getting away from him & that this informant was immediately afterwards assaulted by another of the Irishmen whose name is John Conmee who struck him on the back part of the neck with his fist & with whom he also had a scuffle & got the better of by throwing him down. That Mr.Kinder assisted in keeping the men from this informant & soon afterwards received a violent blow himself from one of the Irishmen across the forehead with a stick but the night being very dark he cannot identify the man who so assaulted Mr.Kinder. That there were about 9 or 10 Irishmen in the street at the time & that they were all endeavouring to force an entrance into the Public House & were very noisy & turbulent.

525/8 Information & complaint of William Slaughter, victualler, 15th Aug. who saith that he is the Landlord of the Crow Public House & that several Irishmen were drinking together at his House last night & that when it was about 9 o'clock he refused to draw them any more beer when several of them became very violent & troublesome; that there were 20 or more of them in number & that he assisted by his wife & several labouring men resident in the neighbourhood who were also drinking in the house at the same time succeeded in turning all the Irishmen out of the House except three. That amongst the men so turned out of the House were three men now present who say their names are James O'Hara, John Conmee & Michael Dyer & that soon after they were turned out into the street they were all very noisy & tumultuous & attempted to break & force the door to make their way into this House & that on Mr.Thos.Kinder's coming to the door & making himself known he opened the door but this informant & his wife were very much frightened & what passed particularly afterwards in the street this informant doth not know.
Presentment of the jury 525/12 concerning James O'Hara, John Conmee & Michael Dyer assaulting William Pheby. Endorsed 'A true Bill. All prisoners plead Not Guilty. Verdict Jas.O'Hara Guilty, John Conmee Guilty, Michael Dyer Not Guilty'.

525/14 *Rough note in pencil, almost illegible.* Regarding proposed inspection of Court House with a view to alteration.

525/15 Bill. Concerning prosecution of James O'Hara, John Conmee & Michael Dyer.   £3..9..2

525/16 Bill of James Deayton, Borough Gaol. 8 entries totalling £5..7..11. Includes 98 days subsistence for John Butler & extra bread for him, 60 days subsistence for James O'Hara & his fees (13..4d)

525/17 Bill of John Deayton, House of Correction. 18 entries totalling £8..0..6. Includes subsistence for number of days as shown:-
John Brittian (21days), Thomas Richardson (5), John Conmee (68), Michael Dyer (68), Wm.Turner (7), Jas.Allway (7), George Godfrey (2), Benj.Bishop (3), Margaret Carter (35) & Benj.Bishop (10).

525/18 Bill. Mr.Deayton had of D.Hirst for John Conmee & Michael Dyer in the House of Correction, 2 round frocks, 2 shirts, 2 pairs of trousers & 2 waistcoats. Total £2..9..0.

525/19 Bill. Mr.Deayton had of D.Hirst for Jas.O'Hara in the Borough Gaol, 1 round frock, 1 shirt, 1 pair of trousers & 1 waistcoat. Total £1..4..7.

525/20 to 22 Bills of George Oakes of St.Peters Ward, James Barnet, J.Barnet and William Scourfield of Middle Ward. Entries mention military and prisoners of war. French and Italian prisoners. 'Attending the water daily all the summer to prevent them bathing by order of the Justices. I have done for 7 years.' Taking James Evans for robbing Mr.Hodges garden at the Chequers, getting him whipped.

525/24 Relief of Paupers, July to Oct.1814.   Paid   7s..0d

SESSIONS ROLL 526, Epiphany 1815   (13th.Jan.)

526/1   Writ proclaiming Quarter Sessions and Gaol Delivery.

526/2   Calendar of prisoners for the Borough Gaol.
John Butler. Remains in gaol.
George Brooks committed 25th.Oct. on the oath of Wm.Turner with having maliciously assaulted & wounded him with a knife. Bailed out.
Joseph Harding committed 3rd.Dec. upon oath by Thos.Chambers with breaking the peace & that he threatened Thos.Chambers.
John Grange committed 20th.Dec. on the oath of Mary Carpenter of the Parish of St.Alban she being delivered of a male bastard child & hath charged John Grange late of the Parish of St.Alban, labourer, with having gotten her with child that is become chargeable to the Parish.

143

526/3   Calendar of prisoners for the the House of Correction. (None).

526/4   List of jurors for the Grand and Petty juries of the Borough

526/8   Presentment of the jury concerning George Brooks maliciously assaulting, cutting & wounding Wm.Turner. Endorsed 'A true Bill. Plea, Not Guilty. Verdict, Guilty'.
Recognisances 526/5, 6 & 7.

526/9   Bill of John Deayton, House of Correction.
14 days subsistence for William Andrews and straw.   6s..3d.

526/10 to 16   Bills and notes concerning relief of paupers, soldiers families and two sailors.

526/11   Bill of Clerk of the Borough from Midsummer to Michaelmas. 51 entries totalling £24..18..2.

526/12   Bill of James Deayton, Borough Gaol. Subsistence, straw etc.

SESSIONS ROLL 527, Easter 1815   (7th.April)

527/1   Writ proclaiming Quarter Sessions and Gaol Delivery.

527/2   List of jurors for the Grand and Petty juries of the Borough.

527/3   Calendar of prisoners for the Borough Gaol.
Caleb Elbon committed 10th.March on the oath of William Moreton & his own confession of stealing a quantity of eathenware & glass.

527/4   Calendar of Prisoners for the House of Correction.
Thomas Peacock committed 28th.March charged on the oath of William Aungier with having been guilty of bad conduct.

527/6   Complaint of William Moreton, china man and dealer in earthen and glass ware, Who saith that earthen ware and glass have at various times been stolen from out of his warehouse in the Borough and that he has reason to suspect that Caleb Elbon the younger, labourer, did steal the same.
Recognisances 527/5.
Presentment of the jury 527/7 concerning Caleb Elbon stealing 2 dozen earthen pint pots valued at 3/- & 6 rummer glasses valued at 3/-. Endorsed 'A true Bill.. Plea, Not Guilty. Verdict, Guilty'.

527/8   Bill of Wm.Scourfield for apprehending Caleb Elbon for felony to gaol. 5/-

527/9   Bill of Benj.Fowler for repairs to the Town Hall & Borough Gaol. 13 entries totalling £3..7..8$^1/_2$

527/10 Bill concerning clothing purchased from Thos.House for prisoners.

527/11 Bill. .....for use in the Borough Gaol 1 pair blankets £1..13..0

527/12 Bill of W.Thornton totalling 10s..6d for mixtures & embrocation for J.Butler & ointment for O'Hara.

527/13 Bill from John Deayton totalling £1..0..2$^1/_2$. Entries include subsistence for John O'Neill, McKenzie, William Smith & Thomas Peacock at 4$^1/_2$d per day and fees of Thomas Peacock of 13s..4d.

527/14 Bill from the Coroner. For taking an inquisition on the body of Ruth Exton who hung herself.   £1..17..0.

527/15 Bill of James Deayton. Borough Gaol. 8 entries, mentions subsistence & fees of Caleb Elbon, straw for Fishers 2 boys. Paid Mr.Mason for taxes for the Town Hall.   Total   £2..19..5$^1/_2$.

527/16 Note.   'Received 3/2. G.W.'

SESSIONS ROLL 528, Midsummer 1815   (14th.July)

528/1   Writ proclaiming Quarter Sessions and Gaol Delivery.

528/2   List of jurors for the Grand and Petty juries of the Borough.

528/3   Calendar of prisoners for the Borough Gaol.
Matthew Putnam committed 8th.April by Thos. Kinder Esq., J.Carpenter Gape & Richard West. Whereas complaint had been made on oath by Francis Searancke Esq., Mayor, that Matthew Putnam, shoemaker, did make use of improper language to him then being in the execution of his office tending the breach of the peace & had called the Mayor a perjured forsworn person & hath otherwise behaved in an outrageous manner defying justice & refusing to find sureties. Bailed Out.
Joseph Sheath committed 1st.July on oath by Ann his wife with having assaulted & beaten her & threatened to do` her further bodily harm.
John MacLean committed 12th.July on the oath of Ann Fensom with having feloniously taken & carried away a pair of shoes her property.

528/4   Calendar of House of Correction, 1st.July 1815. (No prisoners)

528/5   Calendar of House of Correction, 1st.July 1815.
James Hewett alias George Field alias Philip Gibbins committed 26th.May

'as a rogue & vagabond & did use subtill craft to deceive & impose upon His Majesty's sujects.'

528/7 Recognisance concerning a charge against James Higgins by Ann Slater who is with child likely to be born a bastard .

528/9 Complaint of Ann Fensom 12th.July that a pair of shoes were yesterday afternoon hung up in a room of her house on the ground floor which opens on the street called Fishpool St. that she went out of the back door a short time. Upon her return the shoes were stolen. That a person was seen to go into the house by an opposite neighbour Thomas Parrott whereupon pursuit was made & the prisoner John MacLean was taken into custody on suspicion. On further enquiry the shoes were discovered to be in the possession of Thomas Jeffs who had purchased them of the prisoner for 2 shillings.
Recognisance 528/6.
Presentment of the Jury 528/8 concerning stealing a pair of leather shoes value 3 shillings the property of Samuel Fensom. Endorsed 'A true Bill. Plea, Not Guilty. Verdict, Guilty'.

528/10 Bill of William Scourfield for apprehending John MacLean for felony July 14th.1815.

528/11 Bill of the Clerk of the Peace from Easter to Easter. 59 entries totalling £18..7..10.

528/12 Bill of John Deayton. House of Correction. 7 entries totalling £2..1..2½. Includes subsistence for Thomas Peacock, John Taylor, Jas.Hewett & Stephen Hall and the fees of Jas.Hewett.

528/13 Bill of James Deayton, Borough Gaol. 9 entries totalling £3..11..1. Mention made of subsistence for Caleb Elbon & Joseph Sheath. Straw for James Hewett. Fees for Joseph Sheath. Pay to Brown & the 4 Constables for whipping Elbon 13s..6d.

SESSIONS ROLL 529, Michaelmas 1815   (20th.Oct.)

529/1 Writ proclaiming Quarter Sessions and Gaol Delivery.

529/2 Calendar of prisoners for the Borough Gaol. (No Prisoners).

529/3 Calendar of Prisoners. House of Correction. (No Prisoners).

529/4 List of jurors for the Grand and Petty juries of the Borough

529/5 Sworn oath of Catherine Boom 23rd.Aug. That George Stevens of the Abbey Parish did get her with female bastard child delivered 21st.July

and likely to become chargeable to the Parish.
Recognisance 529/6.

529/7   Bill of James Deayton, Borough Gaol. 10 entries totalling £3..14..0.   Including:- subsistence, straw & fees for John MacLean James Cully & William Wilson. Subsistence for Alexander Cobbett & Edward Daws taken on suspicion of being deserters.

529/8   Bill of Benj.Fowler for bricklayers work done at the Town Hall.
£2..3..10.

529/9   Bill of John Deayton, House of Correction.
Concerns straw & subsistence for Benj.Bishop, John MacLean & John Smith.

529/10   Bill of J.Bradshaw for work including repairs at Compter Gaol.

SESSIONS ROLL 530. Epiphany 1816   (12th.Jan.)

530/1   Writ proclaiming Quarter Sessions and Gaol Delivery.

530/2   List of jurors for the Grand and Petty juries of the Borough.

530/3   Calendar of prisoners for the Borough Gaol. (No Prisoners).

530/4   Calendar for House of Correction. (No Prisoners).

530/6 & 7   Recognisances concerning an assault upon Henry Scourfield by Henry Jeffreys.

530/8   Complaint of Joshua Lomax of Childwick, Parish of St.Michaels, who saith that George Marston, baker, hath at various times insulted him in the public market & threatened him and particularly this day hath insulted & abused & behaved in a very disorderly manner and raised a mob in the market following this complainant from place to place & threatening to repeat such ill conduct whenever he meet him wherefore this complainant craves sureties of the peace against him.
Recognisances 530/5.

530/9   Bill of Clerk of the Peace for Midsummer to Michaelmas 1815. 48 entries totalling £21..4..2.

530/10   Coroners Bill £1..17..0 for taking an Inquisition on the body of William Puddiphat who died in a fit..

530/11   Bill of Jno.Boys as Clerk of the Justices.   6s..0d

530/12 to 15 Bills of George Wilkins, Benj.Fowler, William Scourfield and an unnamed person, Constables of Holywell, St.Peters, Middle and Fishpool Wards. Entries mention:- Setting down all the House Keepers names in Holywell Ward. 'Searching after some women for abusing the Mayor.' (Deleted). Taking Patrick O'Conner with bad money and tools. Searching public houses and lodging houses for vagrants.

530/16 Bill of James Deayton, Borough Gaol, totalling £2..17..0$^1/_2$. Entries included subsistence for Thos. Makins & Thos.Shepherd. Fees for George Sharman & Thos.Shepherd, straw & fires.

530/17 Bill of Benj.Fowler for building work.

SESSIONS ROLL 531, Easter 1816   (26th.April)

531/1   Writ proclaiming Quarter Sessions and Gaol Delivery.

531/2   Lists of jurors for the Grand and Petty juries of the Borough.

531/3   Calendar of Prisoners. House of Correction. (No Prisoners).

531/4   Calendar of Prisoners for the Borough Gaol.
Mary Buggs committed 20th.Jan. charged on the oath of John Rogers with having feloniously taken his pocket book from him.
William Brewer committed 23rd.March charged on the oath of John Furness, butcher, with having at various times defrauded him of his employment of carrying & selling milk by keeping the money he received for milk.

531/5   Recognisance concerning Frances Bury(?), single woman, to appear at the Liberty Sessions & abide order under Statute of Elizabeth concerning bastardy.

531/6   The Complainant William Bowra of Gorhambury, Gamekeeper to the Earl of Verulam taken on oath this 9th.March. Who saith that George Wilshire of the Boro', baker, hath at various times used abusive language to him as he has been in the public streets of the town with intent to provoke him to disturb the peace and that he hath reason to think that he will continue such ill usage wherefore he craves sureties of the peace against him.
Endorsed with note of recognisances.
Recognisances 531/7 concerning George Wilshire appearing at the next Quarter Sessions to be of good behaviour to William Bowra of the Parish of St.Michael in the Liberty.

531/8   Recognisance concerning John Rogers, yeoman of Brentford, appearing to prefer a Bill of Indictment against Mary Bugg for felony.

531/9 Recognisance concerning John Furness appear to prefer a Bill of Indictment against William Brewer for embezzlement.

531/10 Bill of James Deayton. Borough Gaol.

10 items totalling £4..17..6½d. Entries include:-

	£.. s..d
1 days subsistence & straw to William Williams	0.. 1..3
Paid Mr.Mason for taxes	0.. 7..9
90 days subsistence to Mary Bugg	1..19..9
To fees of Mary Bugg	0..13..4
35 days subsistence to William Brewer	0..13..1½
To fees of William Brewer	0..13..4

531/11 Sacrament Certificate of Charles Longhurst, Excise Officer.

SESSIONS ROLL 532 Midsummer 1816   (19th.July)

532/1 Writ Proclaiming Quarter Sessions and Gaol Delivery.

532/2 Lists of jurors for the Grand and Petty juries of the Borough.

532/3 Calendar of Prisoners for the Borough Gaol.
Mary Banks committed 4th.May charged with having stolen a £2 Bank of England note the property of David Monk.
Charles Louch committed 11th.June charged on the oath of Wm.Henshaw with having feloniously and privately taken from him a purse containing Bank notes and shillings.

532/4 Calendar of Prisoners for the House of Correction.
William Clark, Private in the 11th.Regt.Light Dragoons, committed 11th.July, upon the oath of Elizabeth Harvey, single woman, with having gotten her with child likely to be born a bastard and to be chargeable to the Parish of St.Alban.
Margaret Hally committed 13th.July and John McGee committed 15th.July as rogues and vagabonds.

532/5 Recognisance concerning William Clark appearing to answer the charge of Elizabeth Harvey.

532/9 & 10 Recognisance concerning William Groves appearing to answer a bill of indictment preferred by Octavius Wooding for assault.

532/14 Instruction from the Mayor, dated 6th.July, to find Wm.Groves to answer an indictment by Octavius Wooding of striking and assaulting him.

532/15 Information and Complaint of William Henshaw of Dunstable. He saith on his oath that on Saturday night last he came into the town of St.Albans it being wet weather he got into a waggon which was standing in the street near the Red Lion for shelter that a young lad of the name of Charles Louch who was a stranger to him got into the waggon with him, that this examinant was rather in liquor and fell asleep in the waggon where he remained until about 4 o'clock in the morning, that Charles Louch left him in the night and upon this Examinants waking he missed his purse containing a Ten Pound and two One Pound Bank of England notes and some silver about 10 or 12 shillings. That this examinant suspects that Charles Louch had picked his pocket and on search being made after him he was taken into custody and this Examinant's purse was found upon him together with a One Pound Bank of England note which he attempted to throw away but was detected in the act of doing so. The other one pound note had been delivered to Absolom Holt for the purpose of being changed. Recognisances 532/11/12.

Presentment of the jury 532/29 concerning Charles Louch feloniously taking one canvas purse, value 2 pence, 1 promissory to value of £10, 2 other promissory notes or Bank notes to the value of £2, 2 pieces of silver or bank tokens to the value of 6s. belonging to William Henshaw. Endorsed 'A True Bill. Plea Guilty'.

532/16 Examination of David Monk late of St.Clements in the Liberty of Westminster now of Northampton, labourer, taken the 4th.May Who saith that the prisoner Mary Banks did on 21st.April steal and take away a £2 Bank of England note, his property, which note being now produced and received from Augustine Brooks to whom the prisoner paid the same this Examinant saith that he believes to be his property. Recognisances 532/13.

Presentment of the jury 532/18 concerning Mary Banks....*Ends mid sentence, no further details given.*

532/17 Information of Cornelius Franklin of the Parish of St.Peter. Who saith that James Woodward of New Barnes Mills in the parish of St.Peter did this day regrate in the public market of the Borough by buying three 'piggs' part of ten and selling the same again in the same market this day and further says that the ten 'piggs' be bought of William Jessop and afterwards sold to Philip Dickens of Colney Heath and one to Mrs.Sharp of Colney St. Recognisances 532/6, 7 & 8.

Presentment of the jury 532/19 concerning James Woodward buying 1 pig from Wm.Jessop for 14s, afterwards regrating in the same market to Ann Sharp for £1. and further that he bought 10 pigs for 14s,each from Wm.Jessop and in the same market did unlawfully regrate one of the 10 pigs to Ann Sharp for £1. Endorsed 'A true Bill. Plea, Not Guilty. Verdict.Guilty'.

Presentment of the jury 532/22 concerning James Woodward buying 2 pigs from Wm.Jessop for £1..8..0 & selling them on the same day to Philip Dickens at £1..6..0. That he bought 10 pigs from Wm.Jessop for 14s each & sold 2 to Philip Dickens at 13s each. Endorsed 'Not A True Bill'.

532/20   Bill of Wm.Henshaw for prosecuting Louch for felony.

3 days attendance.	10..6
Coach from Dunstable & back.	7..0
Expenses.	2..6
Paid into court.	6..0
Paid at the house where apprehended.	3..9
Four witnesses expenses for 2 days.	14..0
Apprehending Charles Louch.	10..0
Stevens the Constable.	5..0
	£2..17..9

532/21   Bill of Clerk of the Peace. Epiphany to Easter inclusive. 39 entries totalling £12..12..2. Entries mention payments to builders for work on the Town Hall & House of Correction, to the Coroner, to James Deayton for the maintenance of prisoners, to the parish constables etc.

532/23   Bill of John Deayton. Subsistence and fees. Entries mention:-
To 36 days Sarah Best, To 9 days and fees for Wm.Clark.

532/24   Bill. A petticoat for Mary Banks in Boro' Gaol (5s..6d), A shift and stocking (7s..6d) and A shift (5s..0d).

532/25   Bill of Wm.Corbett for 10 nails for a pane of glass   2s..0d

532/26   Bill. For repairing 2 pulls to the bell in the Town Hall. 2s..6d

532/27   Bill of James Deayton. Borough Gaol. 8 entries totalling £4..6..2. Mention made of:- 85 days subsistence and fees for Mary Banks and 39 days and fees for Charles Louch.

532/28   Bill of James Fowell. For carpenters work at the Town Hall.

SESSIONS ROLL 533, Michaelmas 1816   (17th.Oct.)

533/1   Writ Proclaiming Quarter Sessions & Gaol Delivery.

533/2   List of jurors for Grand & Petty juries of the Borough.

533/3   Calendar of Prisoners for the Borough Gaol.
Charles Louch. Ordered to be transported for 7 years. Remains under sentence.

533/4   Calendar of Prisoners. House of Correction.
Samuel Fisher committed 2nd.October on the oath of Mary Parratt of the Parish of St.Alban, who was delivered of a male Bastard child likely to become chargeable to the Parish.

533/5/6 Recognisances concerning an assault by William Jessop upon William Powell.

533/7 Bill of James Deayton, Borough Gaol, totalling £4..11..9 Entries
include:-
	£.. s..d
91 days to Charles Louch.	2.. 5..6
2 days to Michael Alley & straw.	0.. 2..0
12 days Matthew Reading committed as a deserter but not owned.	0..10..0
17 days to Thomas Fisher committed as a deserter but not owned.	0..13..9
7 days to James Kieff & straw.	0.. 4..6

533/8 Bill of John Deayton, House of Correction, totalling £2..0..4. Subsistence for 6 named prisoners for: from 4 to 17 days.

533/9, 10 & 11 Bills of John Stevens, Robert Cawston and an unnamed person, Constables of Holywell, Middle and St.Peters Wards. Mention made of:- Flogging Johnson & Langham for theft.

SESSIONS ROLL 534, Epiphany 1817 (16th.Jan.)

534/1 Writ Proclaiming Quarter Sessions & Gaol Delivery.

534/2 Lists of jurors for the Grand and Petty juries of the Borough.

534/3 Calendar of Prisoners for the Borough Gaol.
Beatrice Sparrow committed 13th.Dec.1816 by the oath of Ann Smorthwaite, spinster, with stealing a smelling bottle her property.
Thomas Brown committed 1st.Jan.1817 charged on oath of Thomas Rolfe one of the Churchwardens of the Parish of St.Alban with suspicion of feloniously breaking open the Poor's Box in the Parish Church of St.Alban & stealing the contents thereof. Bailed out.

534/4 Calendar of Prisoners. House of Correction. (No Prisoners).

534/8 Examination of Thomas Rolfe one of the Churchwardens of the Parish of St.Alban taken on oath 1st.Jan. who saith that the Poor's Box in the Parish Church of St.Alban otherwise Abbey Parish was on Friday night or Saturday morning feloniously broken open & some money or property as he believes taken from thence & this examinant hath reason to suspect that Thomas Brown the Parish Clerk did feloniously break the same & steal the property therein contained.
Endorsed with note of recognisances.

534/9 Examination of Thomas Rolfe one of the Churchwardens of the Parish Church of St.Alban taken on 4th.Jan.1817 before us against Thomas

Brown for felony who saith that the prisoner came to him on Saturday morning last & informed him that the Poor's Box was broken open witness saw the box, Brown claims that this is the third time within twelvemonths twice within six months, there was no door broken, there are six Keys, Prisoner has two, Rolfe, Searancke, Greenhill & Turner one each, the Padlocks were unlocked & on the floor, Prisoner admitted that it must be done by somebody who had a secret key, witness informed Mrs.Nicholson, went to Greenhill who went down with him, the secret fastenings were forced there were marks of an instrument, the instrument applied to force it was at each end and where the secret fastenings were, and in his opinion it was done by someone who knew where the fastenings were. On Tuesday Morning he communicated his suspicions to Mrs.Nicholson & searched for the Crow, Sexton said if Brown had not brought it back he must have it, witness brought it from Brown's House compared it & it corresponded as he thought with the indentations in the lids of the Chest, Brown has been Clerk for three years in April last, witness put the Crow in the lower end of the Church, went to Mrs.Nicholson & appointed a Meeting next day but it was put off. On Wednesday witness sent for Brown, he came directly on being sent for, told him he suspected that he was the person, he asked Brown what brought him to the Church on Saturday morning so early in the presence of Mr.Searancke & Mr.Russell he said he could not charge his memory & seemed at a loss, he named the borrowing of a Crow & asked, what time he took the Crow from the Church, he said he did not know or words to that effect, said could not charge his memory with it.

534/10 Examination of Nathaniel Turner, Sexton of the Abbey Church taken 4th.Jan. against Thomas Brown for a felony who saith That about half past 10 o'clock on Friday 27th.Dec. Brown borrowed a Crow, witness fetched it back on Tuesday last, Brown said he had not done with it at his house, he wanted it for something about a post, it was wet & rather rusty, the Glaziers had the Keys on Friday a'noon & he locked the doors about half past four, there were workmen in the Church on Friday, Greenhill's Son was in the Church on Friday, the doors were left open at the time, the Tool house was not locked up, Brown never borrowed the Crow before & did not tell for what he borrowed it.

534/11 Examination of Edward Greenhill, watchmaker, taken 4th.Jan. against Thomas Brown for a felony who saith That he has the management of the Chimes & a key of the Church, in September last he made two secret fastenings for the Chest, he did it entirely himself, no one but Mr.Rolfe knew how it was done. On Saturday last he first saw the Chest about a quarter before 11, Brown came in whilst he was examining it, he found the secret fastening had been forced with great violence, he opened it about three months ago, after the fastenings had been made, there was 4 shillings & $7^3/_4$d in it, it appeared to be forced with an Iron Instrument, he saw the Crow & is of the opinion that it was an instrument of that sort by which the Chest was opened, Brown came in, witness said to Brown they have done us again, Brown said yes & went on, but did not come to examine the Chest,

the point of the Crow now produced corresponded with the impression made on the Box.
Endorsed with note of recognisance.

534/12 Examination of William Greenhill, watchmaker, taken 4th.Jan. against Thomas Brown for a felony who saith That about 9 o'clock on Saturday he went in at the door opposite the Abbey Orchard, took no notice of the Chest & wound up the Chymes, as he was crossing out of the Chancel he saw Brown come off the steps out of the Vestry Room, he came out, the Lobby door was open & the Entrance door besides, he did not say anything about the Chest, he never came out to open the door before, he hid part of the Box from this witness's view as he went out. If he had not been there witness very likely might have seen the Box, Brown did not as the witness knew take any pains to conceal the Box, he has often met Brown before in going to wind up the Chimes.
Endorsed with a note of Recognisance.
Recognisances 534/5/6.
Presentment of the jury 534/15 concerning Thomas Brown, shoemaker, stealing two padlocks value 10 pence in the custody of Francis Searancke, Thomas Rolfe & John Mason. Endorsed 'No true Bill'.

534/13 The Complaint of Ann Smorthwaite taken on oath 13th.Dec.1816 who saith that on Tuesday 10th.Dec. she was possessed of a glass smelling bottle & silver case which she had in a drawer in the parlour of the house of her brother William Smorthwaite, baker, & that the next day she missed her smelling bottle & had reason to suspect that Beatrice Sparrow on occasion of her being in the room had stolen the same whereupon she applied to a Magistrate for a search Warrant & hath been informed that the smelling bottle was found upon her.
Recognisances 534/7.
Presentment of the jury 534/14 concerning Beatrice Sparrow wife of Francis Sparrow of Hertford, late of the Boro', yeoman, stealing one glass smelling bottle value one shilling & one silver case value 10 shillings the property of Ann Smorthwaite. Endorsed 'A true Bill. Plea, Not Guilty. Verdict, Guilty'.

534/16 Bill of Clerk of the Peace. Midsummer to Michaelmas inclusive. 51 entries totalling £24..5..8. Entries include:-

	s..d
Allowance for carriages provided for H.M.Forces.	5..0
John Farell, bricklayers work at Town Hall.	5..0
Edw'd Greenhill repairing bells at Town Hall.	5..0
William Corby, smith, work at Town Hall.	5..0
Copy Sentence of Transportation of	
Charles Louch to go with him to the Hulks.	5..0

534/17 Bill of James Deayton. Borough Gaol. 13 entries totalling £9..8..5. Entries include:-

	£ .. s..d
73 days to Charles Louch.	2 .. 2..7
37 days to Beatrice Sparrow.	1 .. 1..7

4 days Thos.Brown.	0 .. 2..4
Doctor for Wm.Barker, Jas.Crouch &Thos.Daws under an Execution of Court of Request.	0 .. 6..0
To removing Chas.Louch a convict on board the Hulks at Woolwich.	3 .. 5..6
To the fees of Beatrice Sparrow.	0..13..4
To the fees of Thomas Brown.	0..13..4

534/18 Bill of John Deayton. House of Correction. Subsistence and straw for prisoners. These included:- John Oakley (14 days), James Skeggs (14 days) and Benjamin Shipwright (31 days).

534/19 Bill of William Scourfield.

534/20 Bill. Borough Gaol. For 10 Blankets £2.

534/21 Bill of W.Thornton. 14 entries totalling 15s..0d for pills & ointments for prisoners in the Gaol.

534/22 Bill of Luke Cherry, Constable for Fishpool Ward.
5 entries totalling 16s..0d. Entries mention the drawing up of militia, serving warrants, attending hall on licence day.

534/23 Bill. By order of John Bacon, Mayor.	s..d
To a smockfrock.	8..6
To a pair of trousers.	6..6
To a pair of stocking.	2..0
	17..0

534/24 Bill. Rex on the Prosecution of Ann Smorthwaite v Sparrow.	
Expenses of apprehending prisoner.	0..5..0
Indictment.	0..3..6
Crier.	0..1..0
Expenses of prosecutor & witnesses in this prosecution	2..2..0
	£2..11..6

534/25 List of Fees for Borough Gaol. Fees for the last three years. 53 in total.

534/26 List of Fees for House of Correction. Fees for the last three years. 96 in total.

SESSIONS ROLL 535, Easter 1817   (18th.April)

535/1 Writ Proclaiming Quarter Sessions and Gaol Delivery.

535/2 Lists of jurors for the Grand and Petty juries of the Borough.

535/3   Calendar of Prisoners. House of Correction.
Samuel Hartley committed 28th.March 1817 on the oath of Elizabeth Brickland, single woman, of the Parish of St.Alban. She declared herself to be with child likely to be born a bastard and charged Saml.Hartley with having gotten her with child.

535/4   Calendar of Prisoners for the Borough Gaol.
Thomas Hatton committed 31st.March on the oath of Thomas Denham for suspicion of felony and stealing five pieces of leather of the value of five shillings the property of James Denham.

535/9   Warrant to apprehend Robert Upson to answer a bill of indictment preferred by Mary Painter that he is the father of her bastard child.
Recognisance 535/5.

535/10   The complaint of James Denham, cordwainer, 31st.March who saith That five pieces of soling leather of the value of five shillings found concealed in a part of the deponents dwelling and this deponent suspecting that his apprentice Thomas Hatton had stolen them charged him with it which he at first denied but afterwards admitted that he did take them for the purpose of mending his own shoes.
Recognisance 535/6.
Presentment of the jury 535/11 concerning Thomas Hatton stealing five pieces of leather value 5/- the property of James Denham. Endorsed 'A true Bill. Plea, Not Guilty Verdict, Not Guilty'.

535/12   Presentment of the jury concerning William Jessop, yeoman, assaulting William Powell. Endorsed 'A True Bill. Plea, Not Guilty'.
Recognisances 535/7 & 8.

535/13   An account of false weights and penalties 25th.Jan.1817.
Persons convicted:- Edward Landridge, Issac Steabben, William Griffen, James Motton, William Smith, Joseph Newson, John Denham, Thomas Bowstead and Robert Brooks.

535/14   Bill of John Deayton. House of Correction. Subsistence and straw for four prisoners including 25 days to Samuel Hartley.

535/15   Bill of Thomas Harris for glazing & plumbing done at the Town Hall.   £1..18..6

535/16   Bill of James Deayton. Borough Gaol.

The main entries being:-	s..d
7 days subsistence & straw Beatrice Sparrow.	5..4
3 days Wm.Corby & straw.	2..9
Straw to Abel Lines & Thos.Philips under an execution.	2..6
19 days to Thomas Hatton.	11..1

Duplicate of this item 535/18.

535/17   Bill. Borough 'Jail'. For 1 pair Blankets.   15s..6d

535/19   List of Persons Committed to the Borough Gaol. Easter 1814-
Easter 1817.

Name	Date Committed	Offence
James O'Hara	18 Aug.1814	Riotous Assault
George Brooks	25 Oct. 1814	Assault
Joseph Harding	3 Dec.1814	Disturbing the Peace
John Grange	3 Dec. 1814	Bastard Child
Caleb Elbon	10 March 1815	Felony
Matthew Putnam	8 April 1815	Breaking the Peace
William Wilson	29 April 1815	Felony
Joseph Sheath	1 July 1815	Assault
John McLean	28 July 1815	Felony
James Culley	28 July 1815	Base Money
George Sherman	26 Dec.1815	Breaking the Peace
Mary Buggs	20 Jan. 1816	Felony
William Williams	3 Feb. 1816	Breaking the Peace
William Brewer	23 March 1816	Defraud
Mary Banks	4 May 1816	Felony
Charles Louch	11 June 1816	Felony
William Barker	17 Aug. 1816	Under an execution
James Crouch	17 Aug. 1816	ditto
William Barker	17 Aug. 1816	ditto
Job Young	30 Sept. 1816	Breaking the Peace
Beatrice Sparrow	13 Dec. 1816	Felony
Thomas Philips	26 Dec. 1816	Under an execution
Thomas Brown	1 Jan. 1817	On suspicion of felony

Note on the reverse.'Salary Increased to £30 per year.'

535/20   Bill. By the order of J.Bacon, Mayor. For the Borough Jail
             1 pr.Blankets.   15s..6d

SESSIONS ROLL 536, Midsummer 1817   (18th.July)

536/1   Writ Proclaiming Quarter Sessions and Gaol Delivery.

536/2   Lists of jurors for the Grand and Petty juries of the Borough.

536/3   Recognisance concerning William Young, labourer, accused of
being the father of a bastard child upon Mary Denton, spinster.

536/4   Bill of Clerk of the Peace. Epiphany Sessions 1817 totalling
£16..4..0. 51 Entries include:-
Payment of 1/3 the bill of Edward Greenhill for repairing
the bells of the conical Chamber in the Town Hall.   5s..0d
To Messrs. Hillman & Bacon for standard weights
for weighing bread.   1s..3d

Hearing & recording Order that the Salary of the Gaoler be increased from £20 to £30, such increase to be considered in lieu of all fees.

536/5   Bill of James Deayton. Borough Gaol.
Paid to Mr.Mason for 2 quarters taxes.   7..9
Straw for Randall.   1..3
14 days Thos.Bowstead.   8..9
8 days for Thos.Byrne, deserter.   6..0
Straw for John How & Wm.Powell under an execution.   2..0
                                                          £1.. 16..3

536/6   Bill of John Deayton. House of Correction.
Subsistence and straw for 7 prisoners including:-
        To 39 days Samuel Hartley.   £1..4..4¹/₂

SESSIONS ROLL 537, Michaelmas 1817   (11th.Oct.)

537/1   Writ proclaiming Quarter Sessions and Gaol Delivery.

537/2   Lists of jurors for the Grand and Petty juries of the Borough.

537/3   Calendar of Prisoners for the Borough Gaol.
Rebecca Arnold committed 11 Oct.1817 charged on the oath of John Warwick, draper, with having feloniously taken and carried away a piece of cotton handkerchief the property of the John Warwick.

537/4   Calendar of Prisoners. House of Correction. (No Prisoners).

537/6   The Information & Complaint of John Warwick 11th.October who saith that this morning about 11 o'clock Rebecca the wife of John Arnold came into the shop of this complainant situate in the Parish of St.Alban to buy some goods & that whilst she was looking at some goods which this complainant's brother Charles Warwick was showing to her, this complainant was informed by Susan Huckett who was also in the shop that Rebecca Arnold had taken some handkerchiefs from off the counter and put them in her pocket. That this Complainant immediately challenged Rebecca Arnold with the theft which she at first denied but on this Complainant telling her that he would have her searched she immediately drew from her pocket a piece of cotton handkerchief which this Complainant swears is his property.
Endorsed on reverse with a note of recognisances.
Recognisances 537/7, 8 & 9.
Presentment of the jury 537/5 concerning the theft from John Warwick of six cotton handkerchiefs value three shillings and six pence by Rebecca Arnold.

537/10, 11 & 12 Recognisances concerning an assault by William White upon William Clark.

537/13   Bill. King against Arnold.   s..d
         Indictment.   3..6
         Crier.   1..0
         Witness.   <u>5..0</u>
                                                             9..6

537/14 to 17   Bills of John Galer: Constable for Holywell Ward, William Scourfield: Constable, and unnamed constables for Middle Ward and Fishpool Ward. Entries mention:- Being out all day to prevent rioting between the English & Irish.

537/18   Bill of John Deayton. House of Correction.
Subsistence and straw for two prisoners including:- 14 days for Thos.Shepherd.

537/19   Bill of James Spicer, Constable. Attending Statute and fairs.

537/20   Bill of John Farell. For work done at the Town Hall. 11 entries totalling £14..5..10.

SESSIONS ROLL 538, Epiphany 1818   (16th.Jan.)

538/1   Writ proclaiming Quarter Sessions and Gaol Delivery.

538/2   Lists of jurors for the Grand and Petty juries of the Borough.

538/3   Calendar of Prisoners for the Borough Gaol.
Susanna Thompson committed 30th.Dec. on the oath of Ann Smith, widow, with having feloniously stolen out of the dwelling house of Ann Smith 2 plated candlesticks.

538/4   Calendar of Prisoners. House of Correction. (No Prisoners).

538/7 & 8   Recognisances concerning Henry Jeffries, fishmonger & William Field, butcher, being involved in an assault.

538/9   The Information & complaint of Ann Smith, widow, who saith that she 'hath within the space of the last days' *(this last crossed out in ink)* hath since the hour of six o'clock in the evening of yesterday lost out of her dwelling house two silver plated candlesticks which she had probable cause to suspect were feloniously stolen and carried away by one Susanna Thompson she having as this Informant hath been informed and believed offered two candlesticks of the same description for sale and this informant further states that she had probable cause to suspect and doth suspect that the plated candlesticks are concealed in the dwelling house of Robert Thompson the father of Susanna Thompson situate in a place called the Saracens Head yard where Susanna Thompson resides.

The same day a pair of plated candlesticks being produced by Mr.Robert Nicholls which Susanna Thompson now in the custody of Thomas Thacker, the Constable, the said Ann Smith made oath that the same was her property and produced another candlestick which corresponds there with and of which pattern she stated that she has half a dozen more in the whole. Recognisances 538/5/6.

Presentment of the Jury 538/12 concerning Susanna Thompson stealing two plated candlesticks the property of Ann Smith. Endorsed 'Verdict, Guilty'.

538/10 Gaol Visitors Report.

538/11 At a Court Leet or View of Frank-pledge held on Friday 31st.October 1817 the following representation was made by the Jury.

The Jurors this day discovered the Cage to be in the same situation in which it stood at the last Court Leet and they now renew their recommendation to the Magistrates of this Borough (by whose authority they understood the cage was originally erected) that an order may be made at the next Quarter Sessions for it's removal to some more convenient place 'or for it's removal altogether' *(this crossed out)* the same being in the opinion of the Jurors a great nuisance and very obnoxious to the inhabitants of the neighbourhood and to be otherwise ill calculated for the purpose it was intended for.

538/13, 14 & 15 Bills of Thos.Kent for IronWork done at the Bridewell. Ben.Fowler for Brickwork done at the Town Hall and Roger Bradley for Masons work done at the Town Hall.

538/16 Bill of Clerk of the Peace Midsummer to Michaelmas inclusive. 46 entries totalling £16..8..9.

538/17 Bill of James Deayton. Borough Gaol. 8 entries totalling £2..19..10. Entries include:-

	s..d
Paid to Mr. Mason for taxes.	7..9
For sweeping the chimney.	2..0

538/18 Bill of Wm.Thornton. Drugs supplied to prisoners. 19s..6d

SESSIONS ROLL 539, Easter 1818 (3rd.April)

539/1 Writ proclaiming Quarter Sessions and Gaol Delivery.

539/2 List of jurors for the Grand and Petty juries of the Borough.

539/3 Calendar of Prisoners for the Borough Gaol.

Susannah Thompson convicted ordered to be imprisoned in the 'Goal' of this Borough three calendar months. Remains in 'Goal'.

539/4 Calendar of Prisoners. House of Correction.
Thomas Sheppard committed 28th.March 1818 requiring him to find sufficient sureties to keep the Peace especially towards Sarah his wife.

539/5 Recognisance concerning John Reading, carpenter, likely to be the father of the bastard child of Louisa Ashton.

539/6 Recognisance concerning William Hawkins, labourer, likely to be the father of the bastard child of Elizabeth Holliman.

539/8 Warrant for apprehending Robert Tyson, butcher, to answer the charge of Mary Painter that he is the father of her bastard child.

539/9 Complaint & information of George Russell, postmaster, taken on oath 12th.February 1818 who saith that John Mails being a person duly and legally licensed to keep a common Alehouse or Victualling house at the sign of the Valiant Trooper .... being bound by Recognisance .... only to keep good order .... did nevertheless .... neglect to keep good order etc. by keeping the said house open and permitting and suffering Thomas Brewer, John Surety & divers other persons to be drinking & tippling therein at an unreasonable and improper time .... at the hour of one of clock in the morning of same day and several hours immediately before and after that time ...... wherefore Geo. Russell prays the Justice that John Mails be summoned to appear at the next General or Quarter Sessions of the Peace. *(Considerably edited).*
Recognisance 539/7.

539/10 Recognisances concerning John Mails being licensed to keep a common Alehouse or Victualling house at the sign of the Valiant Trooper.

539/11 Information & complaint of Sarah wife of Thomas Shepherd, carpenter, 28th.March who saith that for a considerable time her husband hath treated her with great cruelty and barbarity having frequently beaten and bruised her without any provocation on her part. That he has often held a knife to her throat & threatened to kill her and that for several nights on his going to bed he has stuck a Clasp Knife in a chair by his bedside and threatened to do this Informant an injury with it. That he is almost in the constant habit of getting intoxicated with liquor & that this a'noon in particular he struck her several violent blows on her head and other parts of her body and actually seized her & laid her upon the fire in her lodging room in the Christopher Yard, by which means he very much bruised her loins and that on some of the neighbours interfering he threatened to do them a bodily mischief & this Informant saith that since the ill-usage last mentioned her husband has threatened to spill her blood before night is over & that she is now under great fear & apprehension that he will take the first opportunity of doing her some bodily hurt. Wherefore she craves Sureties of the Peace against her husband & she declares that she doth *('not' has been omitted)* make this complaint out of hatred, malice or ill will towards him but merely for preservation of her life & person from bodily harm.

539/12 Letter & Bill addressed to John Palmer Esq. Rickmansworth.
Sir, I beg leave to send you on the other side the amount of my little Bill
for a business done by order of Mr. Searanke when he was Mayor of Saint
Albans respecting a man name Gibbon alias Field that was tried at the
Sessions & convicted for fraud, your kind 'interfearance' in 'recomending' it
to the Magistrates at your Quarter Sessions will be ever 'greatfully' Ack'd.
by Sir Your Obt. Serv't John Vickery.

May 26th. 1815.   Public Office Bow Street.
John Vickery going by order of a letter from Mr.Searanke, Mayor of St.
Albans to Saint Georges Fields to make enquiries and to find the 'lodgin' of
a man named Phillip Gibbon alias George Field and searching his 'lodgin'.

		£.. s ..d
	To searching his lodgin in St. Georges Field.	0..10..6
	To expenses in enquiries in different parts	
	of Saint Georges Fields to find his lodgin.	0.. 8..6
May 27th.	To coach here to St.A & back coachman etc.	0..14..0
	To expenses travelling one day.	0..16..0
	To one days time as above.	1.. 1..0
		£3..10..0

539/13 Bill of James Spicer, Beadle.

	s..d
Delivering & sticking fair bills at Mich's fair.	5..0
Ditto at Lady Day.	5..0
Attending 2 fair nights at Lady day fair.	5..0
	15..0

539/14 Bill of William Scourfield, Beadle. 6 entries totalling £1..5..0.

539/15 Bill of James Deayton. Borough Gaol.

	£.. s..d
To 90 days subsistence to Susan Thompson.	2..12..6
To straw 3/-. Two fires 6/-. Pens, paper, ink 3/-.	0..12..0
	£3 .. 4..6

539/16 Bill of John Deayton. House of Correction.

	s..d
Paid Mr. Gutteridge for a large Can & 'Bason'.	7..9
Paid Mr. Mason for a large Can.	5..0
	12..9

SESSIONS ROLL 540, Midsummer 1818   (17th.July)

540/1 Writ proclaiming Quarter Sessions and Goal Delivery.

540/2 Lists of jurors for the Grand and Petty juries of the Borough.

540/3 Calendar of Prisoners for the Borough Gaol.
Sarah Simpson committed 6th.June on the oath of John Warwick of having
feloniously stolen a cotton 'shall' value 5/- from out of the shop.

James Grady committed 24th.June on the oath of Wm.Hoggan and Elizabeth the Wife of Thomas Baynes with feloniously taking & carrying away 3 quarten loaves of bread property of Thos. Baynes.

540/4   Calendar of Prisoners. House of Correction. (No Prisoners).

540/8   Information and Complaint of Elizabeth wife of Thomas Baynes, shopkeeper, taken on oath 24th.June who saith that yesterday about 11 o'clock in the forenoon she placed three quarten loaves on a shelf in her husbands shop in Fishpool Street which she intended for one of her husbands customers of the name of Grubb and that before she went to dinner she saw them in the same place:- After she had dined her husband and all the children being from home and no one being in the house besides herself she went into the shop and found William Hoggan (a boy) there who wanted to purchase a half Quarten loaf and that she then missed the 3 quarten loaves before mentioned and told William Hoggan of it upon which he said that a man was in the shop when he came in who was eating some bread and that he had gone down the street -that William Hoggan then showed this Examinant the man who was there in the road nearly opposite the Angel Inn and this Examinant pursued him and overtook him opposite the Black Lion Public House. That she found 3 loaves concealed under his shirt and that she believed all the loaves to be the property of her husband and that she then gave the man in charge of her husband who is one of the Constables of the Boro' and that the same man calls himself by the name of James Grady.
(Same day) William Hoggan (11 years or thereabouts) maketh oath and saith that he went into Mr. Baynes shop yesterday a little before one o'clock in the afternoon to buy a half quarten loaf by his Mothers orders when he saw the Prisoner James Grady in the shop eating bread there who immediately said "I will be off now" -that he immediately went out of the shop and on this witness calling one "Hallo" Mrs. Baynes came into the shop. That this Examinant had no suspicion that the man he had seen in the shop had stolen anything from it but on Mrs. Baynes informing him that she missed 3 quarten loaves he then informed her that a man was in the shop when he the Examinant came in and that he had gone down the street upon which Mrs. Baynes pursued him and caused him to be apprehended.
Recognisance 540/7 & 13. Endorsed on reverse of 540/13 'No True Bill'.

540/9   Complaint of John Warwick, Mercer & Draper, taken this 4th.June on oath saith that this morning about the hour of eleven a cotton shawl value of 5/- was feloniously stolen from his shop (which shop constituted the front part of his Dwelling House). John Warwick a Constable in St. Albans Parish saith he hath just and reasonable cause and doth suspect that Sarah Simpson did steal.....the same - he upon oath says that his Brother Charles Warwick saw Sarah Simpson take up the shawl and she immediately ran away that he followed her out of the shop and challenged her with the theft that she positively denied but after being searched it was found concealed on her arm covered by her own shawl. And thereupon the said John Warwick prayeth that Justice shall be done to the

Prisoner.
Recognisance 540/8 & 12. Endorsed on reverse of 540/12 'A True Bill.
Plea, Not Guilty. Verdict, Guilty'.

540/10 Complaint of Richard Devall, Victualler, taken on oath this 20th.
June 1818 who saith that William Field, butcher, hath at various times
threatened to do him some bodily harm and that he is afraid William Field
will put his threats into execution. Wherefore he prays sureties of the Peace
against William Field.
Endorsed with note of recognisances.
Recognisance 540/5.

540/11 The Information and Complaint of William Weatherly, labourer,
20th.June 1818 who saith that Thomas Dawson, carpenter, and John Fisher,
labourer, did on last Thursday evening about seven of the clock violently
assault and strike this Complainant without any just cause or provocation
and against the Peace. Wherefore he prayeth that Justice be done in the
'premices'.
Endorsed with note of recognisances.
Recognisances 540/6 & 14. Endorsed on reverse of 540/14 'A True Bill.
Plea, Not Guilty. Verdict, Guilty'.

540/15 Bill of Clerk of the Peace. Epiphany to Easter inclusive. 41
entries totalling £13..0..8. Entries include:-

	s..d
Drawing & recording order for the removal of the cage. Sale of materials etc.	10..0
Wm. Thornton for medicines.	5..0
For payment to Wm.Scourfield, Beadle for his trouble in clearing the Borough of Vagrants.	5..0
Payment of 1/3 of bill of Elizabeth Few for carpenters work repairing Town Hall.	5..0

540/16 Bill of John Deayton. House of Correction.   8s..0d

540/17 Bill of James Deayton. Borough Gaol. Entries mention:-
To 28 days to Michael Nolan, deserter. To 49 days to Sarah Simpson. To
32 days James Grady. 2 days to a stranger ordered into custody by the
Mayor. 21 days bread, beer & soap to the Nurse. Paid for shaving
Michl.Nolan by order.

540/18 Bill of John Deayton. House of Correction. Subsistence for two
prisoners.

SESSIONS ROLL 541, Michaelmas 1818   (23rd.Oct.)

541/1 Writ proclaiming Quarter Sessions and Gaol Delivery.

541/2 Lists of jurors for the Grand and Petty juries of the Borough.

541/3   Calendar of Prisoners for the Borough Gaol.
John East committed 14th.Oct. charged on the oath of Andrea Chiesa with having feloniously stolen and carried away three clasp knives the property of Andrea Chiesa. Bail'd out.
John Olney committed 14th. Oct. charged on the oath of Charles Street & Elizabeth Mead with having feloniously stolen and carried away a hat the property of Charles Street.   James Deayton 'Goaler'.

514/4   Calendar of Prisoners. House of Correction.
Elizabeth Holliman committed 25th.July upon the oath of Joseph Parsons, Overseer of the Parish of St. Peters with having been delivered of a female bastard child and chargeable to the Parish Ordered to be imprisoned in the House of Correction six months. Remains under her respective sentence.

541/5   Information and complaint of Charles Street of Luton, servant, taken under oath 14th. Oct. who saith that last night about 9 o'clock he went to the Bell Public House (it being Fair time) and placed his hat under a form in the room & that about an hour afterwards he missed the hat and that the hat soon after produced to him by Elizabeth Mead proved to be the hat which was so lost.
Elizabeth Mead, spinster, being sworn 14th. Oct. saith that she was present at the Dance last night at the Bell Public house & that a silk shawl & a muslin frill her property were stolen out of the room & that suspecting a man who was in the room & who states his name to be John Olney she this Informant pursued him up St. Peters Street & apprehended him near the house of Mr.Fowell with a hat on his head which was afterwards claimed by Charles Street to be his property. That the frill she had lost was found by her in the hat but that her shawl has not been found.
Endorsed with a note of recognisances.
Recognisances 541/9 & 10.
Presentment of the jury 541/12 concerning John Olney, 'laborer' stealing one beaver hat value of ten shillings the property of Charles Street. Endorsed 'A True Bill. Plea, Not Guilty. Verdict, Guilty'.

541/6   Information and complaint of Andrea Chiesa, dealer in cutlery, taken on oath 14th.Oct. who saith that he hired a stall at the late Fair in the Borough in order to expose cutlery & other goods to sale and that the stall was erected in the Parish of St.Peter nearby the house of Mr.Rogers the Surgeon and that yesterday a'noon abt. half past 5 o'clock as he was standing at the stall he saw John East (now in custody) take a knife from the stall and went towards the Market Place. Upon which this Informant pursued him for about twenty yards and on searching John East found three clasp knives in his possession all of which this Informant deposes to be his property.
Endorsed with a note of recognisances.
Recognisances 541/7/8.
Presentment of the jury 541/13 concerning John East, 'laborer' stealing three clasp knives the property of Andrea Chiesa. Endorsed 'A True Bill. Plea, Not Guilty. Verdict, Guilty'.

541/11 Sacrament Certificate of Isaac Piggott, Gentleman.

541/14 Bill. The King against Olney.
Indictment (3/-), Crier (1/6) and 2 days loss of time for each of 3 witnesses
(£2..10..0).

541/15 Bill of William Scourfield.	s..d
Apprehending & committing John East for 'felerny'.	3..0

541/16 Bill. King against East.	9s..6d

541/17 Bill of James Deayton. Borough Gaol. 12 entries totalling
£3..3..0. Entries include:-

	£.. s.. d
To 35 days subs'ce to Sarah Simpson.	1.. 0.. 5
To 7 days Thos.Clark.	0.. 4.. 1
10 days John Olney.	0.. 5..10
Paid for taxes.	0..15.. 6
2 days to John Aveling.	0.. 1.. 2
Straw for John Rogers & John Peele under an execution.	0.. 1.. 0

541/18 Bill of Isaac Piggott.

Inquisition on the body of James Dawes accidentally	£.. s.. d
killed by the falling in of the ground at a gravel pit.	1.. 0..0
Paid jury & constables.	0..17..0
Inquisition taken on the body of William Parsons a prisoner	
who died by the visitation of God in the Liberty Gaol.	1.. 0..0
Paid jury & constables.	0..17..0
	3..14..0

541/19 Bill of John Deayton. House of Correction.	
To straw and 91 days subsistence to Elizabeth Holliman.	£2..16..1

541/20, 21, 22 & 23 Bills of the Constables. A.Glascock,
Thos.Babnes (St.Michaels Ward), John Fowell (St.Peters Ward) and
William Scourfield. Mention made of:-
For being on duty (Nov.5). Carts for Regt.Light Horse, 13 Regt.Light
Horse & 95 Regt.Foot. 2 days Fair and 2 days Mich.Fair.

541/24 Bill of James Spicer, Beadle. Similar to Constables Bill.

SESSIONS ROLL 542, Epiphany 1819   (15th.Jan.)

542/1 Writ proclaiming Quarter Sessions and Gaol Delivery.

542/2 Lists of jurors for the Grand and Petty juries of the Borough.

542/3 Calendar of Prisoners. House of Correction.
Elizabeth Holliman remains under her respective sentence.

Richard Jeffs committed 19th.Nov. on the oath of Mary Webb, singlewoman, for that she hath declared herself to be with child likely to be born a bastard & chargeable to the Parish, Richard Jeffs having gotten her with child.

542/4　Calendar of Prisoners for the Borough Gaol.
William Reed committed 17 Nov. charged with having designedly by false pretences obtained from Edward Langridge one cheese of twenty shillings value with intent to defraud him of the same.

542/5　Jury list for The King against Reed.

542/10　Information and complaint of John Savage taken on oath 9th.Jan. who saith that in the a'noon of Sunday 3rd. Jan. Thomas Hatton, shoemaker, assaulted this complainant as he was walking along the footpath near Mr. Kinder's house striking him over the head against the Peace wherefore this Complainant prays that Thomas Hatton may be apprehended to answer the complaint.
Recognisances 542/6 & 7.
Presentment of the jury 542/13 concerning Thomas Hatton, shoemaker, making an assault on John Savage against the Peace. Endorsed 'A True Bill. Plea, Not Guilty. Verdict, Not Guilty'.

542/11　Information and complaint of Edward Langridge, cheesemonger, taken on oath this 17th. Nov. 1818 who saith that this afternoon about 1 o'clock a man came to this Informant's shop and said he wanted a cheese for Mr.Pocock of Hatchen Green. That this Informant has for some time past been accustomed to supply Mr.Pocock with goods and considered that man so applying for cheese was Mr.Pocock's servant. This Informant without any hesitation sent his servant Joseph Peppercorn with a cheese which weighed about 25 lbs. to the Public House called the Red House where the man desired the cheese to be sent. That this Informant on the return of his servant began to suspect that the cheese had been obtained fraudulently and he therefore hastened immediately to the Red House where he saw the man who calls himself William Reed and asked him if he was really Mr.Pocock's man & many other questions when William Reed told this Informant that his mistress (meaning the wife of Mr.Pocock) had given him a note for cheese and some other articles but he had lost the note and he further stated that he had left his cart at the Woolpack Inn which this Informant immediately went to enquire about and found to be false. That he then went back to the Red House and found William Reed had gone away with the cheese and was soon afterwards discovered at the Trumpet public house where he was taken into custody by the Constable and this Informant further saith that after William Reed was so apprehended & without any promise of forgiveness or other inducement he confessed to the Informant that Mr. Pocock had not sent him for cheese.
Examination of Joseph Peppercorn (servant to Mr.Langridge) taken on oath this 17th. Nov. who saith that about one o'clock in afternoon this day he

took a Derby cheese weighing 25 lbs. by order of Mr. Langridge, his Master to the Red House public house where Mr. Swale resides and that his Master desired him to put it into Mr.Pocock's cart where he would find it there. That the cheese had a paper ticket fastened to it with the name Mr. Pocock, Hatchen Green written upon it and that on seeing the man (Wm.Reed) who had ordered the cheese, he this Examinant offered to deliver the cheese to him but he desired this Examinant to give it to Mr.Swale the Landlord which this Examinant accordingly did and then came away.
Endorsed with note of recognisances.
Recognisances 542/8/9.
Presentment of the jury 542/12 concerning William Reed unlawfully obtaining by fraud one Derby cheese weighing 24 lbs. value twenty shillings the property of Edward Langridge. Endorsed 'A True Bill. Plea, Not Guilty. Verdict, Guilty'.

542/14 Bill of Thos. Thackster, Constable of Middle Ward. £1..5..0.

542/15 Note.
William Scourfield, Beadle will be much oblig'd to the Magistrates for his years 'Salerey' due this Jan'y 1819.

542/16 Note. Similar to previous item.
James Spicer, Beadle......salary from Epiphany to Christmas.

542/17 Bill of Clerk of the Peace. Midsummer to Michaelmas inclusive.
61 items totalling £22..15..1. Entries include:-
'The Assizes being appointed to be held on same day as Quarter Sessions, attended the Chairman thereon who directed same should be adjourned for a week. (6s..8d). Bill of John Warwick for blankets for Gaol and Clothes for prisoners. (5s..0d).

542/18 Bill of James Deayton. Borough Gaol.
Subsistence and straw etc. Mentions:- 2 days to Thomas Tutt, 31 days John East, 62 days John Olney and 59 days William Reed.

542/19 Bill of J.W.Wells.
Additional work done at the Borough Gaol. 12 entries totalling £5..15..11$^{1}/_{2}$
Entries include :-
Removing back of Mrs.Deayton's privy - throwing Debtor's
privy into ditto. Laying additional floor taking up grate etc.
5 days work.   1.. 0..0
Making & hanging a door in partition fitting lining
round ditto in felons sleeping room.   0.. 4..3
Cutting out small doorways in felons - debtors rooms
making & hanging small doors, Putting on bolts to side
door in sleeping room.   0..16..9
Taking down seat & refixing in felons gaol, Fixing a new seat
in debtors room, Putting on lock to women's sleeping room. 0.. 7..6

542/20 Bill of Thos.Chambers & J.W.Wells.
For work done at the Gaol.   £89..10..0

542/21 Bill of John Deayton. House of Correction.
Straw and subsistence for prisoners. Elizabeth Hollinson (91 days). Thos.
Shepherd (30 days) and Rich'd Jeffs (58 days).

SESSIONS ROLL 543, Easter 1819   (23rd.April)

543/1 Writ proclaiming Quarter Sessions and Gaol Delivery.

543/2 Lists of jurors for the Grand and Petty juries of the Borough.

543/3 Calendar of Prisoners. House of Correction. (No prisoners).

543/4 Calendar of Prisoners for the Borough Gaol.
William Reed convicted and ordered to be in imprisoned six calendar
months. Remains in prison.

543/5 Information and complaint of Frances Stephens, spinster, taken
6th.March who saith that as she was going out of the lane called School
Lane last night about 7 o'clock on her way home from the silk mills where
she had been to work she saw a great number of persons assembled together
on the pavement opposite to Mr.Masons house and that before this
Examinant could cross the road she was laid hold of by Samuel Boarder
Jacob Dudley and Joseph Dudley three of the persons so assembled and
others of the said persons whose names this Examinant is unacquainted with
and that Samuel Boarder Jacob Dudley and Joseph Dudley very indecent by
forcing their hands up her petticoats and otherwise assaulted and ill treated
her against the Peace...... wherefore she prays that Samuel Boarder Jacob
Dudley and Joseph Dudley may be apprehended to answer the complaint.
Recognisance 543/13.

543/6 Information and complaint of Joseph White, labourer, taken 27th.
Jan. who saith that last Sunday evening the 24th.Jan. about half past 8
o'clock as he was walking along the footpath in George Street he was
accosted by Samuel Burrows, shoemaker, who asked him if he had not been
insulting his Brother (meaning a young man named Frank Burrows who is
reputed to be silly) and this Complainant replied that he had not whereupon
Samuel Burrows immediately struck this Complainant a violent blow on
the face which caused a great discharge of blood from his nose and brought
him to the ground for which assault this Complainant prayeth that Justice
may be done.
Recognisance 543/12.
Presentment of the jury 543/15 concerning Samuel Burrows assaulting
Joseph White. Endorsed 'A True Bill. Plea, Guilty'.

169

543/7 Warrant requiring the Constables to bring John Smith of Luton before the Justices as a material witness to an assault upon James Barfoot of Luton, dealer in straw plait, by Henry Lee of the Parish of St.Peter, dealer in straw plait.

543/8 Information and complaint of James Barfoot of Luton, dealer in straw 'platt' taken on oath 13th.June 1819 who saith that Henry Lee, dealer in straw 'platt' did this day assault this Complainant in the Parish of St.Peter by striking him over the head against the Peace.
Endorsed with note of recognisances.
Recognisance 543/10.
Presentment of the jury 543/14 concerning Henry Boswell Lee assaulting James Barfoot. Endorsed 'A True Bill. Plea, Not Guilty. Verdict, Guilty'.

543/9 Information and complaint of Francis Searancke, brewer taken on oath 27th.Jan.1819 who saith that this afternoon between the hours of two and three he was violently assaulted in his yard by William Randall, publican, without any good cause or provocation wherefore the Complainant prayeth that Justice may be done to him.
Endorsed with note of recognisances.
Recognisance 543/11.

543/16 Bill for work done in the Borough Gaol.
6 entries totalling £5..15..2, for hooks, bolts and hinges, alterations to a window and for the fixing of iron bars.

543/17 Bill for work done at the Borough Gaol.
6 entries totalling £2..2..11. Entries include:- 2 new framed deal
lights hung in Debtors room & Felons sleeping room etc.   18s..6d
Fixing seat & shelves in women's day room & hanging 2
deal casement lights in a pane.   6s..0d

543/18 Bill for glazier's work done in Borough Gaol. 9 entries.

543/19 Bill of R. Webster. 24 entries totalling £1..13..6 for pills, powders, plasters, ointments, mixtures and embrocations for prisoners.

543/20 Bill of John Deayton. House of Correction.	£..	s..	d
11 days Elizabeth Holliman.	0..	6..	5
84 days Richard Jeffs.	2..	9..	0
7 days James Peacock.	0..	4..	1
28 days Susan Turpin.	0..	16..	4
10 days David Watts.	0..	5..	10
2 days William Randall.	0..	1..	2
1 day John Sharpe.	0..	1..	0
8 days Francis Wykes.	0..	4..	8

543/21 Bill of Samuel Deayton. Borough Gaol.

28 days William Reed.	2..17..2
2 days George Childs.	0.. 1..2
Straw for debtors under an execution of the Court of Requests.	0.. 4..0
Paid taxes.	0.. 7..9
Two fires.	0.. 6..0

SESSIONS ROLL 544, Midsummer 1819   (16th July)

544/1 Writ proclaiming Quarter sessions and Gaol Delivery.

544/2 List of jurors for the Grand and Petty juries of the Borough.

544/3 Calendar of Prisoners for the Borough Gaol.
William Reed remains under his respective sentence.

544/4 Calendar of Prisoners. House of Correction. (No prisoners).

544/6 Be it remembered that on 19th. May 1819 George Macdonald came before me Rev. J. C. Gape residing near the place where offence was committed & informed me that Joseph Stirrup, labourer, on 17th. May 1819 was a pedlar & trading person going to other men's houses travelling on foot carrying to sell and exposing to sale goods & did on the day foresaid as a pedlar ....goods (to wit) earthenware without a licence contrary to the form of the Statute ...... declared that he was not guilty of the offence but the same being fully proved on oaths of Robert Willis and Thomas Lovell credible witnesses it manifestly appears to me that Joseph Stirrup is guilty of the offence and I do hereby convict him and do adjudge that he hath forfeited the sum of Ten Pounds of lawful money.....
Recognisance 544/5 appeal by Joseph Stirrup against the fine for trading as a pedlar without a licence.

544/7 Petition of Michael Genone, cordwainer, sheweth that Thomas Ashbury by Indenture bearing date 12th. May 1818 was bound apprentice to yr. Petit'r in his trade of a cordwainer for a term 7 years from thence next coming and from that time until the present hath continued in yr. Petit'rs sce. but that Thomas Ashbury is of a very ungovernable disposition & neglects his duty towards yr. Petit'r by refusing to perform his lawful orders & commands-That he frequently gets intoxicated with liquor & that he did in particular on Sunday 4th. July inst. assault & ill treat Elizabeth the wife of yr. Petit'r by striking her with his fist. Whereof yr. Petit'r prays that the conduct of his said Apprentice may be enquired into & Justice done.

544/8 Bill of the Clerk of the Peace.Epiphany to Easter inclusive.
44 items totalling £13..19..0.

544/9   Bill of James Deayton. Borough Gaol.   £.. s .. d
            To 93 days subsist. William Reed.   2..14.. 3
            To 2 days Henry Wright.   0.. 1.. 2
            To 5 days Thomas Borthwick.   0.. 2..11
            To 20 days John Goole.   0..12.. 3
            Straw.   0..10.. 0
            Pens, ink & paper.   0.. 4.. 0
            Pd. for horse & expenses going after
            John Goole who had escaped.   <u>0..12.. 0</u>
                                                                        £4..16.. 7

544/10 Bill of John Deayton. House of Correction.   s.. d
            To 24 days pay to Jas. Grissele as a deserter.   18.. 0
            To 5 days subst. Isabella Steward.   2..11
            Straw.   <u>3.. 0</u>
                                                                        £1..3..11

SESSIONS ROLL 545, Michaelmas 1819   (22nd.Oct.)

545/1   Writ proclaiming Quarter Sessions and Gaol Delivery.

545/2   Lists of jurors for the Grand and Petty juries of the Borough.

545/3   Calendar of Prisoners. House of Correction.
Charles Pope committed 21st.July on oath of Elizabeth Hudson she hath declared herself to be with child chargeable to the Parish of St.Peters & hath charged Charles Pope to be the father.

545/4   Calendar of Prisoners for the Borough Gaol.
Ellen Murphey convicted for hawking goods without a licence. Ordered to be imprisoned in the Gaol for three months. Remains in Gaol.

545/5   Offence and conviction details similar to item <u>544/6</u> whereby on the information of Thomas Reed, Ellen Murphy, widow, of St.Michaels Parish was fined £10 for selling goods without a licence.

545/6   Offence and conviction details similar to item <u>544/6</u> whereby on the information of George Brown, Thomas Tooley was fined £10 for trading earthenware without a licence.

545/7   Recognisance concerning Charles Pope being father of the bastard child of Elizabeth Hudson.

545/8   Recognisance concerning James Dolamore being father of the bastard child of Sarah Brooks.

545/9   Bill of Ben.Fowler. 9 entries totalling £3..16..4$\frac{1}{2}$d for carpenters work done at the Borough Gaol. Entries mention:-

.....nailing on iron roofing to privy in sleeping cell at Boro' Gaol.
.....whitewashing inside sleeping cell at Boro' Gaol.

545/10 Bill of William Corby. 12 entries totalling £3..18..2 for hinges, 'nales' copper 'wier', hooks and 'stapels' used in repairs at the Town Hall.

545/11 Bill of the Clerk of the Peace. Midsummer to Michaelmas inclusive. 15 entries totalling £4..13..6. Entries include:-

	s..d
Payt. $\frac{1}{3}$ of the bill of Ben. Fowler for work done at House of Correction.	5..0
Ditto bill of P. Gutteridge for stone & fender for House of Correction.	5..0

545/12 Bill of Isaac Piggott.

	£.. s..d
For Inquisition at the White Hart Inn on the body of Samuel Field accidentally killed by being run over with a cart.	1.. 0..0
Paid Jury & summoning Officer.	0..17..0
For Inquisition on the body of Wm. Hart lying dead at the Woolpack Inn when a verdict was found against Thomas Perdy & George Butler for manslaughter.	1.. 0..0
Paid Jury & summoning Officer.	0..17..0
For Inquisition on the body of Wm. Grubb accidentally killed by the overturning of the Manchester Telegraph Coach.	1.. 0..0
Paid jury etc.	0..17..0
	£5..11..0

545/13 The King against John Goodle.
Expenses paid by Isaac Piggott by order of the Magistrates.

	£.. s..d
Paid Mr. Nicholls for printing 100 handbills to discover the owner of the mare if possible.	0.. 7..6
Paid for distributing & posting the handbills.	0.. 3..0
Paid for advertisement in the County Chronicle & for the paper.	0..11..0
Paid postage of letters to the Mayor of Nottingham & the Mayor of Rochester & the answers received from the Town Clerks of those places & from the Public Office at Bow Street.	0.. 3..6
Paid Mr. Hodson for the keep of the mare beyond the sum of £3..2..0 received of Mr. Nicholls for the balance of the sale by public auction.	3.. 8..0

545/14 Bill of James Deayton. Borough Gaol. Entries mention 66 days to Ellen Murphey (£1..18..6). 27 days to Henry Taylor comm'd as a deserter. 3 days to Wm. Chambers. 4 days to John Jackson. Cleaning the room after the bricklayers (5s..0d).

545/15 Bill of John Deayton. House of Correction.

545/16 Bill of William Scourfield, Beadle.
Similar to previous bills of constables, e.g. 'Attending the streets till 12 o'clock to prevent fireworks (Nov. 5). 2s..6d', etc.

545/17 Bill of William Hawes. Constable of Fishpool Ward.

545/18 Bill of Constable of St. Peters Ward.

545/19 Constables Bill. (Unspecified but presumably Middle Ward).

545/20 Bill of James Spicer, Beadle.

545/21 Bill of William Gregory, Constable of Holywell Ward.

SESSIONS ROLL 546, Epiphany 1820   (14th.Jan.)

546/1 Writ proclaiming Quarter Sessions and Gaol Delivery.

546/2 Lists of jurors for the Grand and Petty juries of the Borough.

546/3 Calendar of Prisoners for the Borough Gaol. (No Prisoner).

546/4 Calendar of Prisoners. House of Correction.
Thomas Lawford & Ann Lawford. Convicted under the Game Laws. Ordered to be imprisoned 3 Calendar Months. Remain in confinement.

546/5 Information and complaint of Ann the wife of James Webb, carpenter, taken on oath 10th.Jan.1820 who saith that this evening between 6 & 7 o'clock William Burgess, surgeon did assault this Complainant in a violent manner by kicking her & otherwise ill treating her without any just cause or provocation in the dwelling house of Mrs. Hannah Kingston situate in the Parish of St. Alban wherefore this complainant prayeth that Justice may be done.
Endorsed with note of recognisances.
Recognisances 546/6/7.
Presentment of the jury 546/8 concerning William Burgess assaulting Ann Webb. Endorsed 'A True Bill. Plea, Not Guilty. Verdict, Not Guilty'.

546/9 Bill of James Deayton. Borough Gaol. Entries include:-
Paid Mr. Edwards for taxes (7s..9d). 18 days to Ellen Murphy (10s..6d).
4 days to Wm.Nix & John Gammel (4s..8d).

546/10	Bill of John Deayton. House of Correction.	£..s..d
	40 days to Ann Lawford.	1..3..4
	2 days to Robert Merton.	0..1..2
	37 days to Thos.Lawford.	1..1..7
	Straw.	0..5..0
		£2.11..1

546/11   Bill of John Deayton. Entries include:-   s..d
         Paid for administrating the Oath.   2..0
         Going round the Boro' to give Publicans Notice.   2..6
         Examining weights and balances.   4..0
         Going round Boro' to give bakers notice.   2..6
         Exam. weights & balances.   4..0

546/12   Bill of Wm.Brown. 1 pr. 9/4 Blankets.   £1..7..0

546/13   Bill of James Fitch. For work done at Liberty 'Gail'.

546/14 & 15   Notes. William Scourfield and James Spicer, Beadles.
Will be much obliged to the Magistrates for an order for the yearly 'salerey'.

SESSIONS ROLL 547, Easter 1820   (14th.April)

547/1   Writ proclaiming Quarter sessions and Gaol Delivery.

547/2   Lists of jurors for the Grand and Petty juries of the Borough.

547/3   Calendar of Prisoners. House of Correction. (No Prisoner).

547/4   Calendar of Prisoners for the Borough Gaol.
John Peel committed 5th.Feb.1820 on the oath of J.T.Lipscomb, Mayor.
Luke Batten, Thomas Hill, & Thos. Kent with feloniously stealing and
taking away out of the well of the Blue Pump in the Parish of St. Peter a
quantity of copper pipes & a brass barrel the property of the Mayor,
Aldermen & Burgesses of the Boro.

547/5   Information and complaint of John Thomas Lipscomb Esq.
Mayor, taken on oath 3rd.Feb. who saith that there is a Pump called the
Blue Pump in the Waste ground in St. Peters Street which with the pipes &
other materials belonging to it the Informant believes are the property of the
Mayor, Aldermen........in their corporate capacity. That about three months
ago John Peele, whitesmith applied to this Informant for leave to repair the
works of the said pump but that this Informant forbid him from
intermeddling with the same & this Informant further saith that he was
totally unacquainted with the said John Peele taking upon himself to remove
the copper pipes & other works belonging to the Pump & believes that
John Peele lately removed & conveyed away some part of the copper pipes
& other works with a felonious intention.
Endorsed with note of recognisances.
Recognisance 547/9

547/6   Examination of Luke Batten, cooper, taken 3rd.Feb.1820 who
saith that he is now in possession of a quantity of copper piping & a pump
barrel which John Peele, whitesmith, hath ack'd he took out of the wall of
the pump called the Blue Pump & left with Thomas Hill at the St.Albans

Turnpike Gate on Thursday evening last 27th.Jan. to be sent to London by the Silsoe Waggon. That this Exam't. believes the pump & the pipes & barrel & other works belonging to it are the property of the Mayor & he suspects that the copper piping & pump barrel were feloniously taken out of the well belonging to the pump by John Peele.

547/7 Examination of witness against John Peele on a charge of felony taken on oath 5th.Feb.1820. Thomas Hill, toll collector saith that this Examinant being on his duty at the St.Albans Turnpike Gate on Thursday 27th.Jan. last John Peele, the prisoner, whitesmith came to the Turnpike about half past 7 o'clock in the evening & brought a heavy parcel tied up in a sack which he requested to leave there for the Silsoe Waggoner who usually passes thro the Turnpike with the waggon every Thursday night about 9 o'clock in his way to London. That this Exam't observed to John Peele that the contents of the parcel looked like the piping of an engine or something of that sort upon which the said John Peele replied that it was nothing of that kind & then he went away saying that he should tell the waggoner to call for the parcel. That this Exam't had the curiosity to cut the sack & see what it contained when he found it was copper & brass 'pipeing' & that suspecting that John Peele had come dishonestly by it he informed Mr. Luke Batten who shortly after passed thro the Turnpike of his suspicion & he delivered the parcel to Luke Batten.
Luke Batten, cooper, saith that on Thursday evening last he received from Thomas Hill the copper & brass piping & the brass barrel now produced. That there are five pieces of piping in all besides the barrel & that this Exam't hath had the same in his custody ever since.
Thomas Kent, plumber, saith that he hath had the well of the Blue Pump examined & that the piping which was placed therein for the purpose of drawing water is missing & that the prisoner John Peele voluntarily admitted to this Exam't that he took the piping & barrel now produced out of the well but alleged that when he carried the same to the St. Albans Turnpike for the purpose of being sent to London, it was his intention to have it repaired by Mr. Phillips or Mr.Braithwaite & to have followed the waggon to London & this Exam't further saith that from the circumstance of the piping being cut into short lengths it could not in this witnesses opinion be the intention of John Peele to have piping repaired but this Exam't believes that same was removed & taken away with the intention to sell it.
Recognisance 547/10.

547/8 Evidence of George Church taken 19th.Feb. who saith that he is a journeyman plumber in the service of Mr.Thomas Kent & that by his Masters orders he went down the well of the pump in St.Peters Street which is called the Blue Pump about a fortnight ago in order to ascertain if any of the pipes or works belonging to the pump were missing. That this witness found the barrel, the bucket, the flaunches or brass collars (which join the pipe to the barrel) & the lower part of the piping to be missing & that the other part of the piping from about the height of three feet from the water

was in the well. And that about a week ago he went down the well a second time for the purpose of trying if the brass barrel which is in the possession of Mr.Luke Batten fitted the lower part of the pipe which was left in the well & found there by this witness and that it matched exactly by the worm or screw which is affixed to the barrel fitting the pipe and this witness saith provided any holes were in the lower part of the piping which went into the water there could be no necessity for taking away the piping to be repaired on that account but if there were any holes in that part which was above the water it would be otherwise, because it would not be air tight.
Recognisance 547/11.
Presentment of the jury 547/12 concerning John Peele feloniously stealing forty pounds weight of copper pipe, value twenty shillings & one barrel, value five shillings the property of the Mayor, Aldermen & Burgesses of the Borough of St. Albans.
Endorsed 'A True Bill. Plea, Not Guilty. Verdict, Guilty'.

547/13 Bill of J. S. Story. Michaelmas to Easter inclusive.
58 entries totalling £18..17..7. Entries include:-

	s..d
Payments to constables, beadles, gaoler, coroner. Drawing out order touching prosecution to be inst'd at next Assizes agst. Thos. Perdy & George Butler for manslaughter.	5..0
Attending the Mayor 'persuing' Mr. Fowlers specif'n of the alter'ns necessary at the Gaol in order to the providing a place of safety for the offenders taken up in the night & subseq't atten'ces thereon.	6..8
Making out list of Magistrates in the present commission of the Peace disting'ng those who have died removed or declined to act.	10..0
Proportion of journey to Rick'th to receive the rest of the records in the hands of Mr. Palmers family belonging to the Liberty checking same with list & giving ack'nt.	10..6
On letter from Lord Sidmouth's Office containing directions to the Magistrates touching the taking of the oaths etc. consequence of the accession of the present King. Pd for printing several copies.	3..4
Several attendances at the Gaol for materials & prep. a report of nos. of prisoners committed in 1819 to the Boro' Gaol the greatest number at any one time & as to many other partics. for Lord Sidmouth at his request.	10..0

547/14 Bill of James Deayton. Borough Gaol.	£..	s	.. d
Pd. Mr. Edwards for Two Qtrs taxes.	0..	7..	9
2 days sub. to Henry Draper, a deserter.	0..	1..	6
70 days to John Peele.	2..	0..10	
5 days Thos. Perdy.	0..	2..11	
ditto George Butler.	0..	2..11	
Removing 2 prisoners to Hertford by 'Haabius Corpius'.	1..16..	6	
Straw etc.	0..15..	6	
	£5..	7..11	

547/15 Bill of John Deayton. House of Correction.
56 days sub. to Thomas Lawford.
53 days to Ann Lawford.
Pd. Mr. Edwards for taxes.
Straw.

£..	s..	d
1..	12..	8
1..	10..	11
0..	6..	6
0..	2..	6
£3..	12..	7

547/16 Bill of John Deayton for examining measures.

547/17 Bill of the Clerk of the Peace. For books for recording proceedings of the Sessions & minutes.

547/18 Bill of Rd. Webster. Medical Acct. for Borough Gaol. 9s..8d.

547/19 Bill of Thos.Narraway.
King v Titmuss. For apprehending Wm.Titmuss with a stolen mare.

547/20 Constables Bill for Providing Baggage Waggons.
13 entries totalling £1..4..6.

547/21 Bill of John Fowell for carpenters work in the Gaol.
3 entries totalling £7..10..0.

547/22 Offence and conviction details similar to item 544/6 whereby on the information of Robert Childs, Ann, wife of Thomas Lawford was convicted of selling two hares to George Wildbore contrary to Statute and fined £10, that is £5 for each hare.

547/23 Offence and conviction details similar to item 544/6 whereby on the information of George Little, Thomas Lawford was convicted of selling to John Osborn one pheasant and two partridges for 5/- contrary to Statute and fined £15.

SESSIONS ROLL 548, Midsummer 1820 (14th.July)

548/1 Writ proclaiming Quarter Sessions and Gaol Delivery.

548/2 Lists of jurors for the Grand and Petty juries of the Borough.

548/3 Calendar of Prisoners for the Borough Gaol.
John Peel committed last Easter remains in confinement.
William Frankall charged on oath of George Wilkins & others with stealing one coachmakers plane, value 5/-.
Daniel Gatlin committed on the oath of George Carlington & John Fordham for obtaining from George Carlington one pound & one shilling part of the Bounty for entering as a Private Soldier under false representation.

548/4 Examination of witness against Wm.Frankall charged with felony. Thomas Southam, carpenter, saith that he is a journeyman to Mr.Eli Pew and that about 7 o'clock last Saturday evening 15th.April the prisoner William Frankall came into Mr.Pew's yard near St.Peters Street with a rule and plane in his house where this witness was attending and offered to sell him the plane for 18d. That the witness offered to give 1/- for it which the prisoner said he would take. And that the witness then paid him a 1/- and received the plane from him. That the prisoner then went away and that the witness observing the letters G. W. upon the plane began to suspect it was stolen in consequence of which he was recommended to go to Mr.Wilkins's the coachmaker and make enquiry about it which he accordingly did and one of Mr.Wilkins's men stating that the plane was his Masters property the witness then went in search of the prisoner and found him in St.Peters Street that the prisoner then offered him 9d. in part of the 1/- back again but he refused to take it and then John Ireland an apprentice to Mr.Wilkins gave the prisoner 1/- which the witness took from the prisoner upon which he delivered the plane to John Ireland for his Master Mr.Wilkins.

John Ireland the younger, apprentice to George Wilkins saith that Thomas Southam came to him last Saturday about 10 minutes after 7 o'clock & produced a plane which the witness immediately recognised to be his masters property and that he then went into St.Peters Street in pursuit of the man who had sold the plane to Southam and that when they came near to the White Horse pond the witness found it to be the prisoner Wm.Frankall who had been working for Mr.Wilkins about 8 or 10 days. That the prisoner then offered Southam 9d out of the shilling which he had received on selling the plane but Southam refused to take it in consequence of which James Pullen who was standing by paid 1/- into his hand which he then gave to the prisoner who on paying it to Thos.Southam requested Southam to deliver up the plane to this witness for his Master.

548/5   Information and Complaint of George Wilkins, coachmaker taken on oath 15th.April 1820 who saith that Wm.Frankall, a journeyman coachsmith in the service and pay of this Complainant did this day according to his voluntary confession made to this Complainant feloniously steal out of the workshop a plane called a Tongning plane of the value of 5/- at the least, the property of this Complainant and that he afterwards sold the plane for 1/- to a man in the service or employ of Eli Pew, carpenter, the name of this man is at the present unknown to this Complainant.
Note. 548/13 No date or heading.

'I am very sorry for the crime which i have comited but I was very much intoxicated at the time and I humble hope you will take it into your merciful considerations the long confinement which i now already suffer as it will be a warning to me as long as i live and as i am a Stranger here and have No one to Speak in my behalf i humble beg to throw myself on the mercy of the Court.'
Recognisance 548/6.

Presentment of the jury 548/14 concerning William Frankall stealing a coachmakers plane called a Tonging plane value three shillings the property of Geo. Wilkins. Endorsed 'A True Bill. Plea, Not Guilty. Verdict, Guilty'.

548/7   Information and complaint of George Carlington a Sergeant in the Chatham Div. Royal Marines taken on oath 24th. June 1820 who saith that this Complainant in the month of November last was stationed at St. Albans on the Recruiting Service and that on or about the 13th. Sergeant James Sefton then a Corporal in the same Div. of Royal Marines brought a recruit to this Complainant who stated his name to be Daniel Catlin and that this Complainant thereupon procured the same Daniel Catlin to be examined and having been declared fit for service he was regularly attested and sworn before .... that he was Daniel Catlin and did not belong to the Militia or to any Regiment in His Majesty's Services or Navy or Marines. That this Complainant did therefore pay Daniel Catlin the sum of One Pound and One Shilling for part of the Bounty .... but it hath since been discovered that Daniel Catlin knowingly did make a false Representation in the Oath so taken by him before the Justice of the Peace insomuch as the Daniel Catlin at that time belonged to the Militia of the County of Hertford ....

John Fordham maketh oath and saith ....and it was the duty of Daniel Catlin to have joined the Militia at St.Albans 27th. May last for the purpose of being trained and exercising according to the Public Notice given for that purpose but he neglected to do so.

Recognisance 548/8.

Presentment of the jury 548/9 concerning Daniel Catlin, labourer well knowing himself to belong to the Herts. Reg. Militia and to be a Private soldier in the same Regt. contrived and fraudulently intend to obtain the County Bounty to wit a large sum of money £1..1..0 by pretending he did not belong to the Militia. Endorsed 'A True Bill. Plea, Not Guilty. Verdict, Guilty'.

548/10   Bill of Mr.G.Wilkins. Expenses for the trial of William Frankall.

548/11   Bill of John Deayton and Charles Cook.
Mentions:-Going round to examine measures. Going round to examine weights & balances. Attendance at Petty Sessions to give evidence in support of information.

548/12   Bill of James Deayton. Borough Gaol. Entries mention:-
4 days subsistence Wm.Kitchener & Jn. Miller. 91 days to John Peel convicted Easter. 21 days Wm. Frankall. 21 days Daniel Catlin. Straw for debtors under Ct. of Requests.

SESSIONS ROLL 549, Michaelmas 1820   (20th.Oct.)

549/1   Writ proclaiming Quarter Sessions and Gaol Delivery.

549/2   List of jurors for the Grand and Petty juries of the Borough.

549/3   Calendar of prisoners in the House of Correction.

Stephen Norris and Joseph Swann (bailed out). Committed 4th.Aug. Who are charged on the oath of Thomas Wood one of the Constables of the Borough with having unlawfully neglected and refused to aid and assist him in the execution of his office.

Thomas Weston. Committed 9th.Sept. Requiring him to find sureties to appear at the next Quarter Sessions and in the meantime to keep the peace especially towards Richard William Brabant, one of the Aldermen of the Borough.

Thomas Whitley. Committed 7th.Oct. as a rogue and vagabond.

Thomas Sadler. Committed 19th.Oct. For not finding sureties for his keeping the peace especially towards Elizabeth his wife.

549/4 Calendar of prisoners in the Gaol of the Borough.

John Peele. Convicted at Easter Sessions. Ordered to be imprisoned in the Gaol for six calendar months. Remains in gaol.

Daniel Catlin. Ordered to be imprisoned in the Gaol for six calendar months. Remains in gaol.

Benjamin Rose. Committed 16th.Oct. Charged on the oath of Jas.Peppercorn on of the Overseers of the Poor for the Parish of St.Peter with having obtained from him by fraud and deceit the sum of one shilling and six pence.

549/5 The Information and Complaint of Thomas Wood one of the Constables of the Borough who saith that he was sent for on Sunday 30th.July to go to the house of John Hodsdon called the Chequers Inn in order to quell an affray. He immediately went there and found several persons to the number of four assembled together in a riotous and tumultuous manner amongst whom was Christopher Manderson a stonemason of the Borough whom he apprehended and took into custody for assaulting John Hodsdon. Finding Christopher Manderson to be very much intoxicated in liquor and to be very violent and ungovernable this complainant informed him that he should take him before the Mayor and thereupon required Charles Pain, Stephen Noris, Joseph Swan, John Fray and Thomas Durrant who were there present, to aid and assist in securing Manderson, but they did unlawfully neglect and refuse to assist and were the means of Christopher Manderson escaping custody.

Recognisances 549/9, 10, 11, 12 & 13.

Presentment of the jury 549/16. Endorsed 'A True Bill'.

549/6 The Complaint and Information of Ann Dolling the wife of William Dolling of the Parish of St.Alban, labourer, taken on oath this 20th.Sept.. This complainant saith that her husband hath for some very considerable time now treated her very ill violently assaulting beating her and threatening to take away her life. That last night her husband swore that he would murder her and she is, from the violence of his temper and his being greatly addicted to drinking, very much afraid that he will --- --- to his bloody threat unless he be restrained by law. This complainant prays surety

not out of malice but solely to guard her life from the effect of her husbands murderous threat.
Recognisances 549/14.

549/7   The Information and Complaint of Richard William Brabant of the Parish of St.Alban taken on oath 9th.Sept. This informant saith that several of the window and window frames belonging to his dwelling house have this afternoon been wilfully maliciously broken and destroyed and that this informant hath reason to suspect that they were broken by Thomas Weston, late of the parish, tailor.

549/8   The Examination of Hilesdon Bayly of the Borough, carrier, taken this 9th.Sept. who saith That about half an hour after two o'clock this afternoon he saw Thomas Weston go from the public house called the Little Red Lion with a stick in his hand towards the dwelling house of Richard William Brabant which is situate about 30 or 40 yards distant and that he immediately broke and demolished the frames and glass of three of the windows in front of the house by striking the stick against the same and that this examinant then forced the stick from his hand to prevent his doing further injury which he was proceeding to do at the time.
George Russell, tailor and draper, sworn the day and year aforesaid saith that hearing a violent breaking of some glass as he stood in his house he went to his outer door and saw Thomas Weston in the act of breaking and demolishing the frames and windows of Mr.Brabants dwelling house with a stick which he held in his hand and that in a violent and mischievous manner.
The Complaint of Richard William Brabant taken 9th.Sept. who saith that in consequence of great mischief done to him this day by Thomas Weston's breaking and demolishing of several of this complainants windows he is fearful that Thomas Weston will do him some further injury to person or property unless restrained from so doing and prays sureties against Thomas Weston for his good behaviour.
Presentment of the jury. 549/8. Endorsed 'A True Bill. Plea, Not Guilty. Verdict, Guilty of the offence, but insane at the time of committing it'.

549/15   Recognisance concerning Israel Shepherd having got Elizabeth Munt with child which is likely to be born a bastard.

549/18   Gaol Visitors Report.

549/19   Bill of the Clerk of the Peace. Epiphany Sessions to Midsummer Sessions inclusive. 47 entries totalling £18..0..1.

549/20   Bill of John Deayton. House of Correction. Mainly for subsistence at 7d per person per day.

549/21   Bill of James Deayton. Borough Gaol. Mainly for subsistence at 7d per person per day.

549/22 Bill of John Deayton & Charles Cook.
For Going round to examine weights and attending at Town Hall.

549/23 Bill of Isaac Piggott.   Entries mention:-
For Inquisition at the White Hart Inn on the body of Elizabeth, wife of Samuel Wilson accidently killed and for inquisition at the Cock Public House when the verdict of the jury was that deceased died by Visitation of God.

549/24 Bill of William Scourfield, Beadle. Entries mention:-
For attending fireworks by order of the Mayor, attending fairs, Attending town to prevent any disturbance of the Irish, attending Statute Nigh, Attending river during summer to prevent their bathing.

549/25 Bill of James Spicer, Beadle.

549/26 Bill. By order of Rev.Dr.Bowen. For Borough Gaol.
Wm.Franket two shirts at 3/6 each and two pr. stockings at 2/3 per pr.

549/27 Bill of John Fowell. For carpentry work at Gaol.   £2..9..8$\frac{1}{2}$

549/28 to 31   Bills of T.Wood, John Austin, John Hartwell and James Cottle, Constables of Middle, Fishpool, Holywell and St.Albans Wards.

Index of persons and places

Brabant, Richard, 67-69, 71, 81, 82; Richard William, 181, 182
Brace, James, 7
Brackley, Charles, 7, 9
Bradley, Roger, 117, 160
Bradshaw, John, 34, 140; J., 147; Richard, 73
Braithwaite, ---, 176
Brandon, William, 57, 58
Brandy Tom. See Coventon
Braw, James, 13
Breech, John 25; John jun., 19; John sen., 19
Brentford, Middx., 148
Brewer, John, 84, 100; Sarah, 95; Thomas, 161; William, 148, 149, 157
Brewers, Jonathan, 67
Brice, James, 8, 9
Brickhill, Beds., 138
Brickland, Elizabeth, 135, 156; Mathew 5-7
Bridges, Hannah, 76
Briton, ---, 76
Brittian, John, 143
Brookes (Brook, Brooks), Augustin(e), 60, 140, 150; George, 143, 144, 157; John, 127, 128, 133; Robert, 156; Sarah 172
Brown, Ann, 104, 105; Elizabeth, 132; Floriana, 94; Francis, 126; George, 172; James, 125; James (alias Watson), 128; Thomas, 90, 104, 152-155, 157; William, 7, 9, 22, 25, 39, 44, 67, 114, 125, 126, 137-139, 175; ---, 26, 121, 126
Bruton, T., 75
Buggs (Bugg), Mary, 148, 149, 157
Bulcock (Bullcock, Bullock, alias Palmer, alias Brown), Thomas, 55-57, 62
Bull & Gate, Kentish Town, 46, 47
Bull, William, 135, 136
Buller, Fredrick William, 31
Bunnage, William, 9
Bunyan, Joseph, 135, 136
Burch, Charles, 118
Burgess, John, 3, 4; William, 174
Burrows, Frank, 169; Samuel, 169
Bury, Frances, 148
Bush, John, 34
Butler, George, 173, 177; John, 85, 137-140, 143, 145

Cain (Cane), Felix, 100, 101, 103, 105, 106; Henry 101
Caldwell, Joseph, 133
Calverly, John, 130
Calvert, Francis, 107; George ,107, 109, 116
Cane. See Cain
Carlington, George, 178, 180
Carpenter, Mary, 143; William, 91

Carr (alias Watson), James, 125, 127
Carter, Margaret, 140, 141, 143; Thomas, 15, 85
Caswell (Cashwell), Joseph, 135, 136, 138
Catlin, Daniel, 180, 181; William, 118, 120
Caulkington, Thomas, 7
Caustin (Cawston), Robert, 82, 152
Chambers, Thomas, 113, 143, 169; William, 173
Chandler, Thomas, 71
Chaplin, Nathaniel, 137, 138, 140
Chapman, Ann 17; Henry 17; William 53
Charlton, Richard, (alias Hodges, John), 15
Chennills, William, 10, 12
Cherry, Henry, 59; Luke, 155
Chester, Ann, 22; James, 22
Chiesa, Andrea, 165
Childs George, 171; Robert, 178
Church, George, 176
Clark (Clarke), Alice, 9; James, 64, 118, 120; John, 57, 59; Mary, 38; Thomas, 33, 42, 64, 166; William, 96 149, 151, 158; ---, Mrs., 59
Claxton, Richard, 113
Clemency, Stephen, 45
Cobbett, Alexander, 147
Cockington, John, 96; Thomas, 8
Cockle, ---, 137
Cogdell (Cogdill), Joseph, 48, 54; Sarah, 48, 49
Cole, James, 33
Coleman, Amelia, 89; Jane, 115, 116, 118, 119; William, 89
Collins, John, 119
Colney Street, Herts., 68, 71
Compere, Thomas, 98
Compton, Henry, 88
Conisby (Cunisbee), James, 88; Thomas, 82
Conmee, John, 140, 142, 143
Connor, Stephen, 122, 123
Conyers, Mary, 89
Cook, Charles, 180, 183; Elizabeth, 72; John, 72, 73, 97; Sarah, 53; William, 91
Cooper, Charles, 102; Sarah, 69. Cf Cowper
Copeland, Thomas, 85
Corbett, William, 151
Corby, William, 16, 126, 138, 140, 154, 156, 173
Cordmen, Elizabeth, 69
Cordwell, John 121; Sarah 138
Corfield, Samuel, 25
Costin, William, 57, 60, 61, 139, 140
Cottle, James, 183
Coventon, Joseph, 46, 47, 63; Thomas, 52, 54

Fleming, William, 46, 47
Fletcher, Joseph, 126; Sarah, 125-127
Fly, John, 9, 13
Ford, T., 46, 47
Fordham, John, 178, 180
Fowell, James, 151; John 166, 178, 183
Fowler, Benjamin, 36, 64, 95, 138, 145, 147, 148, 160, 172, 173; George, 111, 116, 128; --- , 177
Fox, Kepple, 88
Frankall, William, 178-180
Franket, William, 183
Franklin, Cornelius, 150
Fray, John, 181
Frost, --- , 117
Furness, John, 86, 148, 149
Fryston, Water, Yorks., 37

Galer, John, 159
Gammel, John, 174
Gape, rev. Carpenter, 88; rev. James Carpenter, 90, 114, 145, 171; Joseph, 9
Gatlin, Daniel, 178
Gazeley, Thomas, 129-131
Gee, Ann, 38, 39; Edward, 38
Geffard, William, 8
Genone, Elizabeth 171; Michael 171
Geoff. See Gough
George, Prince Regent, 132
Gibbins (Gibbon) (alias Hewett, James, alias Field, George), Philip, 145, 162
Gibbons, Peter, 1, 2
Gibbs, Mary, 76; Thomas, 114
Gilbert, Benjamin, 131, 132, 134; William, 35
Giles, Samuel, 41, 75, 125, 126
Gladman, Joseph, 87, 96
Glascock, A., 166
Godfrey, George, 143
Godwin, Joseph, 9, 10, 12, 13
Goff. See Gough
Gold, Daniel, 2
Golding, Samuel, 57, 60-62, 69
Goodge, John, 52, 53
Goodle (Goole), John, 172, 173
Goodman, Elizabeth, 103
Gore, James, 32
Gosbell, Thomas, 112
Gough (Geoff, Goff), Solomon, 48, 49, 115, 116
Gower, Ann, 137, 138; Elizabeth, 58; Joseph, 58, 98, 104, 105; William, 123, 124; William the younger, 7
Grady, James, 163, 164

Grange, John, 143, 157
Granger, John, 93
Green, Ann, 89; Charles, 63, 77; James, 140; John, 89, 95
Greenhill, Edward, 153, 154, 157; Edwin, 113; William, 154
Gregory, Joseph, 10, 12, 13; Philip, 37, 39, 40; Samuel, 38; Thomas, 26; William, 7, 13, 174
Griffen (Griffin), William, 156; Charles, 81
Grimston, Lord,Viscount James, 84, 105
Grissele, James, 172
Groam, George, 91; Martha, 91
Groghan, (Grogham, Grogan), Owen, 86-88, 91
Groom, Thomas, 73
Grove (Groves), James, 88; William 121, 149
Grover, Thomas, 104, 105; --- :Mrs., 117
Grubb, William, 65, 67, 173; --- , 163
Gutteridge, P., 138,173; --- , 162

Hair, John, 103
Hale, John, 62, 111, 127; William 84, 120; --- , 95
Hall, John, 12; Stephen, 146; Thomas, 83; William 83, 85-88
Hally, Margaret, 149
Halmer, Thomas, 7, 13
Hammond, Elizabeth, 76
Hands, George, 48
Hannel, James, 74
Hannoway, Thomas, 74
Harbridge, Coventry, 3
Harding, James, 63-65, 67, 69; John, 6; Joseph, 53, 143, 157; Thomas, 133
Hares, Robert, 82
Harris, Jeremiah, 78; Thomas, 76, 156; William, 68, 98; --- , 84
Harrison, George 96; John 20, 23, 41
Hart, William, 80, 173
Hartley, Samuel, 156, 158
Hartwell, John, 183
Harvey, Elizabeth, 149; Peter, 20
Haseldine, Samuel, 125
Hatchcliff, Beds. See Hockliffe
Hatcher, John, 70, 71
Hatching Green, Herts., 167, 168
Hatfield, Herts., 2, 72; Bishop's, 113; Hall, 38
Hatton, Thomas, 156, 167
Haughter, William, 140
Hawes, Edward, 61; Lucy, 57, 60-62; William, 174
Hawkesbury, Lord, 88

187

Hawkins, Mary, 49; William, 161
Hayes (Hays), John, 133, 134; ---, Lieutenant, 92, 93; --- , Mrs., 92
Hebbs, John, 124
Henshaw, John, 13, 16; William, 149-151
Herbert, George, 64; Thomas, 116
Hertford, 22, 33, 39, 40, 44, 50, 117, 127, 138, 140, 154, 177; gaol, 20, 52
Hester, Michael, 122, 123
Hevans, John, 5
Hewes (Hews), John, 18, 108; Thomas, 18
Hewett, James, 145, 146
Hexton, Herts., 3
Hicks, Ann, 29, 31; Mary, 31
Higbid, Thomas, 60, 61; William, 10, 60
Higgins, James, 146
Hill, George, 135; James, 122, 123; Thomas, 40, 41, 175, 176
Hilliard, John, 141; --- Mrs., 141
Hillman & Bacon, Messrs., 157
Hilsdon, James, 12
Hirons, rev.Jabez, 22, 23
Hirst. See Hurst
Hitchin, Herts., 3
Hockliffe (Hatchcliffe), Beds., 58
Hodges, John, (alias Charlton, Richard), 15; Richard, 31; --- , 143
Hodsdon (Hodson), John, 181, --- , 173
Hoggan, William, 163
Holliman, Elizabeth, 161, 165, 166, 170
Hollingsworth, Mary, 76
Hollinson, Elizabeth, 169
Holt, Absolom, 150; Mary, 96
Homer, George, 90, 91, 93; William George, 89
Honnor (Honor), George, 31; Henry, 106, 109
Hopkins, Thomas, 72-75, 77, 78, 80
Hornsey, John, 52, 53
Horton (Hortin), Daniel, 107, 108; William, 48, 49
Houghton, William, 93
Houndslow, William, 89-91
House (Howes, Howse), Ann, 70, 71; Thomas, 74 122, 124, 128, 135, 145; William, 11, 67
Howe (How), John, 158; Mary, 96, 127, 128; William, 96, 103
Howel, Mary, 77
Howes. See House
Howlinsaw, William, 91
Huckett, Susan, 158
Hudnal, Francis, 19, 20; Mary, 19, 20; Sarah, 19, 20
Hudson, Elizabeth, 172

Huggins, Charles, 57, 60-62; Jenny, 32; Richard, 15
Hulks, Joseph, 69, 72, 77
Humbley, Thomas, 25, 28, 31
Hunt, Rebecca, 91
Hurrell, Charles, 104
Hurst (Hirst), D., 127, 143

Ing, Richard, 18
Ireland, John, the younger, 179
Irons, George, 67, 78
Ivory, James, 78, 79, 80

Jackson, John, 173; William, 90, 93, 95, 96, 121
James, Edward 50; John 19; William 83
Jeffard, Wm., 21
Jefferies (Jefferies, Jeffery, Jefferys, Jeffrys), Henry, 67, 81, 147, 159; James Dixon, 89; Thomas, 18; William, 64
Jeffs, Richard, 167, 169, 170; Thomas, 146; William, 99
Jennings, John, 83
Jessop, William, 150, 152, 156
Johnson, Thomas, 49; William, 57, 59, 61; --- , 152
Jones, Gabriel, 91; Jemima, 95; John, 45; Peter Henry, 31; Philip, 100, 101; Thomas, 71, 114; Walter, 80; --- , major, 111
Jordan, Mary, 87
Joscelin, William, 68
Jude, James, 82

Keer, Samuel, 125-127
Kelly, Henry, 21; Sarah 48, 49, 50
Kennedy, Patrick, 6, 7
Kent, John, 5; Richard Leonard, 28; Thomas, 87, 160, 175, 176
Kentish, Charles, 53, 67; James, 57, 59; John, 16, 34, 36; Joseph, 26; Joshua, 73; Matthew, 90; Thomas, 61; William, 90; --, 40
Kentish Town. See London
Kible, Richard, 28
Kieff, James, 152
Kilby, Jeremiah, 34; Joseph, 35; Martha, 34; William, 18, 19
Kinder, Ann, 90; Thomas, 9, 10, 11, 16, 46, 53, 66, 82, 84, 88, 93, 135, 140, 141, 142, 145; William, 10, 11, 17; --- , 59, 117, 167
King, James, 24, Mary, 35
Kingham, --- , 126

Kingston, Francis, 2, 92; Hannah, 174
Kippings, George, 25
Kirk, George, 101
Kitchener, William, 180
Knebworth, Herts., 84
Knight, Thomas, 103
Knowles, John, 10, 11, 12, 103

Lacey, Joseph, 96
Landridge, Edward, 156
Lane, John 14; William, 114
Langham, Thomas, 58; --- , 152
Langridge, Edward, 167, 168
Latchford, John, 60; William, 60
Latham, Mary, 89; William, 64, 99
Lawford, Ann 174, 178; Thomas, 174, 178
Laws, Thomas, 54
Lawson, William, 28
Lee, Henry Boswell, 170; Mary, 68
Leeds, Yorks., 1
Leicester, 45
Levermore, John, 39
Lewin, John, 15, 20; William, 131
Lewis, Percival, 36, 39, 44, 45, 50, 78, 119;
    Thomas, 33, 61
Liggins, Edward, 71
Lines, Abel, 156; Henry, 48, 62; Henry jun.,
    47, 49; John, 113; Thomas, 47
Lintot, William, 67
Lipscomb, John Thomas, 175
Little, George, 178
Lloyd, Jane, 34
Loins, Joab, 76
Lomax, Joshua, 147
London, 18, 40, 48, 70, 81, 94, 102, 134,
    176; Basinghall street, 133; Bishopsgate
    street, 3; Bow street, 173; Kentish Town,
    46, 47; Monmouth street, 64; Smithfield
    market, 100; Woolwich, 69
London Colney, Herts., 31, 46, 58, 69, 72,
    76, 99
Long, William, 16
Longford, Mary, 8
Longhurst, Charles, 149
Lottrell, Lt.Patrick, 103
Louch, Charles, 149-152, 154, 155, 157
Lovell, Thomas, 171
Lovet (Lovett), John, 100, 101, 103
Lowe, Jeremiah, 63
Lucas, William, 72, 73, 74; William Nelson,
    34
Lush, Sarah 45
Luton, Beds., 165, 170

Maccarty, Elizabeth, 13

Macdonald, George, 171
McGee, John, 149
McGwyer, John, 50-52. Cf. McQuire
McKarlie, Beace, 6
Mackay, Murdoc, 41
Mackennell (Mackinnell), --- , 134
McLean (Macklan, Mackline, MacLean,
    McLane), John, 145-147; Thomas, 75-77
Macnair, John, 41
McQuire, Ann, 21; Mary, 21. Cf. McGwyer
McTag, Michael, 122-124
Maddams, James, 110
Mails, John, 161
Main, Thomas, 102
Major, William, 3, 4
Makins, Thomas, 148
Maloney, John, 82
Manderson, Christopher, 181
Mannard (Manniard), Sarah, 56; Tabitha, 42,
    43
Mansell, Humphrey, 47, 52, 69, 71; Thomas,
    99, 100
Mansfield, Lord Chief Justice, 5
Mardale (Mardell), Martha, 131, 132, 134
Mark, --- , Mrs., 124
Markee, Ann, 89
Markham, John, 15
Marks, Ann, 59
Marlen (alias Mullins), Ann, 95
Marsh, Nathaniel, 71; William, 140
Marshall, Mary, 80; William ,129, 131
Marston, George, 147; James, 2, 7; William,
    8, 13, 14, 16, 32, 34, 40, 47, --- , 27
Martin, John, 129, 130
Mason, John, 86, 154; K., 36; Michael, 98;
    Richard, 7, 23, 31, 86; Richard junior, 53;
    Richard senior, 101; ---., 145, 149, 158,
    160, 162, 169
Maxwell, John, 34
Mead, Elizabeth, 165; George, 91
Merton, Robert, 174
Messenger, James, 97, 98; Thomas, 65-67
Milemore, Abraham, 24
Miller, John, 180
Mills, Mary, 76
Missenden, John, 53, 54, 96
Missington, --- , 117
Molloy, Patrick, 122, 123; Richard, 122, 123
Monk, David, 149, 150
Moore (More), Cuthbert, 12; Elizabeth, 68;
    Jacob, 107, 108, 112
Moreton, William, 144
Morris, William, 8
Moss, Mary, 72; Richard, 106, 109
Motton, James, 156
Mowbray, Thomas, 123

189

Mullins (alias Marlen), Ann, 95
Munn, Ann, 30, 82; Gazely, 30; May, 30; Thomas, 30
Munt, Catherine, 132; Elizabeth, 182; John, 10
Murphy (Murphey), Ellen, 172-174
Murty, John, 54

Narraway, Thomas, 178
Nash, Elizabeth, 50, 51; Job, 51, 65, 73; Mary, 73
Needham, Abraham, 42, 45
Newson, Joseph, 156; Mathew, 90
Newton, Henry, 92
Nicholls (Nicholl), Robert, 160; William, 56, 99; --- , 173
Nicholson, W.P. 91; --- , Mrs., 153
Nix, William, 174
Nolan, Michael, 164
Norman, James 63
Norris (Noris), Henry 66, 68; Stephen 181; Thomas 25
Northampton, 16, 52, 53
Northchurch, Herts., 48

Oakes, George, 136, 143
Oakley, John, 155
O'Conner, Patrick, 148
Oddey, James, 33
Ogilvy (Ogleby), David, 31, 81
O'Hara, James, 140-143, 145, 157
Oliver, Andrew, 74
Olney, John, 165, 166, 168
Omiar, James, 105
Oneigley, Philip, 82
O'Neill, John, 145
Osborn, John, 9, 25, 28, 33, 43, 49, 50, 52, 53, 178; Sarah 87; --- , 39
Oxton, John, 30

Page, John, 55, 56; Ralph, 1, 2, 4, 8; --- , 117
Pain, Charles, 181; Judith, 116; Thomas, 121
Painter, James, 18; Mary, 156, 161
Pales, Jane, 34; William, 34
Pallin, James, 2, 25, 28
Palmer, Arthur, 37; John, 96, 124, 129, 162; --- , 177
Parkins, Philip, 84; William, 114
Parlar, John, 57
Parrot (Parratt, Parrott), Mary, 151; Samuel, 32, 33, 36; Thomas, 146. Cf. Perot
Parsons, Joseph, 68, 165; Philip, 63, 64, 90; Thomas, 87, 93; William, 166; --- , 67
Peacock, James, 170; John, 70; Mary, 7; Peter, 101; Thomas, 77, 144-146

Pearce, Thomas, 22
Peel (Peele), John, 2, 6, 30, 74, 75, 166, 175, 176, 178, 180, 181; Thomas, 75
Pegrum, Elizabeth, 122
Pellet, Stephen, 91
Peppercorn, James, 181; Joseph, 167
Perceval, James 28; Spencer, prime minister, 132
Perdy, Thomas, 173, 177
Perkins, Ann, 35
Perriam, John, 31-33
Perrin, A., 53
Perrot, --- , 26. Cf. Parrot
Pestell, John, 16
Peters, John, 18, 19
Pett, Robert, 67
Pew, Eli, 179; Joseph, 15. Cf Pugh
Pheby, William 140-142
Philips (Phillips), Thomas, 91, 156, 157; --- , 176
Piggott, Isaac, 73, 99, 166, 173, 183; Thomas, 30
Placket, John, 2; Mary, 2
Platt, John, 21
Pocock, John, 40, 41; --- , 167
Pooley, Abraham, 123, 124
Pope, Charles, 172
Potton, Ann, 21
Potts, Alexander, 76
Poulney (Poultney), Christopher, 25, 29, 34, 42
Poulton, Edward, 8
Powell, John 80; William, 152, 156, 158
Pratt, Thomas, 15
Preedy,James, 119
Price, John, 57, 58; Michael, 73
Proctor, James, 18
Prudden, Elizabeth, 43-46, 48-50, 52; William, 64
Puddephatt (Puddiphat), Elizabeth, 113; Jeremiah, 25; Joseph, 97; Sarah, 97; William, 147
Pugh, Maria, 36. Cf. Pew
Pullen, James, 179
Putnam, James, 64; John, 41; Joseph, 41; Matthew, 145, 157

Randall, William, 170; --- , 158
Ray (Reay), John, 33; Joseph, 22, 82; Thomas, 22
Reade, John, 1
Reading, Berks., 134
Reading, John, 161; Matthew, 152
Reay. See Ray
Redbourn, Herts., 16, 27, 53, 108, 126, 132

190

Wainwright, John (alias Ayre, Joseph), 1, 3, 4
Walker, James, 81; Joseph, 53, 59; Thomas, 3, 7, 9, 47, 50, 51
Waller, William, 106
Wallis, John, 107-109, 111
Walsh, John, 2, Patrick, 2. Cf. Welch
Walton, Edward, 13
Wane, John, 51, 54
Ward, Charles, 21; James, 82; William, 8
Warner, Moses, 11
Warren, Richard, 42, 43; Thomas, 56
Warwick (Warrick), Charles, 158, 163; James, 107, 109-111; John, 107, 109-111, 158, 162, 163, 168
Watlington, George, 122, 132
Watson, George, 126; James (alias Brown), 128; James (alias Carr), 125, 127; Mary, 38, 39; W., 68
Weatherley (Wetherby, Wetherly), John, 48, 49, 118; J., 118; Susanna, 48-50, 52; William, 164
Webb, Ann, 47, 50, 51, 174; James, 174; Mary, 167
Webber, John, 103
Webster, Richard, 178; --- , 141
Weedon, Johnathan, 17; Seth, 57, 58, 62, 63, 69
Welch, Ann, 4; John, 3, 4. Cf. Walsh
Wellingham, --- , 26
Wellington, John, 108
Wells, J.W., 168, 169; William, 3, 4; Winch, 3
West, Richard, 145
Weston, Henry, 93; Thomas, 181, 182
Westwood, Thomas, 127, 128
Wetherly, Wetherby. See Weatherley
Whalley, James (alias Worley), 10
Wheeler, Joseph, 6; Thomas, 11, 56; William, 10, 11, 91
Whitbread, George, 4; William, 94
Whitby, James, 94, 95
White (Whight), George, 7, 9, 13; John, 98; Joseph, 169; Mary, 2, 4; Samuel, 24; Sarah 131, 132; Thomas, 15; Willaim, 57, 61, 158; --- , 59

Whitley, Thomas, 181
Whitmore, William, 91
Whittington (Wittington), Jonathan, 68; John, 83; --- , Mrs., 58
Wight. See White
Wildbore, George, 178; Samuel, 25, 53, 67, 131
Wilde, Charles, 120
Wilkes, John, 30
Wilkins, Edward, 90; George, 148, 178-180; Thomas the younger, 90
Willcox, James, 37
Willes. See Willis
Williams, Thomas, 71, 138, 140; William, 149, 157
Willis (Willes, Wills), Elizabeth, 97, 98; John, 110; Robert, 171; William, 16, 97
Wilouby (Willouby), James, 9; Thomas, 7
Willson. See Wilson
Wilshire (Wilsher, Wilshere), Ann, 92, 130; George, 83, 89-92, 130, 148
Wilson (Willson), Elizabeth, 183; James, 18, 44, 45; John, 3, 4; Samuel, 183; Thomas, 18, 82; William, 62, 147, 157; W., 52
Wimbush, Thomas, 26
Wingrave, William, 54
Witney, James, 53
Wittington. See Whittington
Wolfe, Phebe, 107, 110
Wolley, Admiral, 126; Thomas, 125
Wood, James 129, 130; Thomas, 54, 181; T., 183
Woodbridge, --- , 117
Wooding, Octavius, 149
Woodland, Thomas the younger, 121
Woodrof (Woodroff), John, 129-131
Woodward (Woodwards), Burton, 22; James, 57, 60-62, 69, 150
Woolham, Charles, 99
Worley. See Whalley
Wright, Henry 172; John 68, 76, 102; Johnathan 17

Young, Job 157; William 157

Index of subjects

Admiralty, letter from, 102
aliens, proclamation concerning. 84
army: recruits, 25-27; 103, 123; regiments named, 1, 13, 36, 45, 55, 69, 78, 79, 84, 92, 94, 100, 111, 112, 117, 121-123, 130, 141, 149, 166; soldiers, 1, 13, 25-28, 45, 55, 59, 78, 79, 92, 100, 101, 103, 108, 109, 111, 113, 122, 126, 129, 130, 140, 141, 149, 178, 180; wagons for, 36, 62, 69, 84, 111, 112, 117, 118, 131, 154, 166. See also deserters; militia
assizes, 1, 2, 12, 20, 52, 62, 100, 168, 177

bail, 50, 133, 145
baliff, 40, 56
bank, 134; bank token, 141
baptism certificate forged, 23
bastards, bastardy, 7, 16, 19, 24, 31, 47, 48, 50, 51, 53, 65, 67, 73, 74, 90, 91, 95, 103, 113, 122, 135, 140, 143, 146, 148, 149, 151, 156, 157, 161, 165, 167, 172
bathing, unlawful, 85, 88, 107, 143, 183
Benefit Society, 62
Bethlem hospital, 15
bread, 92, 93, 96, 164; order to prohibit sale of non-standard, 40; scarcity of, 40; weighing of, 130
brewhouse, 135

census. See population
chimney sweeping, 160
corn, proclamation concerning, 70
County Chronicle, 39, 173
court leet, 14, 107, 160
compter. See assizes; court leet; petty sessions; requests

deserters, 17, 21, 34, 37, 41, 45, 50, 54, 67, 71, 81, 83, 88, 91, 93, 94, 97, 101, 121, 147, 152, 158, 164, 172, 173, 177
dogs, stray, 104

Exchequer, estreat roll, 40, 70; standard weights, 40
excise, 57, 149

fairs, 88, 112, 117, 130, 133, 159, 162, 165
Female Society, 120
fine, estreats of, 40, 70
fire, 110
fireworks, 117, 130, 174, 183

gin, 43, 133
gypsies, 130, 136

highway, obstruction to, 14; rate, 90
housholders, listing of, 148

inquests, 25-28, 31, 40, 56, 57, 67, 84, 88, 105, 110, 112, 114, 121, 132, 144, 147, 166, 173, 177, 183

Jubilee Ball, 117, 118

land tax, 61, 115; collection of, 61

levy money, 51, 52
licensing, 68, 75-77, 84, 117, 118, 130, 155, 175; abuses, 161
lodging houses, 68, 69, 130, 148

malthouse 110
marines, 103, 137, 180
medicines, 56, 87, 93, 117, 121, 122, 127, 139, 144, 155, 160, 164, 170, 178
militia, 41, 45, 62, 64, 69, 76, 77, 81, 84, 93, 102, 107, 112, 117, 118, 120-122, 130, 155, 180

navy, 37, 39, 40; deserters, 54, 67, 71, 81, 101; Navy Act, 37, 39, 40; seamen, 81, 136

offences: apprenticeship, neglect of obligations, 42, 171; assault, 1, 2, 5-7, 9, 16, 17, 20-22, 30-34, 41, 43, 47-50, 54, 57, 60-64, 70, 77-83, 85, 91-96, 99, 100, 103-105, 107-109, 116, 119, 122, 123, 133, 135, 141-144, 147, 149, 151, 156-159, 161, 167, 169, 170, 174, 181; breach of peace, 30, 91, 112, 143, 145, 157; breaking and entering, 18, 40; burglary, 40, 41; coining, uttering, 2, 65, 66, 72-74, 78, 83, 85, 86, 88, 89, 133, 136, 148, 157; disorderly conduct, 6, 89, 94, 108, 109, 114, 119, 123, 161; disturbing the peace, 121, 148, 157; drunkeness, 58; embezzlement, 149; false representation, 178; forgery, 22, 23, 125; fraud, false pretences, 6, 10, 12, 29, 57, 58, 62, 87, 133, 134, 148, 157, 162, 167; game laws, breach of, 174, 178; hawking or trading without a licence, 171, 172; highway robbery, 1, 2; insulting behaviour, 124; larceny. See stolen goods;

malicious damage, 181; manslaughter, 173, 177; misbehaviour in service, 85; pawnbroking in breach of statute, 42, 43; public nusance, 85; receiving stolen goods, 59, 61, 125; regrating, 68, 139, 150; refusal to grant billets for soldiers, 103; riot, riotous assembly, 63, 64, 70, 71, 89, 99, 108, 109, 112, 114, 115, 119, 122, 123, 140-142, 157, 181; selling leather mittens without duty, 28; theft. See stolen goods; threatening behaviour, threatening bodily harm, 40, 71, 99, 161, 164; trading on the Sabbath, 90; unlawful assembly, 140; using an unlawful wagon, 96; weights, false, 53, 54, 67, 98, 103, 110, 156

parliamentary election, 23, 99, 112
pawnbroking, 42, 43
petty sessions, 103, 180
pillory, 111
poor (paupers): box broken open, 152-154; churchwardens and overseers of, 19, 23, 37, 38, 50, 51, 62, 64, 68, 72, 73, 80, 87, 103, 107, 122, 124, 126, 165, 181; inquest on pauper, 67; list of, 85; rate, 23, 37, 38, 54, 64; relief, 64, 70, 76, 113-115, 118-120, 122, 125, 128, 132, 134, 136, 139, 140, 143, 144
population, 73, 124, 126, 148; Population Act, 70
printers, 81, 113, 173
prisoners: deaths in gaol, 12, 40, 56, 166; discharged by proclamation, 12, 52, 69, 81, 84, 111, 117; escaped, 138, 172; fee for committment, 40; payment for apprehending, 120, 155; payment for maintenance etc., 4, 13, 33, 36, 37, 45, 47, 49, 50, 52, 54, 62, 63, 69, 71, 74, 75, 78, 81, 82, 86-88, 91, 93, 98, 99, 101, 103, 105, 106, 131, 134-136, 139, 140, 143, 143-149, 151, 152, 154, 155, 169, 170, 172-174, 177, 178, 180, 182. See also medicines
prisoners of war, 45, 84, 130, 143
public houses, search of, 148
publicans. See licensing

rails, removal of, 90
rates, 23, 37, 38, 54, 64, 90
recorder, 39, 119, 132
records of sessions, 95
Requests, Court of, 17, 21, 155, 171, 180
riots, prevention and suppression of, 70, 159.
See also offences

rogues and vagabonds, 6, 13, 33, 71, 133, 135, 146, 149, 181

sacrament certificates, 2, 9, 16, 17, 20, 34, 41, 52, 57, 63, 77, 85, 88, 95, 114, 116, 122, 149, 166
seamen, order in council concerning, 81
search warrants. See warrants
sessions house, court house, 36, 143
smallpox, 16
Society of Good Fellowship, 95, 98, 104, 16, 120, 122, 135
soldiers. See army
stables, 5, 59, 126
stolen goods: apron, 21, 48, 49, 115; bank token, 141; beef, 104; beer, 135; bible, 34; blanket, 55, 96; bonnet, 115, 116; bread, 5, 96, 97, 163; breeches, 37, 41, 44, 45, 64, 127; buttress, 74, 75; buttons, 6; calico, 106; candlesticks, 159, 160; caps, 115; cask, 8; cheese, 131, 167, 168; cloak, 50, 51; copper pipes, 175-177; corn, 57, 59, 125; cotton, 7, 29, 48, 49, 125, 126; curtains, 2, 4; cutlery, 165; dog, 29; earthen ware, 144; fish, 104, 105; fowl, 9, 15; frock, 100; glass, 144; gown, 115, 116; greatcoat, 52, 53, 63, 64; handkerchief, 5, 13, 14, 29, 34, 55, 105, 158; hat, 127, 165; horse beans, 61; Irish cloth, 6, 7; iron chain, 10-14; knife, 100, 101, 165; lead, 4; leather, 156; meat, 46, 47, 60; money, 4, 37, 41, 129, 130, 149, 150; mug, 30; muslin stocks, 14; oats, 17, 18; pattens, 9, 43, 44; pewter pot, 46, 47; pocket book, 148; poor box, 152-154; pork, 47, 57, 60, 61; rafters, 3, 4; ribbon, 137; screws, 74, 75; scythe, 15, 17, 101; shawl, 162, 163, 165; sheets, 55, 106; shift, 38; shirt, 100; shoes, 146; silver salt, 4; smelling bottle, 152, 154; snaith, 17; spoons, 4, 7, 9, 21, 63, 64, 72, 73, 82; staves, 15; stockings, 5, 116; straw, 59; straw plait, 89, 90, 96-98, 127, 128, 131, 132; tablecloth, 7-9, 35; thread, 29; waistcoat, 37; watch, 35, 37, 46; weights, 115, 116; wheat, 65, 66; whips, 10, 11; wood, 87; woollen cloth, 29

taxes, 149, 158, 160, 174, 177, 178; commissioner for, 114
town crier, 166
town hall, 2, 3, 65, 92, 103, 118, 144; attendance at, 68, 117, 128, 183; maintenance and repairs to, 7, 13, 39, 64, 95, 111, 140, 144, 147, 151, 154, 156, 157, 159

197